D0904996

The Rhetoric
of Argumentation

The Rhetoric
of Argumentation

William J. Brandt

The Bobbs-Merrill Company, Inc.
Indianapolis   New York

To Mayflower, Elizabeth, Jane,
and Mr. Um

Preface

It must be said immediately, to avoid any confusion about the purposes of this book, that it has been written for those who would improve their reading. Reading and writing are not utterly dissimilar activities, and portions of what follows should be useful to writers. But this is not a book for writers. It proposes a way of analyzing a certain type of prose, argumentation. This analysis will lead, it is hoped, to more critical reading habits by calling attention to the elements of what is read.

"Argumentation" is of course a very comprehensive, and consequently a rather loose, word. Here we will use it to refer to essays, speeches, learned articles—in short, to all of those modern forms of discourse that have their origin in the classical oration. The common features of these forms of discourse is that they have distinctive parts that relate to each other in a special way. Of course, other forms of discourse—poems, plays, novels—can be said to have parts also; a poet may talk about the *Aeneid* and a small town in Kansas in the same poem, a novel has chapters, and a drama has acts and scenes. But these parts have an immediate relationship to each other, given in experience; they are related by time or in the act of perception. The parts of an argument are not so related. They are always, in some fashion, invented, and their basic relationship is logical rather than perceptual.

Hence, the primary necessity in the analysis of a piece of argumentation is to determine its parts and their relationship to each other. The first three chapters of this book will be concerned with these parts and this relationship. The consideration of these larger structural elements and their relationships will be treated under the general head: "structural rhetoric."

But an essay or speech is more than the organization of large structural elements, since these themselves must have some kind of interior organization. This organization—that is, the ways of manipulating language at the sentence and paragraph levels, by means of figures of speech and various logical devices—is here called "textual rhetoric." Textual rhetoric is considered in Part II. In one sense, we have done no more than provide a glossary that will enable students to talk about prose at this level, with suitable examples provided. But in our experience, the student who learns to use the glossary to this end learns in fact much more. He learns to see prose in an entirely new light.

Although this book takes its inspiration from classical rhetoric and at every point makes use of classical insights as well as classical terminology, we believe it represents a radical innovation grafted onto a very old tradition. Classical rhetorics were without exception prescriptive or descriptive; since they were handbooks for orators, this was a necessity. But the present book is written for readers, and hence it is analytical. The difference is substantial.

It is particularly substantial with respect to what we have called textual rhetoric. The character of discourse below the level of the major structural elements was not a central consideration for classical rhetoricians (only Quintilian and the *Ad Herennium* offer anything like adequate glossaries), because a conscious knowledge of figures and logical devices on the paragraph level and below is of doubtful value to speakers or writers. They will, unconsciously and out of their knowledge of the tradition, employ these figures and devices as they are needed in realizing particular ends. But the reader who is aware of the elements of this figurative texture in prose, by the very fact of his awareness, establishes an active and critical, rather than a passive, relationship to it.

The first two parts (Chapters I through VI) of this book attempt to get at the essence of the argumentative mode of discourse;

what follows is subordinate to these six chapters. Defective argumentation is considered because it is so common, at least outside the law-courts. The type of discourse here called "reportorial" has been included because it is a kind of pseudo-argumentation.

One hears many complaints at the present time about the low level of public discourse, particularly of political discourse. The complaints are surely well founded. The intense concern for one's public image, so characteristic of the mid-twentieth century, necessarily implies a devaluation of the traditional dialogue and its concern for reason. The best way of correcting this tendency is to force upon the image-makers the necessity for more responsible communication. The only practical means of achieving this end is to see to it that those at whom image-making is directed, the passive participants in public discourse, become sophisticated listeners and readers. This book, it is hoped, will contribute something to that sophistication.

WILLIAM J. BRANDT

Acknowledgments

This book was originally undertaken with Professor Leonard Nathan. When he abandoned it, as being too far from his primary interest, poetry, he left to me the spoils. These included the Introduction, virtually as it stands at present, and years of collaboration on the glossary. This is a debt beyond the usual scholarly collaboration. Also, since the book represents ten years of thought and experimentation, students and colleagues have necessarily contributed. Among the former, I must particularly thank Terry Busch, whose insight into the way language works is an unusual gift upon which I drew heavily. My former colleague and still friend, Professor Robert Larsen of the philosophy department at the California State College at Hayward, contributed greatly to the first chapter in spite of his pain at my sometimes cavalier treatment of logic.

Contents

The Rhetoric
of Argumentation

Introduction

A Brief History of Classical Rhetoric
and Rhetorical Theory[1]

Origins. If one defines rhetoric in the simplest possible fashion, as the manipulation of language to create particular effects, then it is obvious that human beings have used rhetoric from a very early time. The *Iliad* and the *Odyssey* presume a sophisticated rhetorical tradition that must have been very old in Homer's day. But rhetoric did not come into Greek consciousness as a particular type of speaking, an art, until the beginning of the fifth century. Appar-

[1] This chapter has been written for students with no knowledge of classical rhetoric, and it necessarily presents a highly simplified account of the subject. For more detailed accounts, the reader is referred particularly to W. Rhys Roberts, *Greek Rhetoric and Literary Criticism* (reprinted; New York: Cooper Square, 1963), Charles Sears Baldwin, *Ancient Rhetoric and Poetic* (reprinted; Gloucester, Mass.: Peter Smith, 1959), and J. W. Atkins, *Literary Criticism in Antiquity* (reprinted; Gloucester, Mass.: Peter Smith, n. d.). Among recent studies, that by George Kennedy, *The Art of Persuasion in Greece* (Princeton: Princeton University Press, 1963), is near to being definitive. It could be supplemented by Donald L. Clark's *Rhetoric in Greco-Roman Education* (New York: Columbia University Press, 1957). The latter also offers a useful bibliography.

3

ently the Greeks of the Sicilian city of Syracuse first recognized that language was made up of norms of diction and word order, on the one hand, and deviations from those norms on the other. Rhetoric, in part, was the analysis and classification of such deviations.

It is no accident that the birthplace of rhetoric, Syracuse, should also be a democracy. The political deliberation that characterized early Greek democracies meant that there was widespread participation in important decisions. But of even more importance, litigants in cases of civil and criminal law were expected to plead their cases in person before the courts or assemblies sitting in judgment. There were ways of evading this practice, but most citizens presented their own cases. Hence, in a classical democracy, one's basic rights, as well as one's status in the community, depended on one's ability to be persuasive in a public situation.

Democracy itself might have led to traditional forms of speech, but it would not have led to a self-conscious art. This was the product of professionals, the *rhetors*. Specialization was no novelty in the Greek city-states; there were merchants and farmers and physicians. It was natural and inevitable that a class of men would arise to help less gifted citizens become more effective in the forum and the law courts: to write speeches, to deliver them, and most importantly, to teach the art of public speaking. Rhetoric as we know it originated with this class of men.

The intellectual climate that characterized classical Greece formed the particular shape of this rhetoric. The most striking fact about these fifth-century city-states was their boundless faith in *logos* (thought, discourse, reason), in the power of the human mind to perceive the real nature of things. But there was more to Greek *logos* than that; there was the implicit assumption that the real nature of things would present itself to man with a certain shape about it. There was a system in nature, or rather, there was a series of systems arranged in an hierarchical order. Hence knowledge, for the Greeks, was the knowledge of systems and was itself necessarily systematic, and therefore approachable through a systematic technique or "art." Each art thus had its own subject, and knowledge about that subject—philosophy, medicine, and so forth—was to a large extent a structure of definitions, although these definitions often included an astonishing amount of close observation.

Rhetoric did not appear on the historical scene so methodically organized; indeed, the Greek conception of knowledge as system took form slowly over a number of centuries. But rhetoric inevitably became an art, modeled on the other arts. In its fully developed form, as represented by Aristotle's *Rhetoric,* it had its own subject matter, the probable. This subject matter distinguished it from philosophy, which was concerned with the demonstrable or true. The art of the probable, unlike other arts, took three forms because it might be applied in three different circumstances (see Part I); it was further divided into parts, according to the different means that an orator might use to persuade his audience that something was indeed probable or improbable. Somewhat later, rhetoricians undertook the analysis and classification of the elements of persuasive speech—words, phrases, and sentences. Rhetoric thus became a complete and self-contained study, an art like the other arts comprising the intellectual and professional life of the ancient world.

Rhetoric in Classical Greece.   Little is known about the first efforts to teach rhetoric, although the names of Corax and Tisias are connected with the persuasive techniques employed in the democratic courts of Syracuse. Our first definite knowledge begins with the arrival in Athens in 427 B.C. of the rhetorician Gorgias of Leontini. He apparently made a great impression on the Athenians; at least, he was important enough to become the star performer, if hardly the hero, of an important dialogue by Plato. Gorgias taught by example, and he concentrated on style. With regard to the structure of argumentation, he apparently taught patterns of rhetoric appropriate to particular cases. His major stylistic devices were antithesis, parallel structure, and rhyme. There is some indication that with these devices Gorgias was attempting to bring into prose the stylistic power of poetic discourse.[2] He also emphasized the importance of appropriateness, of adapting speeches to particular circumstances.

[2] His attention to style, though it anticipates a later Greek preoccupation, was not characteristic of classical rhetoricians, who, as noted above, were chiefly concerned with the larger elements of oratorical discourse.

Oratory flourished in the fifth century B.C., and the works of some of the notable orators of the century, such as Antiphon, Thrasymachus, and Lysias, have come down to us. The teachers of the art of oratory, of rhetoric, also prospered. If we can judge by a teacher's handbook of a somewhat later period, about 300 B.C., the *Rhetorica ad Alexandrum,* their teaching was intensely practical. From the beginning rhetoric had been associated with the schools of the sophists, who taught that only probability was available to man. From this assumption about reality, it might be deduced that everyone was entitled to present his own case in the most probable light and to use any means at his disposal for doing so. This is clearly the position of the *Rhetorica ad Alexandrum,* which baldly sets out to teach the best ways of arguing particular kinds of cases, chiefly those of the law court, paying no attention at all to the rights of the matter. This handbook, typical of the rhetorician's art, unashamedly emphasizes ways of commanding the proper emotional response for the sake of manipulating the judgment of jurors. Such a rhetoric could look, to a moralist like Plato, like the art of "making the worse appear the better."

One of the earliest reactions against the sophistical conception of rhetoric was that of Isocrates. He was not himself an orator; his speeches were literary productions written to be read. Nor was he a theoretician. His interest in rhetoric was moral, and in such "speeches" as "Against the Sophists" and "Panathenaicus" he attempted to give rhetoric philosophical seriousness and political importance. Significantly, he turned to ceremonial oratory to achieve this reform. For in ceremonial oratory he found the noble affirmative stance, inherited from the poets, that rose above the self-interest almost always implied in private litigation and too often underlying political discussion.

Isocrates' high-mindedness is unmistakable, but he cannot be said to have achieved his aim. Ceremonial discourse applied to elevated political purposes simply could not, except on rare occasions, do for Greek culture what Pindar's odes had done; it could not meaningfully affirm community solidarity, perhaps because the sense of community was already dissolving by Isocrates' time. Certainly, his attempts to reassert it seem strained. Signs of Isocrates' failure reveal themselves mainly in a self-indulgent brilliance that calls attention to the speaker at the expense of his subject. Unfortunately, this stylistic indulgence was to become, in exaggerated forms, the model for the declamatory rhetoric of later times.

Isocrates was not alone in finding fault with a rhetoric founded upon principles of expediency. Plato, repeatedly and from many angles, attacked expediency and rhetoric itself, most notably in the *Gorgias.* In Plato's view, rhetoric, far from being an art or science as its teachers had often claimed, is a perversion of discourse, because it promotes a polity in which the search for truth is replaced by satisfaction with probability, and in which opinion is more valued than reason. This criticism of rhetoric is not easily dismissed. The many serious defenses of rhetoric that have been advanced in the last two thousand years are usually attempts to answer Plato, and they almost always make the initial concession to him that rhetoric must in some way be founded on philosophical principles. But even in the best defenses the synthesis of philosophy and rhetoric is apt to be uneasy.

Plato himself, in the *Phaedrus,* attempted to take the curse off rhetoric by uniting it to philosophy. But it was a union that took place in the soul of the orator, who must first be schooled in philosophy and know the truth; then he might properly use rhetoric to persuade his hearers, presumably of lesser philosophic capacities, to this truth. This is hardly a very satisfactory union. Rhetoric remained what it was—the old streetwalker—but now it was to be put to work for the Red Cross.

Aristotle's *Rhetoric* is without question the greatest work ever written on the subject, in spite of the fact that it is built on the same dichotomy between truth and expression as Plato's proposal in the *Phaedrus.* Aristotle brought to the subject an extraordinary eye for what really went on in the rhetorical practice of his day, and an unflagging interest in the relationship between the various objectives that a particular speech might have and the means necessary to achieve those objectives. He was perhaps also the first to discover that logic and rhetoric were not two different modes of argument, that the enthymeme (a syllogism with an implicit major premise) was a major element in public rhetoric, even though it was generally used to establish a probability and not a certainty. The *Rhetoric* is a theoretical treatise of the greatest practical import, since it organizes and classifies the means available to the rhetorician with regard to the end to be achieved. Aristotle's classification was not superseded, although challenged many times, in the classical age.

Aristotle, like Plato, believed that if there was to be a good rhetoric, it had to arise from good intention; and he begins by defending the subject as an art, like medicine, whose quality depends on the ends for which it is employed. Yet it becomes clear soon enough that, for Aristotle, there is no necessary connection between means and ends in the realm of expression. For rhetoric, in Aristotle's analysis, is an instrumental art. It is a morally neutral tool, to be judged only on its effectiveness, with no regard to the motive behind that effectiveness. Thus in a single treatise we have the curious spectacle of finding, on the one hand, attacks on rhetoricians who would pervert their hearers by appealing to emotions instead of reason, and, on the other, explicit and detailed instructions for accomplishing such perversion.

A word must be said of the greatest orator of the classical age, Demosthenes (384–322 B.C.). He is credited by classical authorities with sixty-five orations, written for delivery by himself or others. Most of these were legal, but his political orations are of the greatest interest. The word "philippic," which came to mean any kind of public verbal assault on an individual, originally designated the series of orations by which Demosthenes attempted to alert Athens to the danger posed by Philip of Macedon. What is agreed to be his greatest oration, "On the Crown," turns a technical issue into an impassioned defense of himself and his career. Demosthenes' greatness was personal; he brought nothing new to rhetoric except a fine focus on the objective of the moment, to which considerations of style and personal aggrandizement were subordinated.

The year of Demosthenes' death, 322 B.C., also marked the effective end of Greek democracy. This event was, in the long run, fatal to Greek rhetoric and Greek oratory, since deliberation about public policy offered the best chance for orators to acquire the kind of seriousness they often lacked. There are some impressive individuals known to us during the next few centuries, but on the whole one observes a sharp decline. Schools of rhetoric became associated with particular philosophic positions (Peripatetic, Stoic,

Epicurean), and the rhetoric itself became increasingly academic. Because subjects for oratory tended to become fixed, emphasis shifted to delivery and style. In the late classical period, oratory was perhaps more popular than ever before, but it was oratory directed to display; the same crowds that applauded the traveling entertainers applauded the orators, and for no better reason.

Roman Rhetoric.   Given the public nature of Roman life from earliest times, the profound impression that Greek rhetoric had on Roman thought is understandable enough. Roman rhetoric was based on Greek models, notably the lost handbook of Hermagoras, and remained to the end within the Greek context. Hence discussion can be profitably limited to the two major Latin writers on the subject, Cicero and Quintilian, and one handbook, the *Rhetorica ad Herennium.*

Cicero (106–43 B.C.) has frequently been canonized as a selfless martyr to the Roman republic, and there is no reason to doubt the genuineness of his dedication to an idea of Rome. But he had another major aim in life, to dignify rhetoric by giving it a philosophic basis. The direction that this second aim took diverged from the first aim; ever since, historians have had to deal, somehow, with two Ciceros, one the great partisan of the Republic, the other a not altogether attractive manipulator of the spoken word.

His attempt to give rhetoric a philosophical basis came down to a definition of the orator as first of all a philosopher, even a rather Platonic one. In this effort he was, of course, following a well-worn Greek groove. Good character was to guarantee good rhetoric. But the Roman, and Ciceronian, ideal of good character was something quite different from any Greek ideal. In the figure of the elder Cato, for instance, a kind of moral grandeur is visible that is quite unlike anything in Greek biography. Cicero attempted to create such a character by rhetorical means; the result was, rather oddly, a heavy emphasis on style and delivery. The latter topic dominates his last rhetorical work, *The Orator.* As a result, in practice Cicero is much closer to Isocrates than to Plato, because the tendency of a rhetorical stance chiefly preoccupied with portraying character is to become a form of self-display, not of moral grandeur. The speaker is always in the position of having to *dem-*

monstrate his impressiveness. As an orator, Cicero was consequently inferior to Demosthenes, and he was criticized in his own
time for his grandiloquence and over-elaborateness.

The preoccupation with style that is found in Cicero's *The
Orator* (and which is a heritage of Hellenistic rhetoric) is also
found in the *Rhetorica ad Herennium,* a handbook written about
the second decade of the first century B.C. and for centuries wrongly
attributed to Cicero. Like the earlier *Rhetorica ad Alexandrum*
it is rather narrowly prescriptive. However, it had considerable
authority during the Middle Ages and the Renaissance because of
its supposed Ciceronian origin. It is of interest today chiefly because it includes a lengthy list of rhetorical figures.

The *Institutio Oratoria* of Quintilian (*c.* A.D. 30–96) is the
only document in Latin comparable to Aristotle's *Rhetoric.* Like
Cicero, Quintilian viewed good oratory as the result of good character. But Quintilian also developed, in the first two books of the
Institutes, a systematic educational program that might realize the
ideal orator, whose highest aim would be an eloquence at the service of truth and honor. This is perhaps the most important treatise
on education ever written; it was the fundamental document in
the educational revolution of the sixteenth century.

The most important difference between Quintilian and Cicero, apart from Quintilian's great thoroughness, is hard to pin
down satisfactorily. Quintilian had a kind of humility, a dedication
to service, whereas Cicero was always in danger of believing, if he
did not in fact believe on occasion, that the orator's goodness, his
ethos or character, justified the position that he took. Quintilian,
having gone at length into the problem of educating an orator for
goodness, seems to have assumed thereafter that his rhetoric would
be used for good ends.

But Quintilian was a hopeful man at a time when there was
no hope. In the surviving works of the elder Seneca, probably about
twelve years old when Cicero died (43 B.C.), we can see that Roman
rhetoric was proceeding very rapidly along the same path that
Greek rhetoric had taken, toward public pyrotechnics at the expense of meaning. However, it apparently became more popular
as it became less significant. As the Roman educational system
hardened, under the Empire, into the traditional seven liberal arts,

rhetoric became a fundamental academic discipline, and endowed chairs for rhetoricians became accepted practice in the larger cities. This academic rhetoric aimed at a theatrical brilliance of display through impressive elocution. One of the most cherished gifts among these rhetoricians was the ability to amplify a trivial subject into a marvel, preferably extemporaneously.

These developments had consequences far beyond the confines of public speaking. In the Middle Ages rhetoric continued to be studied even though the classical tradition of public oratory had long since disappeared. One consequence was that rhetoric adumbrated poetic theory and practice. In fact, poetic became synonymous with rhetoric, the rhetoric of late classical display whose influence was compounded because poets in the Roman period— Ovid and Lucan are instances—were likewise trained in rhetoric. And it was such poets, especially Ovid, who were the models of correct practice in the Middle Ages.

The Theory of Classical Rhetoric According to Aristotle. As has been pointed out in the Preface, this book will be chiefly concerned with the usefulness of classical figures of speech in the understanding of argumentation, and this is probably what most of us today mean by "rhetoric." But these figures, in fact, played a relatively minor role in the thought of classical rhetoricians, whose major concern was to organize their art into a coherent and well-defined body of knowledge, possession of which would define the rhetorician. This concern led to an emphasis on the overall structure of the oration and the development of its major elements. Here, as in so many instances, Aristotle's *Rhetoric* provides the best brief outline extant of the classical oration.

Aristotle classified orations according to the three major occasions calling for oratory. First, there were the great public meetings called to deliberate civic policy; these called for *deliberative* oratory. Second, there were the instances of private dispute within the framework of established law, the lawsuits so characteristic of Greek life; these called for *forensic* oratory. Finally, there were those ceremonial occasions in which public speaking was (and is) an affirmation of communal values; these called for *epideictic* oratory. Each kind of oratory, according to Aristotle, had its own particular end, and other important characteristics of each kind followed from that end.

Deliberative oratory was the oratory of politics. According to Aristotle, it urges us to do or not to do something according to whether it will be expedient or harmful. About deliberative oratory little needs to be said, except that it would seem to have offered the best opportunity for the development of a responsible oratorical tradition, and that it was overwhelmed by the other two modes.

Forensic oratory was, as has been said, the oratory of the law courts; its subject is justice and injustice, and it necessarily attacks or defends something or someone.

The forensic was probably from the beginning the most important oratorical mode. This is understandable; few men would have occasion to speak on matters of public policy, but a great many men might be involved, at one time or another, in lawsuits. The *rhetors,* as professionals and men chiefly concerned with what was profitable, naturally laid heavy stress on forensic oratory. However, the dominance of forensic oratory was a misfortune, as Aristotle himself pointed out. Deliberative oratory might be involved in complicated questions of the past, but it was chiefly aimed at influencing the public choice between relatively few alternatives. By comparison even an ordinary legal case is immensely complicated. First, it must determine past facts; it must discover the one law, amid many laws, appropriate to those facts; it must estimate intention; it must consider mitigating circumstances. Second, by the witness of Aristotle, the jury in a legal case was much more susceptible to irrelevant matters than was the assembly hearing a political debate; this weakness added a complicating dimension to forensic oratory. Lastly, it is (and perhaps has to be) a maxim in law cases that every man is entitled to present his own case in the best possible light, and hence moral sanctions are at a minimum in forensic oratory. All of these particular circumstances could make forensic oratory seem very remote from the search for truth proposed by the philosophers, and insofar as rhetoric as a whole was identified with forensic oratory it inevitably appeared to be an essentially vicious and antisocial activity.

Epideictic oratory, according to Aristotle, had as its end praise or blame. It was the only type of oratory that did not ask of its

audience some kind of judgment; members of the audience were
spectators, presumably because they shared the sentiments of the
speaker even before he began.

Epideictic oratory is an attempt to do at length in prose what
had formerly been done in poetry. In preclassical Greece, poetic
recitation had played an important part in public life. Greek
tragedy grew out of this public poetry, for instance. The standard
object of such poetry was praise, very often of the winner of some
athletic contest, as we see in the odes of Pindar. But this poetry
also performed an important civic function; in praising an individual, it necessarily reaffirmed at the same time the traditional
values upon which such praise was based. It was thus an affirmation
of community solidarity.

Epideictic oratory, in taking over this poetic function, inevitably took over something of the diction of poetry. Insofar as the
transfer of elements of poetry into prose extended the possibilities
open to the orator, there was gain. One of the best-known and most
impressive orations in the world, Pericles' "Funeral Oration," is
epideictic. (So is Lincoln's "Gettysburg Address.") But this kind
of public speaking also has its dangers; it is not primarily argumentative but ceremonial, and the orator who was not particularly
awed by the ceremonial occasion could see in an epideictic oration
a handsome opportunity for personal display. Such display became
more and more the rule; sometimes the occasion itself was created
merely as a pretext for oratorical pyrotechnics.

In the long run, the deliberative, the forensic, and the epideictic could not be kept apart. The stance of praise or blame, for
instance, was appropriate on occasion in the deliberative and the
forensic situations, and all oratory inevitably adopted the techniques, and the vices, of the epideictic mode on such occasions.
Forensic oratory was even more of an influence on the deliberative.
Being more complicated, it was more interesting; Aristotle laments
the dominance of the forensic and then proceeds to spend most of
his time on it, as his less high-minded predecessors had done. The
influence of epideictic and forensic modes of argument on the deliberative mode surely contributed to the decline of oratory as an
honorable art, and perhaps the dominance of these two modes
contributed to the decline of the body politic as well.

Inevitably the Aristotelian division of rhetoric into three

modes became too narrow as soon as rhetorical structures were applied to subjects outside of the political and legal realms; praise or blame, guilt or innocence, expedient or not—these do not exhaust the arguments of men. Nor, as has been pointed out, do they describe mutually exclusive oratorical modes. Nevertheless, the Aristotelian question is probably the best way to approach a piece of argumentation: to what sort of judgment is it ultimately directed? This question is especially relevant to political oratory, in which the ostensible object is often not the real one. The Calhoun speech analyzed in Chapter III, for instance, appears on first inspection to be deliberative; Calhoun seems to be asking of his northern opponents a judgment about the desirability of a certain course of conduct. Closer inspection reveals that his speech is not deliberative at all, but epideictic; its real objective is to solidify the southern community around a particular political position.

The Elements of Oratorical Practice.   Classical rhetoricians, approaching their art in terms of the chronological development of a particular oration, worked from conception to delivery. They did not all agree about this development, of course, particularly in the matter of emphasis, and the type of oration was also taken into consideration. But it was generally agreed that the processes that fell within the orator's art were five in number; they were traditionally called: (1) Invention, or the investigation into the nature of the issue to be argued and ways of arguing for it; (2) Arrangement, or the effective division and distribution of the parts of the composition; (3) Elocution, or the choice of the appropriate style to be used; (4) Memory, or the methods for fixing the speech in the mind; and (5) Delivery, or the preparation of the voice and body for the actual performance.

INVENTION.   What invention meant to the classical rhetoricians is not always entirely clear. In general, the term meant, first, an analysis of a particular case in order to reduce it to the issue that could be argued most effectively, and second, the search for means of argument or proof. Arguments were of two kinds. The first was "inartistic," in that it did not belong to the "art" of rhetoric, and consisted of what we would call evidence—witnesses, contracts, oaths, laws, and confessions. Classical rhetoricians were chiefly concerned with the second, "artistic" proofs. These involved a search for topics or commonplaces, that is, more or less general statements or categories from which to draw arguments applicable to a particular situation or case. These arguments were again subdivided into inductive proofs and deductive ones. Aristotle associated the inductive proof in rhetoric with the example. Inductive logic proved by considering all examples relevant to a case, but might establish probability with less rigor than deductive logic. Deductive arguments appeared in rhetoric as enthymemes—syllogisms lacking one premise, usually the major. (See Chapter I, "The Syllogism in Argumentation," for a discussion of this logical figure.)

The aim of this preliminary thought was the discovery of a probable argument, since, if proof were possible, no argument would be necessary. Aristotle very rigorously and very thoroughly classified the kinds of topics and enthymemes appropriate to different circumstances in an analysis that should be better known; it is still very useful. Deliberative oratory, he pointed out, was concerned with the topic of the expedient, since politics is the art of achieving our ends. The deliberative orator's enthymemes, consequently, should be concerned with the expedient and inexpedient. Forensic oratory was concerned with the topics of justice and injustice, and had enthymemes appropriate to such an interest. Epideictic oratory dealt with the topics or commonplaces of honor and dishonor, by means of praise and blame.

It should perhaps be noted that the topic—for Aristotle a descriptive category that provided the grounds for argument—became later, particularly with the triumph of the rhetoric of display, a stock subject matter or theme to be cleverly amplified. Thus some hero, or flower, or mythical character became a prescribed topic for the academic orator to develop and ornament. Such topics became the ready-made subject of poets trained in the sophistic rhetorical tradition. And it is perhaps for this reason that, in later periods, especially in the Middle Ages, invention received only the most perfunctory and mechanical attention. Since the matter of proper topics had been, so to speak, long ago settled, the real concern became style—the means of amplifying or ornamenting what was given by tradition.

ARRANGEMENT. A traditional lore concerning the arrange-

ment of public speeches existed long before rhetoricians system-
atized the subject. The characters in the *Iliad* and *Odyssey* who
speak before public assemblies do so very artfully, beginning with
a preamble, moving to some sort of argument, and drawing an
appropriate conclusion. The demands of the fourth-century law
courts obviously made for more complex arrangements, but long,
formally organized speeches were still necessary, since the size of the
juries prohibited interchange between jurymen and contestants.

The parts of an argument, and their effective ordering, is an
important consideration in rhetoric today, and will be considered
in detail in Chapter II. The basic rhetorical structure, as it was
developed in the classical age, was composed of four parts. The
function of the first part, the *exordium,* was chiefly to project a
character for the orator, an *ethos,* which would persuade the audience to trust him. Next came the *narratio,* which was defined as a
statement of the facts of the case (since this structure was designed
for use in law courts), to serve as a background for the major arguments. These arguments were developed in the central part of the
oration, the *confirmatio;* it was in this part that the inventions,
described above, were chiefly to be found. Finally came a *peroration* which recapitulated the *confirmatio* and concluded the speech.
It was generally recognized that this peroration was the proper
place for direct emotional appeals for a favorable judgment, for
what was called *pathos.*

ELOCUTION OR STYLE.   This third part of the orator's art was
enormously elaborated in the Hellenistic Age; it ranged from the
manner in which to phrase an argument to questions about the
quantity of vowels. Two consequences particularly emerged from
this concern. First, a concern for style was clearly behind the elaborate lists of figures of speech, of which the glossary of Chapter V is
an abridgment. And second, a concern for style led to the doctrine
of the three styles, high, middle, and low, which was important to
later literary theory. Oratory had been concerned from the beginning, of course, with appropriateness. Later, this concern hardened
into the doctrine of decorum, whereby the style of any speech had
to be suitable to the speaker, the subject, and the audience. In the
period of the decay of oratory, style—meaning chiefly copiousness,

brilliance, and ornamentation—was the major concern of rhetoricians.

MEMORY. The importance of memory in classical rhetorical theory reflects, again, its legal orientation. The study included elaborate techniques for fixing speeches in the mind, such as associational systems and more sophisticated structural arrangements. In the Hellenistic Age, when the greatest value was placed on ex tempore speaking, it became customary to memorize long passages that could be adapted to a variety of situations and subjects with the least amount of adjustment.

DELIVERY. Classical rhetoricians worked out all of the techniques for effective platform manner that later came to be included under elocution: appropriate gestures, the use of the eyes, vocal expression, posture, and movements.

This approach to a subject, based on a conception of human arts which is at least very schematized by twentieth-century standards, is apt to seem strange to a modern student. But it needs to be remembered that for many centuries oratory was the royal road to success in Greece and Rome, and as a consequence it commanded the intense interest of a great many able men. Nor, at least in the best periods, was this interest theoretical; it was directed to understanding the best ways to bring about a very specific end, the persuasion of a particular audience. A great deal of what these men discovered can be of great value to students of all forms of verbal communication in our own day, if they will but pay attention to it. These discoveries can be of particular value to the student of argumentation, whatever form it takes. A public speaker today has much the same problems as did an orator in Periclean Athens. A writer of essays today will have many of the same problems.

The classical doctrines about oratory boil down, in a sense, to a vocabulary appropriate to argumentation. This vocabulary can help us to be more conscious of the processes behind speaking and writing; this increased consciousness is the function of any specialized terminology. Unfamiliar as classical terms may be to us, if we take them seriously we begin to see into the workings of verbal discourse at its most basic level.

Part I

Structural Rhetoric

Although the term "rhetoric" was used in classical times to denominate a number of different oratorical considerations, it chiefly referred to two: structure and style. Style, early recognized as a crucial element in persuasion, entailed the study of the manipulation of language in its smaller units. This part of rhetoric, which we have called "textual," was concerned to discover the variations possible in word choice and word order, and the effect of such variations on audiences. Style was thus largely concerned with words, sentences, and paragraphs. But in the classical period it would seem that far greater attention was paid to the other major part of rhetorical study—to the analysis of the large structural segments out of which an oration was built, and their proper disposition. The subject of this second study we have called "structural rhetoric."

The distinction between structure and style was not considered basic in the classical period because in oratory these two major parts of rhetoric are complementary. But this complementary relationship does not always hold. Textual rhetoric is quite obviously characteristic of all discourse—of poetry, drama, and fiction as well as of oratory. It is, in fact, omnipresent in human communication. But structural rhetoric is seldom usefully applied to poetry or the narrative arts.[1] It is applicable chiefly to oratory and to the modern descendants of oratory—essays, scientific articles, editorials, and so forth.

This discontinuity between structural and textual rhetoric points to a fundamental distinction in human discourse. All discourse can be roughly apportioned between two categories. Poetry, drama, and prose narrative together make up a category of discourse which can be called "imaginative." In contrast, all other forms of verbal communication can be lumped under the catchall category of "direct discourse."

In proposing such broad and' inclusive categories, one must emphasize, of course, their rough-and-ready character. It must be expected that some writers (notably modern novelists writing essays) will attempt to incorporate both forms of discourse into the same structure, and that there will be story-essays that really lie someplace between the two kinds of discourse. But this inevitable ambiguity will distress only those Platonists who think categories are prior to the objects they encompass.

Yet the distinction, however rough, is essential to the understanding of direct discourse, since these two ways of writing actually require two very different mental operations from the reader. This fact can be readily confirmed by one's own experience, if one has the patience to observe that experience. The little quatrain, "Western Wind," provides a conveniently brief illustration of the character of imaginative discourse:

> Western wind, when will thou blow?
> The small rain down can rain,—

---

[1] This is not to suggest that poetry or narrative is without structure. But the particular kind of structure that characterizes argumentation is different in aim and kind from those of imaginative literature. It is also true that a certain kind of oratory—the epideictic—can move very close to, and perhaps derives its structure from, poetic discourse. It is further true that some literary types employ an argumentative structure. One need only cite hortatory poems like Pope's *An Essay on Man* and the oratory in plays like *Julius Caesar*.

Christ, if my love were in my arms
And I in my bed again![2]

Any student whose natural perceptions have not been atrophied
by years of abstractions will agree, after a few moments of reflection, that he "understands" the poem—that he is comfortable with
it, that it has meaning for him. But if he is asked to paraphrase it,
his response will be something else again. A new kind of effort is
needed, which he may or may not be able to manage successfully.
And the reader who is aware of his own responses to the second
request will be aware of shifting mental gears, from one kind of
mental effort to another. He is being asked to move from one kind
of experience to another. Or more precisely, he is being asked to
abandon primary experience for a secondary, derivative statement
about that experience.

The understanding that is the proper response to imaginative
literature is, unfortunately, one of those root concepts that cannot
be reduced to simpler terms, and hence it is impossible to explain.
What it means can be roughly paraphrased in this fashion: when
we understand something (as literature teaches us to understand),
we perceive it as possessing some sort of internal order, and as
being somehow contiguous and relevant to our own experiential
ordering. At its best, perhaps, literature does more: it implies that
its own order is a part of some larger order that human beings can
only intuit because it remains on the periphery of their consciousness.

This understanding is only possible within the experience itself. In the very act of paraphrasing a poem or a novel, we move
outside the experience and we violate it in so doing. It is an old
cliché that a good poem is unparaphrasable. This is true, but not
because of the complexity of the poem. Adequate paraphrase is im-

---

[2] We have used the traditional punctuation and reading of the
poem. A new reading of the poem, based on a new reading of the manu-
script (Richard Griffith, *Explicator*, XXI [May 1963], 9), may well get us
closer to the unknown author's intention, but as poetry it is inferior. This
may be an example of a careless or inept editor making a good poem out
of a bad one.

possible because it is an attempt to translate one order of experience into a radically different order.

The relevance of this distinction is obvious. All argumentation is a kind of paraphrase; reader and writer both must stand outside the experience in question and attempt to characterize it. The writer may aim at a greater or lesser degree of abstraction, but in every case the mental activity, which he and the reader after him put forth, is different *in kind* from the corresponding activities demanded by imaginative literature. Furthermore, argumentative thinking is probably always a secondary process, a reduction from some sort of intuited understanding that takes place first.

The fundamental distinction, then, among kinds of discourse arises from the different positions assumed by the reader with respect to the subject matter. Imaginative discourse invites the reader, by an act of the imagination, to experience the subject for himself. Direct discourse, with which this book is concerned, is a statement about the subject matter by the writer to the reader, both of them being outside it. Their radically different structures arise from this distinction.

But a further distinction must be made within direct discourse. As a writer of direct discourse I can, if I choose, propose merely to inform the reader about my subject—the Grand Canyon, the organization of the Russian politburo, or whatever. In other words, my subject can be simply *one term*. There may be an infinite number of details, and I very probably will have some sort of judgment implicit in my discourse, but if I am asked what the piece of writing is about, I must answer merely "the Grand Canyon" or whatever. This kind of discourse is usually called *exposition*, but since this term has become ambiguous by reason of a century or so of use, it will here be called *reportorial writing*.

Traditionally, however, direct discourse did not aim at merely giving information; its object was to persuade the reader to some sort of explicit judgment. A judgment involves not one term but two, and they must be connected to each other in a way that is ultimately logical. "This man is guilty"; "The United Nations functions to reduce tensions"; "The conspiratorial character of the Communist party justifies extraordinary methods of exposure"— each of these sentences connects two terms in a specific way, and each of them might be the theme of an extended piece of direct discourse. Such discourse can usefully be called *argumentation.* Obviously it includes law briefs, learned or scientific articles, and essays as well as speeches.

The relationship between reportorial writing and argumentation is a curious one. Reportorial writing is, today at least, probably more common than argumentation, and at first sight it seems that it ought to be the simpler or more basic type. As a matter of fact, in its organization at any rate, it is clearly a derivative genre. Reportorial writing is actually a kind of pseudo-argumentation, in that the whole art of this form of discourse is to give the illusion that one's subject has the logically related parts of an argument. Accordingly, we have relegated reportorial writing to the last section of this book.

Argumentation, as has been said, has parts, some of which bear a logical relationship to each other. However, the logic of argumentation is not exactly that of the logician, and hence it will be useful to begin with a simplified consideration of how logic relates to argumentation.

Chapter I

The Means of Persuasion
in Argumentative Discourse

The essence of argumentation is the establishment of a convincing connection between two terms. In argumentative discourse, this connecting of terms takes place on two levels. On the primary level, the essay as a whole is engaged in making a judgment, in establishing a specific relationship between two terms. This basic judgment is in effect a structural element of the essay. But the writer of argumentation is also habitually engaged in making assertions, or judgments, and supporting them on the paragraph level; an essay or speech may include dozens of such specific arguments. In this chapter it will be convenient to confine ourselves to paragraph level argumentation, leaving the structural argument for the next chapter.

Simple analysis makes it apparent that there are three means available for establishing a relationship between two terms. First, we can move down from the level of abstraction at which the argument is primarily pitched toward immediate experience. For instance, we can support the abstraction "college students do so-and-so" by calling attention to the behavior of particular college students. This kind of connection is ordinarily called *induction*. Second, the relationship between two terms can be argued by juxtaposing them against two other terms of the same order of abstraction; this is argument by *analogy*. Finally, two terms can be related to each other by being related, in turn, to a third term that stands for a larger class of objects or concepts than either of the first two, and is hence of a higher order of abstraction. The result is the argumentative equivalent to the *deduction* of the logician. Of these three, the analogy, a comparatively minor method of establishing relationships, can be left to the glossary. Induction will require some discussion in this chapter, but deduction is fundamental in several respects to argumentative discourse and will require the most attention.[1]

The Syllogism in Classical Logic

As will be seen, the writer of argument uses a kind of logic substantially different from that of the logician. Nevertheless, he depends very heavily on a basic structure of the logician, the *syllogism*. This, in turn, is best understood by a somewhat simplified consideration of the logician's account.

The classical syllogism runs,

> All men are mortal.
> Socrates is a man.
> Socrates is mortal.[2]

A syllogism consists of three and only three statements. The first statement is the *major* premise, the second is the *minor* premise, and the last the *conclusion*. But the fact that there are three statements does not mean that there is a syllogism; the above

---

[1] This chapter stays fairly close to the logician's point of view, which is not to say that the following is a logician's account of logic. Over and over (see the following note for example) logical distinctions irrelevant to rhetoric have been obscured or ignored. Logical figures as techniques for changing levels of abstraction (which is perhaps the most meaningful way for the rhetorician to look at them) are considered briefly in Chapter V, pp. 120–123.

[2] A logician would describe this classical instance as a *subsumptive inference,* since the syllogism, defined rigorously, deals only with classes of objects. Such a terminological distinction is of course irrelevant to the study of rhetoric.

example is a syllogism because these three statements share three terms in a certain way.

We can most readily understand this relationship if we begin by observing that the syllogism of the logician, as represented by the above example, is a *classifying* device. The two terms of the major premise must designate *classes* of objects or whatever; the statement itself asserts that all the members of one class belong at the same time to another class. It is not necessary that the second class be larger; it may be the same size, as if we were to say, "All men are rational." It obviously cannot be smaller. The minor premise then adds the further fact that a third term, Socrates, belongs to the class of things that has already been asserted to belong to some larger (or coincident) class. This being the case, it follows that he must belong to the larger class.

These relationships are traditionally illustrated by the device of the circles, as follows:

When I say, "All men are mortal," I put the class of men into the class of mortals.

With the second statement, my minor premise, I locate Socrates within the class of men.

Simple inspection then enables me to assert that Socrates also belongs to the larger class of mortals. His position within the class of "mortals" is assured by his position within the class of "men."

Variations are possible. Propositions may be constructed with limiting terms such as "only" rather than inclusive ones such as "all" ("Only men are mortal"). But these propositions may readily be reduced to the standard form.

Syllogisms may also be constructed to support negative conclusions. The major premise in this case will assert a lack of relationship: "No human being can live without sustenance." (It should be noticed, again, that this is a class relationship.) To draw a picture of this statement, I must draw two separate circles, in this fashion:

My minor premise then need simply locate a specific individual, or a smaller class of individuals, within the first circle: "Mayflower is a human being," or, "College professors are human beings." Again, simple inspection leads to the conclusion—being in the first circle, Mayflower cannot possibly be within the second circle too. The conclusion is that "Mayflower cannot live without sustenance." It should be noted that, in a negative syllogism, it is perfectly proper to posit a class of individuals that does not, in fact, exist—"creatures who live without sustenance."

The syllogism is a form by which relationships are determined. Hence, the first question to be asked about a syllogism is not whether its conclusion is true, but rather, does it establish genuine class relationships? The first judgment about a syllogism is not whether the conclusion is *true* or *false* but whether the argument —the relationship between terms that is proposed—is valid or invalid. (Syllogistic truth will be considered later.) This validity is assured by proper form.

In the first place, there must be three, and only three, terms to be related. In practice, this means that a term must not change its meaning in the course of the argument. This difficulty is often demonstrated by the following specious argument:

> No cat has nine lives.
> One cat has one more life than no cat.
> One cat has ten lives.

The conclusion is reached here by playing with words. In the first statement, "no cat" means "not one of the class of all cats." But as the term is used in the second premise, it has to be a pseudo-proper name, a "no-cat." One cannot return to the major premise after reading the second premise and substitute "no-cat" for "no cat" (not any cat). Hence, the syllogism really contains four terms, and no conclusion can properly be drawn.

But the more important source of difficulty in logic arises from the necessity for an "all-or-none" class term at a particular place in the syllogism; in the basic form, this all-or-none term is the subject of the major premise. This is not difficult to understand if it is remembered that, in this form, this noun is the middle term. It joins the major and the minor premise because it appears in both of them, but not in the conclusion. (A rhetorician might prefer to see it as the term that is introduced to permit him to join the two terms of his conclusion.) Obviously, in one premise or another, either as subject of the major or object of the minor, it must include all of the members of the class or classes that are to be joined, or none of them. Otherwise, one could not be sure that the individual in the smaller class, which one is attempting to relate to the larger, is not in fact outside that larger class. Thus, in the first syllogism, if there are a few men who are not mortal, then I have no certain way of knowing whether Socrates is among these exceptions or not, and I cannot certainly draw any conclusion about him. In the second syllogism, if there is even one human being who can live without sustenance, then it is at least possible that that one is Mayflower.

Or, to look at it another way, if one begins with the conclusion of a syllogism (as rhetoric by and large does), one can see the syllogism as providing a linking term, a middle term, between the particular terms in which one is interested. Suppose that I wish to argue that a particular person is fascist. I have no direct evidence of membership in fascist organizations or fascist activity, and hence I can only relate the terms, "X" and "fascist," by relating them both, in an appropriate way, to a third term. I might come up with "believes in racist theories" as the term that would provide my link between the two. I might then assert:

> Those who believe in racist theories are fascists.
> X believes in racist theories.
> X is a fascist.

But this would not be a valid syllogism unless I were able to say, "All those who believe in racist theories are fascists." If some were fascists and some were not, the term would not serve my purpose, to link "X" with "fascist." If the linking term were, "Some who believe in racist theories," "X" might well belong to those who so believe but are not fascists.

What the student needs particularly to watch is that the *middle term,* the one common to the major and minor premises, be more inclusive than the subject of the conclusion and less inclusive than its object. If the above syllogism were stated, "All those who believe in racist theories are fascists, X is a fascist, and therefore X believes in racist theories," the conclusion would be invalid, because the middle term, "fascists," does not meet this criterion. The circles diagram will make this clear.

x

By locating "X" in the larger circle of fascists, I do not necessarily locate him in the smaller circle of "those who believe. . . ." On the other hand, if I were to say, "Only those who believe in racist theories are fascists," the syllogism would be valid, because the "only" would reverse the relationship of the circles.

Valid, not necessarily true. Logic is a method of establishing relationships. The relationships themselves do not tell us anything about the truth of the conclusion proposed. A syllogism is valid if its propositions are correctly related; its conclusion is true only if, in addition, its premises are true.

THE ANALYTIC SYLLOGISM AS TRUTH

However, there is still something peculiar about the analytic syllogism (or the subsumptive inference, as in the above example), although history shows that these deductive forms have been extraordinarily interesting to philosophers after truth. But what does a formal structure have to do with the nature of reality? Let us say that I have constructed a valid syllogism out of true premises: how can the formal structure guarantee the truth of the conclusion? How do I know that the relationship deduced in my conclusion actually holds in the real world? The answer must be that if the syllogism is absolutely airtight, if it is demonstrative, it must be because the conclusion is somehow implicit in the premises. When I assert that "All men are mortal," my inclusion of Socrates in the class of mortal things is already implicit. A nonsense example will clarify the difficulty. Suppose I wish to argue that Mr. Um, a kind of Schnickempu, is green. My syllogism might run:

> All Schnickempu's are green.
> Mr. Um is a Schnickempu.
> Therefore, Mr. Um is green.

This is a valid syllogism. But the trouble with it as a truth-finding device is that to establish that *"All* Schnickempu's are green," I would have had to examine all of them—including the one I am interested in, Mr. Um. But, this being the case, the syllogistically established conclusion is a study in futility. Most analytic syllogisms pretending to a demonstrative conclusion suffer from this defect.

The remainder suffer from another defect. Consider the following syllogism:

> All green objects are, in the matter of
>   color, between yellow and blue.
> This is a green object.
> Therefore, This is between blue and yellow.

Since it is a part of the definition of green that it lies between yellow and blue, to say that an object is green is to say, by that fact, that it lies between yellow and blue. Again, the syllogism simply makes explicit a relationship already present in one of the premises, and again it is of dubious value.

It is perhaps worthwhile to consider one other form of the classical syllogism. It goes as follows:

> All radicals are socialists.
> Some radicals are Boy Scouts.
> Some Boy Scouts are socialists.

We can draw the relationship proposed by the first premise in the usual way:

But the third circle, proposed by the minor premise, must be drawn differently; it must interlock with the first two.

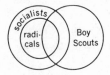

It follows, then, that the conclusion is valid, since if some Boy Scouts are radicals, they are necessarily socialists.

The "some" syllogism is surely more apt to be talking about the real, experienced world than the "all-or-none" syllogism, since most statements worth making are generalizations that permit exceptions. But the "some" syllogism does not really escape the limitations of the "all-or-none," since the major premise would have again required the inspection of all members of the class in question, "radicals" in this case, for the syllogism to be true, and this inspection would necessarily have to include the very group in question, "Boy Scouts." If it is established by inspection that some Boy Scouts are socialists, why bother with the syllogism?

THE SORITES (sòri′tez)

The sorites is a complex extension of syllogistic reasoning, in which a series of syllogisms is strung together, with the conclusion of one becoming the major premise of the next. Sometimes, however, these conclusions will be unexpressed, as in the following example:

> All bearded people are beatniks.
> All beatniks are unstable.
> All unstable people are mentally ill.

All mentally ill people are objects of sympathy.
All bearded people are objects of sympathy.[3]

The unexpressed conclusions are easy to see. The first two premises lead to a valid conclusion (because the middle term, "beat-
niks," is distributed at least once, in the minor premise), "All
bearded people are unstable." This then becomes the major premise, unexpressed, which together with the third statement, "All
unstable people are mentally ill," leads to a new conclusion, "All
bearded people are mentally ill." This conclusion is then turned
into a major premise, to which statement four is a minor and the
fifth statement is both conclusion for the last implicit syllogism and
the whole sorites.

The sorites is very important to argumentation because moving too slowly (and thus losing the reader's attention) is a very
serious crime in writing, at least as serious as moving too quickly.
The sorites permits the writer to omit obvious steps that would
slow down his argument if they were made explicit.

THE ENTHYMEME

The enthymeme is another variation on the form of the syllogism, being simply a syllogism with one premise (usually the major)
omitted. An example might be, "One's country is worthy of loyalty
because it is instrumental in bringing one up." This obviously implies some sort of prior principle, a major premise, so that the
whole syllogism, implicit in the enthymeme, would run:

Anything instrumental in bringing one up is worthy of loyalty.
One's country is instrumental in bringing one up.
One's country is worthy of loyalty.

The major premise, or missing premise, of an enthymeme is easy
to find if one remembers that a syllogism can have only three terms.
The conclusion of the enthymeme will define two of them: "One's
country" (A); "Worthy of loyalty" (B). The reason, the "because
clause" in the example, will couple one of these terms—"It" equals

[3] The examples in this chapter are of course merely illustrative; the
author makes no claim for their probability.

"A"—with a new term, "Instrumental in bringing one up" (C). Thus an enthymeme asserts that "AB because AC." The missing premise must be "BC" or "CB," suitably distributed. The terms do not have to bear this specific relation to each other, of course; the point is rather that the conclusion and given premise will necessarily include three terms, one of them used twice. The missing premise will consist of the other two terms suitably joined.

The enthymeme is far and away the most common logical figure in argumentation. Again, the reason is that it makes for brevity. Furthermore, the function of the syllogism in argumentation is to move from that which is conceded by the audience, the major premise, to that which is problematic, the conclusion. If the audience does not accept the major premise, then the argument is in vain anyway. The enthymeme simply takes that premise for granted.

The "If-Then" Syllogism.   One frequently finds, in argumentative discourse, a sentence or sentences marked by the conjunctions "if-then": "If Socrates is a man, then he is mortal." In many instances, as in the foregoing one, these "if-then" statements are actually a form of the syllogism. A syllogism, and consequently, an argument, is present in such structures when three, and only three, major terms are being related to each other, and these terms stand for larger and smaller classes of objects.

A simple example of this form of syllogism would be, "*If* all Americans have at least an eighth-grade education, *then* they are able to read a modern newspaper; *but* all Americans have at least an eighth-grade education, and *therefore* all Americans can read a modern newspaper." In this instance, the "if-then" statement is clearly a formal variant of the classical model, as can be seen when it is reduced to the circles diagram:

In classical terms the syllogism would be formulated in this fashion:

Everyone who has had an eighth-grade education can read a newspaper.
All Americans have had an eighth-grade education.
All Americans can read a newspaper.

The middle term, connecting "all Americans" and newspaper reading, is "everyone who has had an eighth-grade education," and this middle term is larger than the first and smaller than the second. The syllogism is valid.

A word of caution is necessary. Modern logicians are very interested in certain logical structures, the *hypothetical, alternative,* and *disjunctive* syllogisms and their variants. These logical structures are also signalled on many occasions by an "if-then" form. But, as they are described by logicians, they are irrelevant to argumentation. They consist of propositions, not terms, and the rules concerning the middle term are not considered applicable. What has been said above about "if-then" syllogisms does not apply to these structures, which do not ordinarily occur in discourse anyway.[4]

Conclusion.   The study of classical logic is the study of the ways in which terms can be validly related to each other; it was never, in itself, a study of how to know the truth. But the immense amount of energy devoted to the subject, and its prominent role in education until a century or so ago, suggests that expectations for that study were high—that it was to be, in fact, at least a means to truth. There is today a very general suspicion that this traditional faith in deductive logic was mistaken; if certainties are available to man, they will be achieved by some other means. But classical logic is nevertheless of extraordinary importance. We need to discuss our differences with others even if we can never establish this or that point of view as eternally true; the structure of the syllogism, with its various permutations, is a major instrument in such discussions.

[4] Perhaps the best introduction to these modern logical structures is to be found in Morris R. Cohen and Ernest Nagel, *An Introduction to Logic* (London: Routledge and Kegan Paul, 1963, and New York: Harcourt, Brace and World, Inc., 1962), pp. 96–109. It is perhaps also the most useful introduction to the subject of logic generally.

Classical logic may have been, finally, one of the great illusions of philosophy, but argumentation cannot do without it.[5]

The Syllogism in Argumentation

Syllogistic reasoning is omnipresent in argumentation, but it characteristically appears there in distorted and abbreviated forms. The abbreviation is forced on the writer of argumentation because he must live in terror of boring his audience by asserting the self-evident and therefore the trite. Sometimes the self-evident is a conclusion, as in the following passage from Lincoln's "Cooper Institute" Speech of 1860:

What is conservatism? Is it not adherence to the old and tried, against the new and untried? We stick to, contend for, the identical old policy on the point in controversy which was adopted by "our fathers who framed the government under which we live"; while you with one accord reject, and scout, and spit upon that old policy, and insist upon substituting something new.[6]

The argument, embedded in an *antithesis* (see the Glossary), is easy to see: Major premise, "Conservatism is adherence to the old"; Minor premise, "We, and not you, adhere to the old." It would be supererogatory to draw the conclusion, "We, and not you, are conservatives."

But this same kind of ellipsis is habitual even where the logical form is not obvious. At the beginning of Paine's "The American Crisis, No. 1," for instance, he exclaims:

What we obtain too cheap, we esteem too lightly; it is dearness only that gives every thing its value. Heaven knows how to put a proper price

[5] It should be pointed out that not all of the statements that appear, on simple inspection, to be syllogistic are in fact so. Apparent enthymemes are discussed in the Glossary, p. 122.

[6] Abraham Lincoln, *Speeches and Letters* (New York: E. P. Dutton, 1949), p. 149.

upon its goods; and it would be strange indeed if so celestial an article as *Freedom* should not be highly rated.[7]

The argumentative quality is not nearly as apparent here as it is in Lincoln's speech, although inspection reveals that it is an argument. The first sentence proclaims twice in different ways a major premise: "Only difficulty in achieving gives value." The second sentence is the minor premise, "Heaven has made freedom of great value." But Paine does not draw the conclusion to which these premises commit him, that "Heaven has made freedom difficult in achieving." (He goes on, instead, to argue that freedom is really at issue.) He is able to omit this conclusion because the reader who is only vaguely aware that he is being argued with will nevertheless intuit the proper conclusion.

It should be noted that it is not merely the pressure of a hostile or indifferent audience that forces the writer to be elliptical at times in his logic. Paine's essay is clearly epideictic in that it is chiefly designed to restore flagging confidence in believers rather than to win new recruits. Yet Paine, too, must foreshorten.

The passages quoted above are somewhat eccentric in that they abbreviate by omitting the conclusion of the syllogism. One of the premises is more commonly the omitted member. Furthermore, in an overwhelming number of instances, the omitted premise will be the major premise. Here, for instance, are two enthymemes proposed at the same time because they both depend in a general way on the same major premise:

The nature of man is intricate; the objects of society are of the greatest possible complexity; and therefore no simple disposition or direction of power can be suitable either to man's nature, or to the quality of his affairs.[8]

Here the implied major premise has to run, "Nothing simple can

[7] Thomas Paine, *The American Crisis* (London: James Watson, 1835), p. 3.

[8] Edmund Burke, *Reflections on the Revolution in France,* Part I, Ch. iv, Sect. 4, Library of Liberal Arts, No. 46 (Indianapolis: Bobbs-Merrill, 1955), p. 70.

be adequate to intricacy or complexity." The first two clauses quoted, then, are two minor premises and the clause after the "therefore" is the conclusion to both of them.

This particular shape of the enthymeme, from minor premise to conclusion, is not, however, the most common. The enthymeme ordinarily runs in the other direction, as in the following example:

> We left our observer confronting his task of personality analysis, intent upon finding the most economical ways of discovering the inter-relationship of traits under various environmental conditions. We left him dissatisfied with the results of observing a trait in one recurring situation, because he saw that he had no means of exposing the systemic reactions of the personality as a whole.[9]

The major premise has to be, in effect, "Anything that does not permit the exposing of systemic reactions is unsatisfactory to our observer." The minor premise is the "because clause," "Observing a trait in one recurring situation does not permit . . ." and the conclusion, "Observing a trait is unsatisfactory." In other words, the enthymeme in argumentation usually runs from conclusion to premise.

The importance of these structures is indicated by the number of words in the language functioning ordinarily to signalize them. A contemporary logician has offered the following, admittedly incomplete, lists of such terms:

Premise-Conclusion	*Conclusion-Premise*
therefore	since
which shows that	for
proves that	because
hence	for the reason that
thus	in view of the fact that
so	on the correct supposition that
indicates that	assuming, as we may, that
consequently	may be inferred from the fact

[9] Harold D. Lasswell, "Person, Personality, Group, Culture," *A Study of Interpersonal Relations,* ed. Patrick Mullahy (New York: Grove Press, 1949), p. 329.

Premise-Conclusion	*Conclusion-Premise*
you see that	may be deduced from
implies that	as shown by
entails	as indicated by
allows us to infer that	as is substantiated by
I conclude that	
we may deduce that	
points to the conclusion that	
suggests very strongly that	
leads me to believe that	
bears out my point that	
from which it follows that[10]	

One also finds, not infrequently, the "if-then" syllogism in argumentation. Woodrow Wilson argued, in defense of the League of Nations:

> If Germany had known—this is the common verdict of every man familiar with the politics of Europe—if Germany had known that England would go in, she never would have started it. If she had known that America would come in, she never would have dreamed of it. And now the only way to make certain that there will never be another world war like this is that we should assist in guaranteeing the peace and its settlement.[11]

The bones of logic, the premises and conclusion, are apparent here, but one should note how very far the passage is from its implicit syllogism. At first glance, the best way to set up the major premise would appear to be as follows: "Only if Germany thought England would not go to war would Germany go to war," and similarly with the statement about America. This would establish the basis for a valid syllogism. But the explicit conclusion of the last sentence enormously extends the generality of the syllogism it presumably follows from, and reverses it, so that the syllogism's implicit major premise would have to be, "All the major powers must commit

[10] Monroe C. Beardsley, *Thinking Straight: Principles of Reasoning for Readers and Writers* (Englewood Cliffs, N. J.: Prentice-Hall, 1950), pp. 15–16.

[11] "For the League of Nations," *Famous Speeches in American History,* ed. Glenn R. Capp (Indianapolis: Bobbs-Merrill, 1963), p. 181.

themselves to repel aggression if there is to be peace." The minor premise, "The United States is a great power," would then lead, approximately, to the conclusion urged.

In other words, the argumentative syllogism is very apt to extend itself in ways not visualized by the logician. This characteristic will be discussed shortly, but here it might be pointed out that this extension does not necessarily invalidate argumentation. Most readers with the advantage of hindsight, for instance, would probably agree that Wilson's argument was a very good one indeed.

The sorites (described on p. 31) is habitually included in discussions of logical forms, but it is, in practice, an argumentative figure and not a logical one. The argumentative sorites, however, almost always appears in a form that only a logician could unscramble with confidence. Here is a comparatively simple example, by James Madison, drawn from the *Federalist Papers:*

No man is allowed to be a judge in his own cause, because his interest would certainly bias his judgment, and, not improbably, corrupt his integrity. With equal, nay with greater reason, a body of men are unfit to be both judges and parties at the same time; yet what are many of the most important acts of legislation, but so many judicial determinations, not indeed concerning the rights of single citizens, but concerning the rights of large bodies of citizens? And what are the different classes of legislators but advocates and parties to the causes which they determine? Is a law proposed concerning private debts? It is a question to which the creditors are parties on one side and the debtors on the other.[12]

One can begin the unscrambling with the following analysis:

Conclusion: No man is allowed to be a judge in his own cause.
Minor premise: To be judge in one's own cause leads to bias and corruption.
Major premise (implicit): No man is allowed to be biased and corrupt.

---

[12] *Selections from the Federalist,* ed. Henry S. Commager (New York: Crofts Classics, 1949), p. 11.

Such, at any rate, is the gist of it. If, then, we take the conclusion proposed above as a new major premise, we can add as minor premise, "A group of men is not allowed what is not allowed a single man," with the obvious conclusion following, "No group of men is allowed to be a judge in their own cause." This, in turn, becomes a major premise with the new minor added, "Important acts of legislation are judgments." It follows (again, roughly) that "No group of men is allowed to make important acts of legislation." But Madison isn't through yet. Given the conclusion thus arrived at as a new major premise, he has a new minor ready, "Classes of legislators are groups of citizens" (in effect), and so on.

This seems unfairly complicated, but actually it is not. The human mind, paying attention to what is going on, is able to make these connections with relative ease. As a matter of fact, the sorites is perhaps more common in ordinary discourse than it is in argumentation. When a mother, confronted by a dirty child, exclaims, "Elizabeth, you are going to be the death of me," she enunciates a sorites that they both follow with ease. It would go something like this:

Major: All careless things lead to dirty dresses.
Minor: Elizabeth is a careless thing.
Conclusion: Elizabeth leads to dirty dresses.

Major: All things leading to dirty dresses increase labor.
Minor: (Conclusion of previous syllogism.)
Conclusion: Elizabeth increases labor.

Major: All things that increase labor shorten life.
Minor: (Conclusion of previous syllogism.)
Conclusion: "Elizabeth, you are going to be the death of me."

Perhaps the simplest way to understand a sorites such as the above is to think of it as connecting two terms, the demise of the mother and the peculiar character of the child, by a chain of intermediate terms—dirty dresses, carelessness, increased labor.

THE CHARACTER OF THE ARGUMENTATIVE SYLLOGISM

Several characteristics which distinguish the argumentative syllogism from the logical form are by now apparent. In the first place, argumentative syllogisms are habitually distorted and ab-breviated. They are distorted because they must be adjusted to meet larger structural requirements; they are abbreviated because the skilled writer always tries to avoid losing the interest of his audience, and the self-evident is by definition dull. But behind both of these necessities is a larger one: the necessity for movement. The reader of an argument expects to get somewhere, and he ex-pects every paragraph, even every sentence, to be a part of his prog-ress to that somewhere. Any time he senses the failure of momen-tum toward some meaningful conclusion his attention flags. The writer's arguments, such as those quoted above, must be manipu-lated to preserve the sense of momentum.

For the same reason, the necessity for movement, most argu-ments are cluttered up (from the logician's point of view) by ma-terials not strictly relevant to the syllogistic structure—by defini-tions, by evidence, by distinctions. Here is a typical passage—this one concerning the First World War:

It would all have been quite simple had there been some solid rea-son for the war, had Austria bluntly demanded a Protectorate in Serbia, or Germany claimed some concrete prerogative, some strongpoint or slice of territory either in Europe or abroad. (As France did, as soon as war broke out, with her demand for the return of Alsace-Lorraine; as Russia did with her claim to the Straits.) Such demands would have been a mat-ter of dispute but also and therefore a matter for discussion. The dis-cussion might have failed initially, and war have broken out, but it could always have been resumed once it was established whether or not the demands could be satisfied by military action. But there was absolutely no definable area of disagreement and therefore no problems to be solved, the solution of which would mean peace.[13]

The syllogism behind this passage is sufficiently transparent; it would go something like this:

Major premise: Only defined objectives permit of negotiation.
Minor premise: The Central Powers did not have defined ob-jectives.
Conclusion: The Central Powers could not negotiate.

[13] Herbert Luethy, "The Folly and the Crime," *Encounter,* March 1965, pp. 17–18.

But the passage quoted does much more than present this simple structure.

The passage begins with the minor premise, but it is asserted in its obverse, "had the Central Powers had defined objectives." The validity of this premise is urged by the parenthesis which points out that others involved did define their objectives. The third sentence ("Such demands . . .") is perhaps best described as a kind of definition of the word "negotiation" as something presuming dispute as a subject of discussion. The fourth sentence introduces a qualification ("defined objects do not prevent war") but it also asserts the contrary of the conclusion of the syllogism. The last sentence is a more-or-less straightforward assertion of that conclusion.[14]

All of this complexity results, again, from the pressing necessity for movement. Without this necessity, it might have been more orderly to have begun the argument by a careful definition of terms, to have specified the evidence for their statements, and finally to have presented in a severely syllogistic form the relationship of those statements. But by the time the writer reached his syllogism, the reader would have been long gone.

One further important characteristic of argumentative logic must be pointed out, and the above passage will serve nicely to illustrate it. That characteristic concerns the objective of argumentation. What does the writer mean by his implied major premise, "Only defined objectives permit of negotiation"? Is it to be read as a logician's statement, as a high-level generalization permitting of no exceptions? Surely not. In the context of argumentation, the author does not mean to claim universality. It is a probability statement. And so with the other statements in the passage.[15]

The point is that the whole convention of argumentation presumes that the proper object of discourse is probability. This is very important for the reader of essays and speeches to remember.

---

[14] The student will perhaps have noticed that the overall structure of the passage is "if-then-but-therefore"—a variation of the syllogism discussed earlier.

[15] Classical rhetoricians invented a name for the syllogism accompanied by proof; they called it an *epichireme*. But the distinction between a plain, ordinary syllogism and an *epichireme* yields no insight and therefore seems hardly worth drawing.

There is no essay or speech that cannot be overthrown by a determined searcher looking for exceptions to the statements made. Lincoln's "Gettysburg Address" could be ripped apart by a student with no more logic than has been presented in this chapter. The tradition of argumentation presumes the existence of readers and listeners who are willing to accept probability as a law of life, and who are willing to give conditional assent to probable statements if they indeed seem probable.

This does not, on the other hand, mean that the syllogism and its variants are simply structural principles to be used or abused at the writer's pleasure, that there cannot be bad arguments. The statements that a writer of argumentation makes can be only probably true—they are generalizations that permit exceptions. But his terms must hold still for him and not change their meanings, he must distribute his middle terms as well as probability permits, and he must draw genuine relationships from his form. The matter of failures in argumentation will be considered at length in Chapter VII, but it is important here to recognize that the lack of certainty, by logical standards, implicit in argumentation does not mean that argumentation cannot be seriously defective in its own terms. Most of it, as a matter of fact, is defective. One of the substantial advantages of an elementary knowledge of the syllogism is that it permits a conscious evaluation of the degree of concession that a writer deserves.

Inductive Logic in Argumentation

The term *induction,* or *inductive logic,* refers to a strategy that is easy enough to understand (although the strategy involves thorny philosophical problems). An inductive statement asserts that a particular connection exists between two terms on the basis of observation of some sort. I could perhaps argue the truth of the statement, "All dogs are flea-bearing organisms," by finding some middle term to join fleas to dogs, but the simpler procedure would be a direct examination of dogs. This would be an *inductive* procedure.

It should be noted that, again, we are concerned with class terms. "All dogs have fleas" is a statement to be verified by induction. But the term would probably not be applied to a statement such as, "Jane has fleas."

Even so briefly stated, it is obvious that induction is at least as troublesome to the logician as deduction. How can I *induce* the fact that "All dogs have fleas" unless I have examined all dogs—all dogs whatsoever? And if I should engage in that troublesome enterprise, how can I be sure that a dog will not be born tomorrow without fleas?

In the above example, the problem seems trivial, but exactly the same considerations, the unobserved examples and possible future deviations, must apply to scientific conclusions, which are manifestly inductive also. "All instances of iron are drawn by magnets" is open to exactly the same reservations as the statement about dogs and fleas. There is always the possibility, even if it is a highly improbable possibility, that *some* instance of iron, now or at some time in the future, will unaccountably resist the blandishments of the magnet. Hence even that most scientific of philosophers, Rudolph Carnap, concedes that the statements of science are merely (what denigration!) probable statements. With such problems do logicians concern themselves.

The writer of argumentation avoids the disappointments that have come upon the logician by reducing his initial demands upon discourse and life itself. He expects induction to lead to certain conclusions no more than he expects deductive logic to do so. It is a method of persuasion that may win assent but never compel it.

But induction in argumentation is not merely a softer and less rigorous variety of logical induction; ordinarily the basic assumption it makes is quite different. Logical induction makes its generalizations probable (at least theoretically) by pointing to objects: A_1 is X, A_2 is X, A_3 is X . . . and therefore A is X. Argumentative induction does not really work in this fashion at all. A few examples will show how it does work. In the first, William James is arguing against the Associationist theory, which equates good with pleasure and pain:

The more minutely psychology studies human nature, the more clearly it finds there traces of secondary affections, relating the impressions of the environment with one another and with our impulses in quite different ways from those mere associations of coexistence and succession which are practically all that pure empiricism can admit. Take the love of drunkenness; take bashfulness, the terror of high places, the tendency to seasickness, to faint at the sight of blood, the susceptibility to musical sounds; take the emotion of the comical, the passion for poetry, for mathematics, or for metaphysics—no one of these things can be wholly explained by either association or utility. They *go with* other things that can be so explained, no doubt; and some of them are prophetic of future utilities, since there is nothing in us for which some use may not be found. But their origin is in incidental complications to our cerebral structure. . . .[16]

The second passage is from Lincoln's First Inaugural Address, in which his primary aim was to reassure the southern states:

Apprehension seems to exist among the people of the Southern States that by the accession of a Republican administration their property and their peace and personal security are to be endangered. There has never been any reasonable cause for such apprehension. Indeed, the most ample evidence to the contrary has all the while existed and been open to their inspection. It is found in nearly all the published speeches of him who now addresses you. I do but quote from one of those speeches when I declare that "I have no purpose, directly or indirectly, to interfere with the institution of slavery in the States where it exists. I believe I have no lawful right to do so, and I have no inclination to do so." Those who nominated and elected me did so with full knowledge that I had made this and many similar declarations, and had never recanted them. And, more than this, they placed in the platform for my acceptance, and as a law to themselves and to me, the clear and emphatic resolution which I now read. . . .[17]

The third is from a defense of the humanities by Howard Mumford Jones:

Every profession claims the right to be judged by something better than its failures; and men of learning, in assessing their contribution to the general welfare, claim only the same right they cheerfully accord to

---

[16] "The Moral Philosopher and the Moral Life," *Essays in Pragmatism* (New York: Hafner, 1948), p. 67.

[17] *Speeches and Letters* (New York: E. P. Dutton, 1949), p. 165.

religion, medicine, science, and the social sciences. There was only one Greek genius named Socrates, and Athens put him to death, but we continue to judge Athens not by the jury that condemned the philosopher but by the philosopher who died in obedience to the laws of his countrymen.[18]

The one thing these passages have in common is that they make no attempt to marshal evidence in the fashion that logicians' accounts of induction presuppose. The most formal of the three, that by Lincoln, states the fact he would deal with, the apprehension of the South, denies it, and then supports his point by an example drawn from one of his speeches, by the presumed acquiescence of his party, and finally by a plank from his party's platform. It is as though he makes his point by drawing one example each from three possible categories of examples. William James must work harder to make his point; he piles up a long list of exceptional situations to refute associationist theory. But again there is nothing to suggest that the list pretends to be exhaustive, and the very miscellaneous character of his examples (a matter of deliberation at some level) actually works against any sense of an orderly marshaling of all the evidence. But the last example of induction is most peculiar of all—an important point supported by one single reference.

The fact is, in none of these examples does the author even pretend to tabulate objects in themselves. Argumentative induction is, in its essence, an appeal to the experience of the reader. The writer of argumentation does not use induction declaratively, to establish once and for all a generalization about the world of things; for him it always carries an interrogative note: "Isn't it your experience that . . . ?" He may use one example, or three, or twenty, but they are habitually directed, not to the world of things, but to the reader's experience of that world.

Of course, argumentative induction does not invariably bear this character; a speaker or writer may use statistics or appeal to specific facts in a way that makes it apparent that they aim at a kind of logical proof. It perhaps seems perverse to suggest that apparently demonstrative induction needs to be watched even more closely than experiential induction, but this is the case. Argumentation bears a peculiar relationship to fact. Demonstrative induction is usually confined to questions of existence: there were so many people who did such and such in 1947, so many submarines were sunk in World War I, and so forth. But the major problem that a writer of argumentation faces is not the establishment of the existence of this or that, but the establishment of connections. The use of demonstrative induction can easily confuse this problem; a lot of evidence establishing the existence of something can lead the reader to overlook the fact that the important matter of the relation of that existence to something else may only have been asserted, not shown. Because data these days seem to carry in themselves a powerful persuasiveness for us, sometimes we are contented with a mere catalog, if long enough, when no less than a sound argument should have satisfied us.

Conclusion

The student of rhetoric needs to know the basic structures of the logician, but it is equally important that he not mistake their function. Argument, from beginning to end, is necessarily directed to persuasion because its subject matter prohibits definitive certainties. The logical structures that this form of discourse uses do not transcend in this respect the discourse itself; both are limited to probabilities.

This consideration does not mean that these structures require less attention of the reader. All arguments, deductive or inductive, are not equally good; a great many do not deserve our assent, even our qualified assent. Furthermore, a great many deductive structures in argumentation are pseudo-structures; they do not actually make the connections between terms. These pseudo-structures will require our attention later, but the student needs to be reminded of their existence at this point.

At this time, we should perhaps mention that what the argumentative essay accomplishes (and very often it is doubtful that it accomplishes anything substantial at all) probably depends less on its logical structures than its success in presenting a point of view. But this consideration, too, must be postponed, because it is necessary, first, to see the overall structure within which the writer of argumentation organizes his materials, including his logical ones.

Chapter II

The Parts
of an Argument

In the introduction to Part I, it was pointed out that argumentation is a form of direct discourse, and the mark of direct discourse is that both reader and writer stand outside the subject to be considered. Many of the problems characteristic of argumentation arise from this position with respect to subject matter. The first problem to be considered is structural; an argumentative essay always consists of discrete parts that the writer can never wholly get into satisfactory adjustment to each other.

All writers, of course, have structural problems. No matter what their form of discourse, they must select and arrange. But the writer of poetry or fiction or drama—i.e., of imaginative discourse —always has the experience itself as his criterion of successful structure, and the materials that present themselves to him for selection are coordinate in their relationship to that experience. This coordination with reference to the particular experience is, in fact, what is meant by organic structure.[1]

[1] A consideration of the organic form of poetry from a rhetorical point of view would perhaps shed some light on this common literary conception, which is at present very vague. Perhaps it will suffice here to point out that a poem is organic when it creates a single whole impression for the reader, however many parts making up that whole can be distinguished by analysis. The writer of argumentation cannot even aim

There is no possibility of constructing an argument organically, since judgment, not experience, is its objective. This judgment is built up of different kinds of mental operations that cannot, in sum, be coordinate. The writer must set up his own position while, very often, refuting another. He must often use induction to support a deductive structure. He must habitually limit and direct the conclusion the reader is to draw. These different mental activities must be formed, somehow, into a coherent argument, but regardless of the skill of the writer they remain discrete parts quite unlike the elements into which a story or poem can be analyzed.

Cicero, like other classical rhetoricians, recognized these different parts of an argument, and he proposed a six-element classification of them:[2]

1. The *exordium,* the introductory section in which the speaker got the auditors into the proper frame of mind.
2. The *narratio,* which presented the relevant information—in a legal speech, the facts of the particular case relevant to the issue.
3. The *partitio,* a technical section of a speech which attempted to divide up the facts into those which were agreed upon and those at issue. The *partitio* also made explicit the orator's subsequent organization.
4. The *confirmatio* or proof, which laid out the central argument or arguments.
5. The *reprehensio,* which was the rebuttal of the opponent's arguments.
6. The *peroration,* or conclusion, which summed up the case and appealed to the audience's sympathies if possible.

These terms remain useful ones. In addition, one classical rhetorical figure is best regarded as a part of the oration's structure:

7. The *prolepsis (praesumptio),* in which the line of discourse is interrupted to answer objections that might be raised.

---

at a single impression. The form itself requires of him tasks that have no logical or inevitable connection with each other, and that, as a consequence, will never fuse into a whole for him.

[2] *De Inventione* I. xiv. 19 ff.

Some of these things every modern essay must do, and it may do all of them. Articles in social science journals, particularly, are apt to perform all six traditional functions separately and close to the order outlined by Cicero. But other modern forms of argument tend to conflate. The *partitio,* when it is preserved at all, will almost invariably be found as a part of the *exordium.* And the *confirmatio* or proof has become the central section of the essay; the *narratio, reprehensio,* and *prolepsis* are often or usually mere interruptions in the movement of the *confirmatio.* It seems desirable, then, to regard the classical analysis of the oration as a specification of the functions that an essay or speech may have to perform, within the simple division into introduction, argument, and conclusion.

The Exordium or Introduction

As every writer knows, the beginning is the hardest part of any argument to write. This is because it must do so many things at one time. However, all of them can be subsumed under two major necessities: the writer in his introduction must define himself and he must define his problem.

The requirement that the writer define himself is peculiar to argumentation, although it arises, as do the structural problems implicit in the direct form of discourse, from the fact that the writer of argumentation always stands, with the reader, outside the subject under consideration. In poetry or fiction, we must not be aware of the poet as something separate from his poem. It is, of course, the poet's or the novelist's experience that is the subject of imaginative literature, but it is the writer's job to make us experience it for ourselves.[3]

[3] This is not to say that the poet and his reader are wholly inside the poem. In fact it might be argued that both have to be inside and outside at the same time. That is, the poem, in giving the quality of an experience, does two things at once: first, it "lives" the reader through the experience as a participant. Second, it orders the experience in such a way that the reader can see its wholeness, as from the outside. Thus the reader of poetry is ideally situated for comprehending an experience

The writer of argumentation stands in a different relationship to his material from the writer of imaginative literature. He has stepped outside it to talk about it. He is a presence, and he must be defined. As a consequence, the prose-writer in the twentieth century has exactly the same problem as did the orator in fifth-century Athens; he must set himself up for his audience. It is a little embarrassing to read Aristotle's lengthy discussion, at the beginning of Book II of the *Rhetoric*, about the kind of character the orator must create for himself. We believe that people should be, not seem. Nevertheless, the writer of argumentation must establish a kind of presence at the beginning of an argument—himself or an idealized version of himself.[4]

He must do so if for no other reason than to establish credentials that will guarantee that his arguments will fall into the range of what is acceptable to his audience. When, as in *The Apology*, Socrates refuses to make any emotional appeal, he is not just asserting that his case must stand or fall on good logic. He is also trying to persuade his audience to accept his unusual and exalted conditions for judging the validity of arguments. Most writers and speakers, however, take a more comfortable position, one that is easily shared by the audience, for the contract that demands the least of the latter tends to be the most appealing. Thus the popularity of

---

without losing its immediacy. In our normal lives, to experience immediately means we gain intensity, at the cost of comprehension of the whole of any experience; whereas to comprehend that whole means we must sacrifice intensity and directness. Poetic form aims at giving both immediacy and comprehension at the same time. It is worth noting, however, that in the wide spectrum of poetic discourse, certain poets, like Pope, prefer comprehension to immediacy; others, like Rimbaud, immediacy to comprehension. It follows that the former approaches closer to formal argumentative discourse and the latter toward a highly personal one—telescoped, fragmented, and intentionally mixed. Most poets fall somewhere between these extremes.

[4] This requirement lessens, of course, as the relationship between readers and writer can be presumed to become more intimate. Lionel Trilling or Cleanth Brooks writing for a journal of literary criticism might introduce themselves in a very minimal fashion. The necessity for an ethos is also diminished by the degree of urgency of the argument. Woodrow Wilson, proposing a declaration of war to the United States Congress, practically dispensed with the introduction of himself.

the opening joke in the contemporary speech, which, though it seldom has anything to do with what follows, is a way of telling the audience to relax because they are in the presence of a good-humored speaker who, no matter how serious later, is basically amiable and not about to make excessive demands on their attention or to ask them to follow him into some extreme view. Yet whatever position is taken, whatever ethos the speaker or writer attempts to create, it must be established before a sympathetic response can be hoped for. Of course, the difficulty in establishing an effective ethos is in proportion to the already-existing relationship between speaker or writer and audience. A famous figure before an already sympathetic audience need not work very hard. Mr. Truman, in the presidential campaign of 1948, was frequently greeted at railroad stops with "Give 'em Hell, Harry!" The ethos in this instance was already firmly established. Before a hostile or indifferent audience, the candidate would have to work much harder, and perhaps even alter the ethos that is characteristically attached to his name. In any case, the necessity of establishing an ethos is always present in the rhetorical situation, though each situation, because it is in some sense novel, calls for a different approach.

There are various possible responses to this necessity. Perhaps the most common response is to establish oneself in relationship to a coterie. For example:

Stimulus generalization (SG) is an empirical phenomenon which has, of late, been seeing heavy duty as an explanatory construct in many disparate situations. It has been used in theoretical explanations of discrimination learning (Spence, 1936) of transposition (Spence, 1937), verbal learning (Gibson, 1940), psychoanalytic displacement (Miller, 1948), the behavior of brain-damaged individuals and schizophrenics (Mednick, 1955, 1958a).[5]

This type of introductory paragraph is characteristic of scholarly journals also: "X is important, as A has pointed out, and B; how-

[5] Sarnoff A. Mednick and Jonathan L. Freedman, "Stimulus Generalization," *The Psychological Bulletin,* LVII (1960), 169; reprinted in *Contemporary Research in Learning,* ed. John R. Braun (New York: D. Van Nostrand, 1963), p. 69.

ever C has said. . . ." Such catalogs of authorities do not offer any usable information, nor do they have any value as bibliographies (even if an opening paragraph were not a funny place for a bibliography). The paragraph quoted above is perhaps an exception, but such lists habitually include old chestnuts which no one has read for years. The real function of these introductory lists of authorities is to establish the writer as someone inside the particular coterie for which he writes. Consequently, he is a trustworthy person. He not only knows the amenities, but is willing to abide by them. In short, these catalogs do what Aristotle says must be done at the beginning of an oration (or an argument); they establish an ethos.

But the ethos established by formula is very restrictive; once the writer has established himself solely by a relationship to a coterie, or assumed the character imposed on him by a public role (as in preaching), his freedom of movement is sharply restricted. Hence even in such formulas one sometimes sees an impulse to establish something more. In the above passage, for instance, the informal cliché, "seeing heavy duty" (really a worn-out *abusio;* see the Glossary), reflects an impulse on the part of the writers to loosen up the formula by admitting the accents of ordinary speech.

Essays are in general free of formulas for ethos and hence the writer is able to establish himself for the reader with much greater latitude. Here are two brief introductions illustrating the range of stances that a writer can adopt. The first is from Ayn Rand's *For the New Intellectual:*

> When a man, a business corporation or an entire society is approaching bankruptcy, there are two courses that those involved can follow: they can evade the reality of their situation and act on a frantic, blind, rage-of-the-moment expediency—not daring to look ahead, wishing no one would name the truth, yet desperately hoping that something will save them somehow—or they can identify the situation, check their premises, discover their hidden assets and start rebuilding.
>
> America, at present, is following the first course. The grayness, the stale cynicism, the noncommittal cautiousness, the guilty evasiveness of our public voices suggest the attitude of the courtiers in the story "The Emperor's New Clothes" who professed admiration for the Emperor's non-existent garments, having accepted the assertion that anyone who failed to perceive them was morally depraved at heart.

Let me be the child in the story and declare that the Emperor is naked—or that America is culturally bankrupt.[6]

The second passage opens Adlai Stevenson's first Harvard Lecture, published as *Call to Greatness:*

Great movements and forces, springing from deep wells, have converged at this mid-century point, and I suspect we have barely begun to comprehend what has happened and why. In the foreground is the mortal contest with world communism, which is apparent, if the means of dealing with it are not always apparent. But in the background are the opaque, moving forms and shadows of a world revolution, of which communism is more the scavenger than the inspiration; a world in transition from an age with which we are familiar to an age shrouded in mist. We Americans have to deal with both the foreground and the background of this troubled, anxious age.

It is easy to state our ends, our goals, but it is hard to fit them to our means. Every day, for example, politicians, of which there are plenty, swear eternal devotion to the ends of peace and security. They always remind me of the elder Holmes' apostrophe to a katydid: "Thou say'st an undisputed thing in such a solemn way." And every day statesmen, of which there are a few, must struggle with limited means to achieve these unlimited ends, both in fact and in understanding. For the nation's purposes always exceed its means, and it is finding a balance between means and ends that is the heart of foreign policy and that makes it such a speculative, uncertain business.[7]

To set himself up for an audience a writer must establish three things, as the passages quoted above clearly show. First, he must establish some sort of relationship with his audience. Second, he must establish an attitude toward his subject. And third, he must establish some sense of himself—of the kind of person that he is, or that he chooses to be thought. These objectives can be accomplished simultaneously, of course.

The above passages represent radically different answers to

[6] Ayn Rand, *For the New Intellectual* (New York: New American Library, 1963), p. 10.
[7] Adlai E. Stevenson, *Call to Greatness* (New York: Atheneum, 1962), pp. 1–2.

these three problems, especially interesting because they show how the problems are coordinate. The answer to any one implies the answer to the other two. Nor is it usually possible to see one element as more critical than the others.

The most striking feature of the introduction by Miss Rand is the relationship to audience that it proposes; it is the relationship of the prophet to those requiring enlightenment. But this in turn is perhaps merely a function of her attitude toward her subject. If the modern choice is a clear one between blind expediency and the recognition of a fairly simple problem, then it is difficult to see what Miss Rand could do but proclaim the self-evident choice. But to proclaim a self-evident course where no one in his right mind could possibly choose the second course, is automatically to assume the mantle of a prophet.

By these responses to the first two necessities, Miss Rand obviously fulfills the third; she defines the kind of person she is, at least for the purposes of this particular book. The reader's impression is confirmed by the nature of the analogy used and by the unreservedly declarative tone of the passage.

There is an ethos problem in the writing of any book whatsoever. To write for the perusal of others, or to address them publicly, is to presume some sort of expertness. But this is an uncomfortable presumption, particularly in the twentieth century, and it can easily alienate large segments of one's audience, particularly those who feel they know almost as much as the writer does. (It is easy to see why Miss Rand's call is for new intellectuals; the old ones ordinarily lack confidence in prophets.) The late Ambassador Stevenson avoids this hazard by two means. In the first place, he disclaims the role of expert by insisting on the complexity of the problem, that neither he nor anyone else has a clear-cut solution. At the same time, he establishes a kind of claim to speak and not merely listen—few people quote the elder Holmes, even for purposes of humor. In the second place, he establishes a dialogue-like relationship with his audience: "We Americans," and not merely the readers, have a problem. In assuming this relationship with his audience, of course, he accomplishes the second objective of an introduction: he establishes the approach he will take to his subject —tentative, exploratory, suggestive.

But Mr. Stevenson in the above passage has also defined himself. The reader knows, by Mr. Stevenson's insistence on the complexity of the problem, that he is sensitive and thoughtful; by his relationship to his audience, that he is unpretentious; by the colloquial quality of his language, that he insists upon being a man and not an official; by his implied rejection of the role of politician, that he is candid.

These two passages do not exhaust the possibilities open to the writer of argumentation; they represent, rather, extreme positions. Few writers would care to assume the mantle of prophet so forthrightly as does Miss Rand. At the same time, there have been few major figures in modern politics so obviously pained by his public role as the late Ambassador Stevenson. Both postures, all postures, have advantages and limitations. Miss Rand absolutely destroys, by the first page of her book, the possibility of communicating with those who are unwilling to concede a kind of authority to her, although her popularity suggests that a great many people are looking for the authority of a prophet. Mr. Stevenson's diffidence was surely responsible, in part, for the fanatical enthusiasm he commanded among intellectuals, but it was perhaps responsible, also, for his failure to win the presidency. Different audiences read the postures that one must take in different ways.

But some sort of posture there must be, except in very unusual situations.[8] Consequently, all of these introductions, every introduction, will be rhetorical in the fullest sense of the word because introductions necessarily attempt to create persuasive relationships. The introduction by Miss Rand might appear to have avoided this rhetorical function by ignoring the audience, but this only creates a particular kind of persuasive relationship.

Writers must set themselves up for their audiences in the exordia of their essays, but they must do more: they must set up the subject or problem with which they propose to deal. Certain writers (A. N. Whitehead is an example) often choose to proclaim baldly their thesis at the end of the exordium.[9] This approach has the merit of simplicity, but it also has severe disadvantages. In the first place, it sacrifices suspense. The reader who does not know where an argument is going, quite, is more likely to stay with the

[8] See note 4, p. 52.
[9] See A. N. Whitehead, *The Aims of Education* (New York: Mentor Books, 1953), p. 14.

writer until he has said what he wants to. Worse, the thesis in the
exordium sets up discontinuities. As will be seen in the next section, the body of an argument will ordinarily contain at least one
step-by-step progression to the conclusion—the thesis. To proclaim
this thesis also at the beginning puts the writer at the wrong end
of the progression, and some scrambling is usually necessary to get
back to the beginning again. Thus there are good reasons, aside
from modern convention, for raising the issue in the exordium,
rather than stating a conclusion.[10]

The three introductions quoted above represent three very
common ways of setting up the problem of a particular discourse.
The Mednick-Jonathan introduction is actually, and obviously, the
beginning of a *praeteritio* (see the Glossary) as well as evidence of
status. Inevitably, as it reviews studies already done, it moves to the
one that has not been done—the subject of the article. It thus defines the subject of the paper by setting up, and implicitly rejecting,
other possibilities.

The *praeteritio* is not particularly effective in introducing an
argument, since it closes off possibilities before the issue is properly
defined and therefore reduces the problem to its minimal scope
without necessarily giving it precision. Furthermore, it does not do
much to generate interest. Its implicit argument is that such and
such ought to be done because it has not been done. This is not a
particularly exhilarating prospect for the potential reader. The
usefulness of this strategy is simply that it is always available. The
essayist, or speech writer, can always construct an introduction to
the essay that he did write out of the notes he collected for ones he
did not.

Miss Rand's introduction might be called dramatic, in that its
function is chiefly to dramatize what is to follow, to insist, as force-
fully as possible, that there is a problem without specifying what
it is to any great degree. As with the *praeteritio,* there is the danger
in this approach that the reader will not be given enough information to hold his attention, and it is also possible with a dramatic
introduction that he will resent deliberate mystification.

---

[10] The student who allows his thesis to get into his exordium will
almost invariably be led to illustrate, rather than argue, the point he
wishes to make.

Mr. Stevenson's introduction is built on a very traditional figure, the *structural distributio* (see the Glossary). The *structural distributio* can work in one of two ways. Ordinarily it is used to refute the argument of an opponent without seeming to attack the particular virtue he has chosen to defend. (The Glossary has an example of this kind of *distributio*.) But it can also be used, as here, to insist on some sort of redefinition of interest. Stevenson delivered this series of lectures in 1954, at the height of the McCarthy era. Many were convinced at this time that communism constituted an immediate problem of overwhelming importance. In his introduction, Stevenson had to make the necessary concessions to this widespread feeling at the same time that he insisted discreetly on the superior significance and interest of more fundamental problems. (These were to be, of course, the subject of his essay.) He met this necessity by distributing current problems between the immediate but superficial challenge of communism and the deeper issues raised by modern history.

We have illustrated, then, three possible solutions to the problem of introducing one's subject: the *praeteritio,* the *structural distributio,* and the dramatized problem. These solutions, of course, do not exhaust the resources available to the writer. The essays considered in subsequent chapters illustrate two further possibilities, the "they say, but . . ." introduction, setting up a point of view in opposition to which one's own can be developed, and the use of a *narratio* to define a problem. The formal devices are probably helpful to the writer, but no device is indispensable. The important thing is that a problem be set up. It is the reader's curiosity about the problem that sustains him in the reading of the essay. Moreover, the writer by defining his problem initially lays down clear guidelines that direct his own further moves toward a conclusion. For both the reader and the writer a sense of inevitability in moving from problem to solution is all-important.

The Body of the Essay

Underlying the basic structure of an essay (or speech) is an agreement between writer and reader so universally taken for granted that neither may be aware of it. This agreement is that the essay *move*. An essayist proposes, in his exordium, a problem (rarely a thesis). The reader, it must be assumed, reads the balance of the essay because he is interested in the resolution of that problem. The writer's task is to so connect the parts of the body of the essay that the reader feels himself always advancing toward the resolution in which he is interested.

Discourse moves insofar as the reader perceives some kind of sequential, additive connection between its parts. Imaginative literature may depend on one or more of a variety of connections—chronological, spatial, free association, and so forth. Chronological or spatial connections may be used in argumentation occasionally. But, because the essay will be aimed ultimately at a judgment of some sort, and this judgment will necessarily be an abstract statement, the essential structure of an essay, the elements upon which the sense of movement primarily depends, will be logical. In other words, it is the *confirmatio* which must function as the backbone of an argumentative essay or speech.

CONFIRMATIO

An argumentative speech or essay bears that character because it is designed to persuade listeners or readers to assent to a particular proposition, the *argument* of that particular speech or essay. This argument will be a statement asserting that a particular relationship exists between two particular terms. The argument of the Stevenson book whose introduction was quoted above, for instance, might be paraphrased as follows: "The complexity of the forces acting on the world today *(first term)* requires *(proposed relationship)* a flexible and pragmatic approach, as well as patience, from the United States *(second term)*." The relationship between such a thesis and the conclusion of a syllogism (Socrates is mortal) is obvious; both of them propose to relate two terms in a particular way.

But the relationship between a syllogism and the argument of an essay or speech extends further. Aristotle observed long ago that the classical orator's arguments were actually truncated syllogisms, or enthymemes. The arguments that constitute the point of entire essays and speeches are also almost inevitably the conclusions of explicit enthymemes. To put it another way: lurking in almost every essay that is not clearly expository there will be found a clause that bears an explanatory relationship to the main argument. In the Stevenson book, for instance, the second chapter clearly sets up such a clause: "because these problems do not permit of clear-cut and final solutions."

But it should be noted that we are not talking about the relatively simple enthymemes, used by the way, which were discussed in the previous chapter. The enthymeme that constitutes the major argument of an essay will be a *structural enthymeme;* its parts will constitute a major part of the essay itself, the *confirmatio.* In the Stevenson book, for instance, the function of the whole first chapter is to set up the first term, to persuade the reader that the forces acting on us today are indeed complex. The second chapter is engaged in showing that these problems do not permit of clear-cut solutions, the third that these two facts require of us a flexible and pragmatic approach. This structure is simpler than that usually encountered in modern essays and speeches, but in any case the first question to be asked about any essay or speech is, "What is the point of the essay, and what is the supporting reason for it?" The answers to these questions will constitute the skeleton of the *confirmatio.*

Why arguments should be so overwhelmingly of this nature is not entirely clear. In part, perhaps, this logical structure of argumentation is conventional. We write essays having this structure because we have been taught to think in this fashion. But perhaps there are better reasons. The object of an argument is to persuade, and the crux of the problem is not, ordinarily, to establish valid terms but to establish a persuasive relationship between them. In all of human experience, terms give much less trouble than relationships between terms. What the added premise does is to lessen the relational gap between terms. Thus, the Stevenson book actually argues from "the complexity of forces" to "do not permit clear-cut solutions" to "requires a flexible and pragmatic approach." The advantage of this procedure is clear; one large and ambiguous relationship is broken up into two smaller, more easily managed, relationships.

But the structural enthymeme of the essayist functions for him in another way. It should be noted that the reason supporting the conclusion in an enthymeme works because it implies a prior principle and hence a syllogism. Stevenson's book, for instance, depends on the assumed premise that "problems that do not permit clear-cut solutions require a flexible and pragmatic approach." This principle is surely more obvious, more likely to command assent, than the conclusion of the essay depending on it. The writer arguing an enthymeme has a departure point, an implied major premise, functioning as a point of agreement. In their presumed assent to the major premise, the writer and the reader are at one. The enthymeme functions to lead the reader from that point of agreement to a further, and perhaps novel, conviction by revealing conclusions implicit, but by no means self-evident, in the major premise when it is applied to particular cases.[11]

The *confirmatio* of an argumentative essay will, then, ordinarily consist of the definition of fundamental terms, of arguments (non-structural) that attempt to establish the validity of these terms as ways of looking at experience, and of attempts to relate these terms convincingly to each other. The structure that gives these various functions a logical relationship to each other will be an enthymeme. There is, of course, no law that prohibits an author from declaring his major premise, but authors seldom do it.

The structural enthymeme of an essay or speech will not be really comparable to the enthymeme of the logician. The major difference will lie in the kind of relation between major terms that is proposed. As noted in the previous chapter, the essence of the logical figure is that a single, simple relationship between terms be established, signified by "is," "if-then," "more than," and so forth. The relationships found in argumentation are almost never of this variety. The relationship proposed by the Stevenson thesis, for instance, is not simple equivalence nor quantitative difference; "requires" implies a unique sort of relation unknown to logic. The argumentative enthymeme could be put into logical form, of course, but only at the expense of meaning.[12]

[11] See below, page 64, for a further discussion of this point.

[12] Any deductive or inductive argument can be recast as a class argument. But, some classical logicians to the contrary, such reduction significantly alters arguments because it takes the action out of them. It should be noted that attempts to so reduce them almost invariably turn them into sorites. (See above, pp. 31 ff.)

To put it another way: a logical proposition has classification as its end; this individual belongs to this class, or this class belongs to this larger class. Aristotle to the contrary, this is not really what the rhetorical argument, the thesis, proposes to do.[13] The goal of a thesis, or argumentative enthymeme, ordinarily is the establishment of a particular and specific relationship between two terms (i.e., "requires"), and these terms will be coordinate concepts, not class terms.[14] The *specific, active* character of the verb signals the difference between logic and rhetoric in this respect, and proves conclusively that class relationships are not ordinarily the subject matter of argumentation.

Nor does the speechmaker or essayist proceed in the manner of the logician. The logician hopes to demonstrate; the essayist hopes only to persuade. As a consequence, the essayist moves by connecting concepts in a fashion quite different from the orderly procedure of the logician. The essayist builds a bridge of concepts or terms, each joined (hopefully) to what has gone before and each moving a step closer to the conclusion. He is also usually more anxious to conceal the skeleton that he is engaged in embodying than he is to emphasize it.

The mark of an argumentative essay is, then, that its basic structure will be constructed from an enthymeme—namely, the elements of a proposition together with the reason for believing that proposition to be true, a "because clause." There will usually be other elements in the body of the speech or essay, particularly if it is of any length, but they will ordinarily be subordinate to the basic enthymeme.

A fully developed argumentative structure will be examined in the next chapter, but here it will perhaps be useful to see, in an elementary way, just how an enthymeme can become an element of structure. The opening paragraphs of the first chapter of Sir

[13] Although it is perhaps the case that in legal argumentation (with which Aristotle was chiefly concerned, of course) class arguments are more common.

[14] The word "concepts" is here used to indicate ideas not reducible, through class terms, to one another, as say "Willy Loman's character" to "tragic fear" or "Labor Unions" to "Economic Progress."

Julian Huxley's *Knowledge, Morality and Destiny* illustrate this very well:

TRANSHUMANISM[15]

1. As a result of a thousand million years of evolution, the universe is becoming conscious of itself, able to understand something of its past history and its possible future. This cosmic self-awareness is being realized in one tiny fragment of the universe—in a few of us human beings. Perhaps it has been realized elsewhere too, through the evolution of conscious living creatures on the planets of other stars. But on this our planet, it has never happened before.

2. Evolution on this planet is a history of the realization of ever new possibilities by the stuff of which earth (and the rest of the universe) is made—life; strength, speed and awareness; the flight of birds and the social polities of bees and ants; the emergence of mind, long before man was ever dreamt of, with the production of colour, beauty, communication, maternal care, and the beginnings of intelligence and insight. And finally, during the last few ticks of the cosmic clock, something wholly new and revolutionary, human beings with their capacities for conceptual thought and language, for self-conscious awareness and purpose, for accumulating and pooling conscious experience. For do not let us forget that the human species is as radically different from any of the microscopic single-celled animals that lived a thousand million years ago as they were from a fragment of stone or metal.

3. The new understanding of the universe has come about through the new knowledge amassed in the last hundred years—by psychologists, biologists, and other scientists, by archaeologists, anthropologists, and historians. It has defined man's responsibility and destiny—to be an agent for the rest of the world in the job of realizing its inherent potentialities as fully as possible.

4. It is as if man had been suddenly appointed managing director of the biggest business of all, the business of evolution—appointed without being asked if he wanted it, and without proper warning and preparation. What is more, he can't refuse the job. Whether he wants to or not, whether he is conscious of what he is doing or not, he *is* in

[15] From Julian Huxley, *Knowledge, Morality and Destiny* (New York: Mentor, 1960), pp. 13–14. (Originally published as *New Bottles for New Wine* [London: Chatto and Windus, and New York: Harper and Row, 1957].) Reprinted by permission of A. D. Peters and Company.

point of fact determining the future direction of evolution on this earth. That is his inescapable destiny, and the sooner he realizes it and starts believing in it, the better for all concerned.

5. What the job really boils down to is this—the fullest realization of man's possibilities, whether by the individual, by the community, or by the species in its processional adventure along the corridors of time. Every man-jack of us begins as a mere speck of potentiality, a spherical and microscopic egg-cell. During the nine months before birth, this automatically unfolds into a truly miraculous range of organization: after birth, in addition to continuing automatic growth and development, the individual begins to realize his mental possibilities—by building up a personality, by developing special talents, by acquiring knowledge and skills of various kinds, by playing his part in keeping society going. This post-natal process is not an automatic or a pre-determined one. It may proceed in very different ways according to the individual's own efforts. The degree to which capacities are realized can be more or less complete. The end-result can be satisfactory or very much the reverse: in particular, the personality may grievously fail in attaining any real wholeness. One thing is certain, that the well-developed, well-integrated personality is the highest product of evolution, the fullest realization we know of in the universe.

These paragraphs can be briefly paraphrased as follows:

Paragraph one—What is the relationship of the human consciousness of evolution to the evolutionary process? (This is necessarily a question because the function of the paragraph is introductory, which is to say that it sets up a problem. The paragraph can confine itself to this single function because Sir Julian has defined his ethos and his relationship to his subject in the preceding preface.)

Paragraph two—Evolution is the realization of ever-new possibilities, the newest being the possibilities implicit in human awareness. (Notice that this paragraph is essentially a definition; at least half the paragraphs in an argument will ordinarily have this character.)

Paragraph three—The new understanding of the universe has defined man's responsibility and destiny. (The paragraph actually has two functions; the first sentence is a vague sort of definition, the second connects this definition to man.)

Paragraph four—Man's position makes his responsibility for evolutionary direction inevitable. (This paragraph is actually an extension of the previous one, in that it emphasizes the connection merely asserted previously.)

Paragraph five—The obligation implicit in man's control of evolution is full development of human potentiality. (This paragraph, like the second, is again a kind of definition.)

What is the enthymeme in this passage? Perhaps the best way of getting at it is to ask, "What is Sir Julian urging upon us to this point?" Obviously, the action urged is to be found in the last paragraph, and might be paraphrased, "We ought to pursue full human development." But this section is not merely an incitement to action, it is an argument, and this argument lies in the combination of paragraph five with paragraphs three and four; Sir Julian's point is that, "The powers implicit in an understanding of the universe ought to be used to promote the fullest development of human possibilities." But why? This section is a complete argument because it answers that question; the second paragraph asserts, in effect, "because evolutionary direction is toward the fullest realization of all possibilities." (A reader not inclined to agree with Sir Julian might doubt that evolutionary direction can properly be appealed to for a moral sanction, for an "ought.")

In short, this section of Sir Julian's essay is a unit of discourse because its subsections have a real, a logical, relationship to each other in that they are the parts of a logical figure, of an enthymeme. It is this relationship, also, that gives the section its movement.

But two characteristics of this enthymeme must be noted. First, it has the form but not the logical rigor of a logical enthymeme. One should note particularly the shift in terminology, from "all possibilities" in the "because clause" or minor premise to "the fullest development of human possibilities" in the conclusion. If one were to seek rigorous logical form from the passage, it would turn into a kind of sorites, with a good many intermediate steps taken for granted.

Second, the argument does not follow the order of the thesis statement; we have the subject of the conclusion last ("the powers implicit in an understanding of the universe"), preceded by its object ("fullest development of human possibilities"). Some disorder is almost always observed in the elements of an enthymeme because the writer has to be concerned with the relation of one section of the essay to another, and because he will ordinarily aim at some sort of climactic movement, in which the more important concepts are introduced as late as possible into the argument. In the Huxley essay, for instance, the section following that quoted is a lengthy consideration of human possibilities; to have gone into this consideration as it came up and then completed the syllogism would have not only been awkward, but also would have preempted the climactic effect of detailing actual human possibilities at the end of the argument.

To this point, we have been speaking of the *confirmatio* as if it were composed of the parts of a single enthymeme. In longer speeches and essays, at any rate, this is almost never the case. In the first place, one or more of the other parts of the body of an essay, briefly discussed below, will almost always be interwoven into the enthymatic structure. In the second place, there will ordinarily be several major arguments, and hence several structural enthymemes in a single body. At times these will be organized serially, as in the Calhoun speech analyzed in the following chapter: an enthymeme will establish a conclusion that will then become the point of departure for a second enthymeme. More commonly, the body of an essay will, in its essentials, consist of several enthymemes, based on different major premises but supporting in a general way the same conclusion. An essayist, for instance, may initially set up an argument to refute the commonly accepted interpretation of a particular phenomenon, follow up with a long *narratio* reviewing the facts, after which he might set up two parallel arguments, both establishing his own point of view from somewhat different perspectives. In such a structure, of course, the first, third and fourth sections would each be built on its own structural enthymeme.

OTHER PARTS OF THE BODY OF AN ESSAY

A *confirmatio* is, by definition, an indispensable part of an argumentative essay or speech. This is not the case with the *reprehensio,* the *narratio,* or the *prolepsis.* Furthermore, these other parts of an essay are difficult to illustrate in isolation, since their function is usually apparent only in the context of the *confirmatio,* into which they are ordinarily integrated.[16] Some form of *narratio,* for instance, is very common in an argumentative essay, whenever the writer inserts a large section of description or analysis of the material in question. But modern authors, particularly, habitually break up this material and distribute it between elements of the *confirmatio* to avoid loss of movement. The *reprehensio* and the *prolepsis* are commonly dealt with in the same fashion; they are incorporated into the structure of the *confirmatio* if at all possible.

It should be pointed out, again, that this description of the body of an essay is not prescriptive, and one does find essays in which the *narratio* and not the *confirmatio* constitutes the bulk of the body of the essay. The *confirmatio* in this case may be repeated several times in the course of the *narratio* or it may constitute a relatively short section at the end. But such structures are, if not rare, at least uncommon, and they make for little difficulty. Most essays, by far, will generally fall within the scope of the description proposed above.

Peroration or Conclusion

The obvious function of the peroration, of course, is to assert the thesis that the essay or speech has been engaged in making credible. In speeches, this thesis will ordinarily have been proposed several times prior to the peroration. In essays, where greater concentration on the part of the reader can be assumed, it is customary to withhold the full statement of the thesis until this point. Of course, the statement of the thesis may well be accompanied by a review of the main topics in which the evidence for one's position is maximized and the evidence against it reduced as far as credibility permits.

But this concluding section can have two other functions. First, it can safely make overt emotional appeals; the reader, having

---

[16] All are adequately illustrated in the analyses of particular essays which make up Chapters III and VI. The *narratio* is considered at length in Chapter IX, pp. 268 ff.

been convinced intellectually, will not resist incitements to action or confirming arguments of an exaggerated character. As the essay analyzed in Chapter VIII shows, more or less open emotional appeals at this point are as appropriate in a social science article of the twentieth century as they were in a Greek oration.

Second, a peroration will sometimes be found to contain a kind of double conclusion. This occurs when the concrete thesis the writer wishes to argue does not coincide with the point really at issue. If one wants to argue for the propriety of a particular government action, for instance, the appropriate argument may concern the propriety of a whole category of government actions, because the propriety of this large category is really at issue. In such an instance, the essay will properly concern the large category; having demonstrated propriety for the class, he can in his peroration merely apply his general thesis to the particular case without further argumentation. The peroration, then, may assert not merely what the essay or oration has argued but also a specific application of that general thesis.

Conclusion

The essay writer, or orator, will ordinarily have a central judgment to make; this will be the real point of writing. But there will also be tasks tangential to this point that he must do in writing (in the exordium) and there may be other points that it would be strategic to make. In addition, the central point itself will necessarily consist of parts that must be dealt with one at a time. The essayist's job is, somehow, to make some sort of whole out of these various tasks.

The reader who would approach an essay or speech critically needs to recognize, in the first place, that it is necessarily composed of parts. The terms of structural rhetoric can be of inestimable value to this end. But then he needs to be able to see what point the essay aims at, and the means by which the writer makes the point. He needs to find the enthymeme.

Chapter III

The Structural Analysis of a Speech

It has been pointed out that an argument, although it is logical in its basic structure, does not proceed logically, as it were—does not work from premise to conclusion in the way that logic itself does. This is because the argument must be adapted to persuasive strategies, and also because it will ordinarily have much more to do than lay out an enthymeme. It will frequently have to include matters that are irrelevant to the enthymeme, such as the *reprehensio*, the *narratio* or the *prolepsis*. It must work continually at definitions or redefinitions, which necessarily break up any formal logical structure. And it must establish connections that are, in many cases, by no means self-evident. This all entails considerably more than the assertion of a simple enthymeme.

There is no body of regulations by which the essayist or speechwriter may determine what element belongs where. An essay, as a structure, is successful if it always moves, or gives the illusion of moving, toward its conclusion. The only way one can discuss movement in an essay or speech, however, is to look at specific examples.

The following example is a speech. Speeches ordinarily are much more loosely organized than essays. In part, this looseness is inherent in the form. Spoken discourse must be immediately intelligible; the reader cannot look back at what has already been said nor does he have time to reflect upon what is being said. Hence a speech must make heavy use of devices to recall wandering thoughts, of very explicit transitions, of summaries and forecasts—devices that can be used more sparingly in written discourse because the reader can regulate the speed of movement of thought to suit himself.

But the looseness of many speeches is also partly a matter of convention. Particularly, the public speaker of the last couple of centuries has been allowed a great deal more latitude in the matter of what properly belongs in his discourse than we would ever concede to an essayist, for no other reason than that we have tacitly agreed to allow him such latitude. This concession is especially apparent in political oratory, which only approaches the relative unity of the essay when the importance of a particular subject to the general welfare requires that the orator stick to that subject. Such was the case when Calhoun delivered the following speech (by proxy) in March 1850. Senator Calhoun was ill and obviously at the end of his political career; the speech represented his last statement on the issue that had been his chief concern for twenty years, North-South relations.[1]

1. I have, Senators, believed from the first that the agitation of the subject of slavery would, if not prevented by some timely and effective measure, end in disunion. Entertaining this opinion, I have, on all proper occasions, endeavored to call the attention of both the two great parties which divide the country to adopt some measure to prevent so great a disaster, but without success. The agitation has been permitted to proceed, with almost no attempt to resist it, until it has reached a point when it can no longer be disguised or denied that the Union is in danger. You have thus had forced upon you the greatest and the gravest question that can ever come under your consideration: How can the Union be preserved?

2. To give a satisfactory answer to this mighty question, it is indispensable to have an accurate and thorough knowledge of the nature and the character of the cause by which the Union is endangered. Without such knowledge it is impossible to pronounce, with any certainty, by what measure it can be saved; just as it would be im-

[1] From John C. Calhoun, *Speeches of John C. Calhoun, Delivered in the House of Representatives, and in the Senate of the United States* (New York: D. Appleton and Company, 1861), pp. 542–573.

possible for a physician to pronounce, in the case of some dangerous disease, with any certainty, by what remedy the patient could be saved, without similar knowledge of the nature and character of the cause which produced it. The first question, then, presented for consideration, in the investigation I propose to make, in order to obtain such knowledge, is, What is it that has endangered the Union?

It has been pointed out that a speaker or writer in his introduction must do three jobs: he must introduce the subject or problem, he must define himself by creating an ethos, and he must set up some kind of relationship to his subject. As regards the introduction of the subject, these two paragraphs are sequential, in that the first introduces the general problem of the whole speech, the second, the first element of that problem. The other two jobs are roughly distributed between the paragraphs also.

The first paragraph is largely given over to an introduction of himself by Calhoun. He does not, it should be noted, adopt the role of southern spokesman, which in fact he was, and this makes for nagging problems later. He sets himself up, instead, as an impartial judge of the dispute. He is, personally, a man of good will, striving for an equitable settlement. His professed attitude toward his audience is nicely ambiguous; his tone is certainly that of a man addressing his equals, yet he does not identify himself with them. (". . . I have, on all proper occasions, endeavored to call the attention of both the two great parties . . . to adopt some measure. . . .")

His attitude toward the subject is somewhere between that of Ayn Rand and the late Ambassador Stevenson; he is judicial without being prophetic. He certainly intends to present the truth of the matter, but he does not intimate that it is a truth only visible to himself. Like Miss Rand, he also attempts to give force to a rather dull presentation of the subject with a *comparison* (see the Glossary): ". . . just as it would be impossible for a physician. . . ."

The body of the speech is best understood by breaking it up into several large chunks.

3.   To this question there can be but one answer: that the immediate cause is the almost universal discontent which pervades all the States composing the Southern section of the Union. This widely

extended discontent is not of recent origin. It commenced with the agitation of the slavery question, and has been increasing ever since. The next question, going one step further back, is—What has caused this widely diffused and almost universal discontent?

4. It is a great mistake to suppose, as is by some, that it originated with demagogues, who excited the discontent with the intention of aiding their personal advancement, or with the disappointed ambition of certain politicians, who resorted to it as the means of retrieving their fortunes. On the contrary, all the great political influences of the section were arrayed against excitement, and exerted to the utmost to keep the people quiet. The great mass of the people of the South were divided, as in the other section, into Whigs and Democrats. The leaders and the presses of both parties in the South were very solicitous to prevent excitement and to preserve quiet; because it was seen that the effects of the former would necessarily tend to weaken, if not destroy, the political ties which united them with their respective parties in the other section. Those who know the strength of party ties will readily appreciate the immense force which this cause exerted against agitation, and in favor of preserving quiet. But, great as it was, it was not sufficient to prevent the widespread discontent which now pervades the section. No; some cause, far deeper and more powerful than the one supposed, must exist, to account for discontent so wide and deep. The question then recurs, What is the cause of this discontent? It will be found in the belief of the people of the Southern States, as prevalent as the discontent itself, that they cannot remain, as things now are, consistently with honor and safety, in the Union. The next question to be considered is, What has caused this belief?

5. One of the causes is, undoubtedly, to be traced to the long-continued agitation of the slave question on the part of the North, and the many aggressions which they have made on the rights of the South during the time. I will not enumerate them at present, as it will be done hereafter in its proper place.

6. There is another lying back of it, with which this is intimately connected, that may be regarded as the great and primary cause. This is to be found in the fact that the equilibrium between the two sections, in the Government as it stood when the constitution was ratified and the Government put in action, has been destroyed. At that time there was nearly a perfect equilibrium between the two, which afforded ample means to each to protect itself against the aggression of the other; but, as it now stands, one section has the exclusive power of controlling the Government, which leaves the other with-

out any adequate means of protecting itself against its encroach-
ment and oppression. To place this subject distinctly before you, I
have, Senators, prepared a brief statistical statement, showing the
relative weight of the two sections in the Government under the
first census of 1790 and the last census of 1840.

7. According to the former, the population of the United States. . . .

8. According to the last census. . . .

9. The result of the whole is to give the Northern section a predominance in every department of the Government, and thereby concentrate in the two elements which constitute the Federal Government—majority of States, and a majority of their population,
estimated in federal numbers. Whatever section concentrates the
two in itself possesses the control of the entire Government.

10. But we are just at the close of the sixth decade, and the commencement of the seventh. The census is to be taken this year, which must
add greatly to the decided preponderance of the North in the House
of Representatives and in the electoral college. . . .

11. Had this destruction been the operation of time, without the inter-
ference of government, the South would have had no reason to
complain; but such was not the fact. It was caused by the legislation
of this Government, which was appointed, as the common agent of
all, and charged with the protection of the interests and security of
all. The legislation by which it has been effected, may be classed
under three heads. The first, is that series of acts by which the South
has been excluded from the common territory belonging to all the
States as members of the Federal Union—which have had the effect
of extending vastly the portion allotted to the Northern section, and
restricting within narrow limits the portion left the South. The next
consists in adopting a system of revenue and disbursements, by
which an undue proportion of the burden of taxation has been imposed upon the South, and an undue proportion of its proceeds
appropriated to the North; and the last is a system of political
measures, by which the original character of the Government has
been radically changed. I propose to bestow upon each of these, in
the order they stand, a few remarks, with the view of showing that
it is owing to the action of this Government, that the equilibrium
between the two sections has been destroyed, and the whole powers
of the system centered in a sectional majority.

12. The first of the series of acts. . . .

13. I have not included the territory recently acquired by the treaty
with Mexico. . . .

14. Such is the first and great cause that has destroyed the equilibrium between the two sections in the Government.
15. The next is the system of revenues and disbursements. . . .
16. This, combined with the great primary cause, amply explains why the North has acquired a preponderance in every department of the Government by its disproportionate increase of population and states. . . .
17. But while these measures were destroying the equilibrium between the two sections, the action of the Government was leading to a radical change in its character, by concentrating all the power of the system in itself. The occasion will not permit me to trace the measures by which this great change has been consummated. If it did, it would not be difficult to show that the process commenced at an early period of the Government; and that it proceeded, almost without interruption, step by step, until it absorbed virtually its entire powers; but without going through the whole process to establish the fact, it may be done satisfactorily by a very short statement.

Even on first reading it is apparent that an argument of some kind is being made; the paragraphs are related in that one leads to the next. But the argument itself is not immediately apparent. The major points in this passage might be paraphrased as follows:

1. The Union is endangered by southern discontent. (¶ 3)
2. This discontent is caused by loss of equilibrium between the two sections. (¶ 6)
3. The preponderance of the North has been achieved by unfair means. (¶ 11)

The relationship of these subsections to each other is rendered ambiguous because Calhoun does not draw any conclusion at the end of this section. This failure is perhaps due to the role that he created for himself. His promise, implicit in the introduction, was to analyze the threat to the Union as an indifferent observer. The section just quoted, however, is obviously not indifferent analysis; it is justification. To draw the conclusion implicit in it would surely threaten, in some fashion, the ethos he has created for himself.

But the statement that answers best to the function of this whole section, as outlined, would go something like this: "The loss of equilibrium between the states (¶ 6) has occasioned southern discontent (¶ 3) because it has been unnaturally achieved (¶ 11)." The rest of the material in this section is development of, and support for, this central structure.

But Calhoun's treatment of this section is worth a closer scrutiny. He begins with the object of this thesis, "southern discontent," and establishes it in a short paragraph while pointing out that it had historical causes. Clearly he regarded this situation as self-evident. Paragraph four is a *reprehensio* in that it refutes an opinion not his own. A speaker or writer is habitually confronted with explanations of events that are, in his eyes, not true. Ordinarily these contradictory explanations are simply ignored. But there are occasions, such as this one, when it seems unwise to ignore them. On such occasions, recourse may be had to the *reprehensio*. These may occur at any position in an essay or speech, but ordinarily they will be introduced as soon as possible to minimize the interruption of one's own argument. It should be observed that this paragraph ends with the simple reiteration of the statement ending the previous one; Calhoun is reestablishing the point from which he was drawn by the *reprehensio*.

Paragraph five illustrates a common writing problem. Surely, in Calhoun's view, the major cause of southern discontent was agitation against slavery. But he wanted to discuss this at length later on in the course of his speech. So he can only pass it by here quickly, and rather awkwardly, with a mere reference.

The statement that sets up the subject of his thesis, "the loss of equilibrium between the states," is a statement for which he can bring evidence, and consequently he supports it by an appeal to experience, by a *narratio*. But a *narratio* is a different order of discourse from an argument, and, like the *reprehensio*, it interrupts argumentative movement. Calhoun takes both of these facts into consideration. Paragraph six ends with a sentence whose function is to signal the different order of discourse, the *narratio*, to follow: "To place this subject distinctly before you, I have . . . prepared a brief statistical statement. . . ." And then, to minimize the interruption, he breaks the rather long *narratio* into two sections, paragraphs seven and eight and paragraph ten, interrupted by a provisional summary. His object is to keep the audience from getting lost in the *narratio*.

The third subsection of the argument (the "because clause" of the thesis) presents yet another sort of problem. The point is that the North has gained its preponderance unfairly. If it had done so by one method, there would be no problem. But it did not; Calhoun singles out three methods, and three of anything are difficult to handle in an argument. This difficulty can be seen if we think of a five-paragraph essay. Movement prescribes that such an essay go, "one-two-three-four-five," with the numbers representing paragraphs and the dashes real connections between them. But a five-paragraph essay containing three reasons would have to be visualized in this manner:

As the diagram shows, paragraphs two, three and four are not logically related to each other at all; they are only related to paragraphs one and five individually. The problem of the writer confronting more than one "reason" for something is to organize all of the reasons into one structural unit and to maintain some sense of logical movement as he enumerates them.

Calhoun deals with this awkward problem by being very specific. Most of paragraph eleven which introduces this section is an explicit preview of the three reasons coming up. The first two of these reasons are set up with "sign" sentences (¶ 12 and ¶ 15) which function merely to indicate a reason coming up; paragraphs fourteen and sixteen simply indicate the end of each section. (Such great concern about a "reasons substructure" is due in part to the fact that this is a speech—speeches are harder to follow than essays.)

It should be observed that Calhoun argues for his first two points by introducing further *narratio*. The third point, however, is of a different order than the first two and requires a different kind of proof. He wants to argue in this paragraph that governmental action "was leading to a radical change in its character" (¶ 17). He explicitly declares that this is not to be handled by a *narratio* ("The occasion will not permit me to trace the measures . . ."). Instead, beginning in the next paragraph, we get an argument of the type described in Chapter I, an enthymeme. This is in turn extended by a sorites. The passage is as follows:

18. That the Government claims, and practically maintains the right to decide in the last resort, as to the extent of its powers, will scarcely be denied by any one conversant with the political history of the country. That it also claims the right to resort to force to maintain whatever power it claims, against all opposition, is equally certain. Indeed it is apparent, from what we daily hear, that this has become the prevailing and fixed opinion of a great majority of the community. Now, I ask, what limitation can possibly be placed upon the powers of a government claiming and exercising such rights? And, if none can be, how can the separate governments of the States maintain and protect the powers reserved to them by the constitution—or the people of the several States maintain those which are reserved them, and among others, the sovereign powers by which they ordained and established, not only their separate State Constitutions and Governments, but also the Constitution and Government of the United States? But, if they have no constitutional means of maintaining them against the right claimed by this Government, it necessarily follows, that they hold them at its pleasure and discretion, and that all the powers of the system are in reality concentrated in it. It also follows, that the character of the Government has been changed in consequence, from a federal republic, as it originally came from the hands of its framers, into a great national consolidated democracy. It has indeed, at present, all the characteristics of the latter, and not one of the former, although it still retains its outward form.

19. The result of the whole of these causes combined is—that the North has acquired a decided ascendency over every department of this Government, and through it, a control over all the powers of the system. A single section governed by the will of the numerical majority, has now, in fact, the control of the Government and the entire powers of the system. What was once a constitutional federal republic, is now converted, in reality, into one as absolute as that of the Autocrat of Russia, and as despotic in its tendency as any absolute government that ever existed.

20. As, then, the North has the absolute control over the Government, it is manifest, that on all questions between it and the South, where there is a diversity of interests, the interest of the latter will be sacrificed to the former, however oppressive the effects may be;

as the South possesses no means by which it can resist, through the action of the Government. . . .

The basic enthymeme of this sub-argument, developed through the first six sentences of paragraph eighteen, is readily reduced to an "if-then" statement: "If the federal government claims the right to decide the extent of its powers (and to enforce its decisions), then the separate states cannot maintain their constitutional powers." If this statement in turn were reduced to standard syllogistic form the implicit major premise would be, "No constitutional powers can be maintained against a government deciding the extent of its own powers." The conclusion of this initial enthymeme is repeated in the first half of another statement with a further "then" deduction: "But, if they have no constitutional means of maintaining them against the right claimed by this Government, [then] it necessarily follows, that they hold them at its pleasure and discretion. . . ." The major premise of the last statement is really a definition, "Any governmental structure in which one element holds all power at its discretion is not a federal republic."

The following paragraph, nineteen, is a part of this section, but its function is rhetorical rather than logical; it is a good example of *redefinition* (see the Glossary), in which Calhoun moves through a series of sentences from the moderate "decided ascendency" to "the Autocrat of Russia." This is not done logically; it is done by a series of statements, each a little more extreme than the last.

As is clear by this time, the last two paragraphs depend for their force on the first, implicit major premise from paragraph eighteen, "No constitutional powers can be maintained against a government deciding the extent of its own powers." It is this major premise that leads us ultimately to "the Autocrat of Russia." And its implications are peculiar. Someplace, somehow, there must be a governmental agency that decides the limits of all power, including its own. In the system Calhoun would propose, the several states decide the limitation of federal power and hence of their own power. Would not they necessarily be Russian autocrats by his own major premise? Does not the premise necessarily dissolve all governments holding ultimate authority into absolutisms?

As was pointed out, this whole argument, paragraphs eighteen through twenty, has been ostensibly introduced simply to support Calhoun's contention that one of the ways in which the North has achieved unfair preponderance has been by a change in the federal government's conception of its function. Calhoun was sufficiently skillful as a rhetorician, surely, to recognize in this a dangerous overbalance of his own: how many of his audience, listening or reading, would remember that this lengthy argument served merely to support the third element of a series? Not many, surely. Then why did he handle it in this fashion?

If one looks closely, it is clear that this argument is introduced into the speech for its own sake, and hence constitutes a *paralipsis* of sorts (see the Glossary). The argument is irrelevant to the ostensible issue, how the union might be saved, but it has an impact of its own. It was consequently introduced in a disguised fashion, ostensibly as a reason for another point. This is apparent if one looks at the series of reasons given for the unfairness of northern predominance:

1. Exclusion of the South from the territories.
2. Unfair system of revenues and disbursements (a reference to high tariffs benefiting northern industry).
3. A strengthening of the authority of the federal government.

The third reason is not parallel to the first two; the first two purport to describe discriminatory measures directed against the South, the last a change in the character of government.

But all of paragraph twenty has not been quoted. The paragraph concludes with a lengthy section of transition, introducing the next section of the argument:

> . . . But if there was no question of vital importance to the South, in reference to which there was a diversity of views between the two sections, this state of things might be endured, without the hazard of destruction to the South. But such is not the fact. There is a question of vital importance to the Southern section, in reference to which the views and feelings of the two sections are as opposite and hostile as they can possibly be.
>
> 21. I refer to the relation between the two races in the Southern section,

which constitutes a vital portion of her social organization. Every portion of the North entertains views and feelings more or less hostile to it. Those most opposed and hostile, regard it as a sin, and consider themselves under the most sacred obligation to use every effort to destroy it. Indeed, to the extent that they conceive that they have power, they regard themselves as implicated in the sin, and responsible for not suppressing it by the use of all and every means. Those less opposed and hostile, regard it as a crime—an offence against humanity, as they call it; and although not so fanatical, feel themselves bound to use all efforts to effect the same object; while those who are least opposed and hostile, regard it as a blot and a stain on the character of what they call the Nation, and feel themselves accordingly bound to give it no countenance or support. On the contrary, the Southern section regards the relation as one which cannot be destroyed without subjecting the two races to the greatest calamity; and the section to poverty, desolation, and wretchedness; and accordingly they feel bound, by every consideration of interest and safety, to defend it.

22. This hostile feeling on the part of the North towards the social organization of the South long lay dormant, but it only required some cause to act on those who felt most intensely that they were responsible for its continuance, to call it into action. The increasing power of this Government, and of the control of the Northern section over all its departments, furnished the cause. It was this which made an impression on the minds of many, that there was little or no restraint to prevent the Government from doing whatever it might choose to do. This was sufficient of itself to put the most fanatical portion of the North in action, for the purpose of destroying the existing relation between the two races in the South.

23. The first organized movement towards it commenced in 1835. . . .

24. Neither party in Congress had, at that time, any sympathy with them or their cause. . . .

25. As for myself, I believed at that early period . . . that agitation would follow, and that it would in the end, if not arrested, destroy the Union. I then so expressed myself in debate, and called upon both parties to take grounds against assuming jurisdiction; but in vain. . . .

26. What has since followed are but natural consequences. . . .

27. Such is a brief history of the agitation, as far as it has yet advanced. Now I ask, Senators, what is there to prevent its further progress, until it fulfills the ultimate end proposed, unless some decisive measure should be adopted to prevent it? Has any one of the causes,

which has added to its increase from its original small and contempt-ible beginning until it has attained its present magnitude, dimin-ished in force? Is the original cause of the movement—that slavery is a sin, and ought to be suppressed—weaker now than at the com-mencement? Or is the abolition party less numerous or influential, or have they less influence with, or control over the two great parties of the North in elections? Or has the South greater means of influ-encing or controlling the movements of this Government now, than it had when the agitation commenced? To all these questions but one answer can be given: No, no, no. The very reverse is true. In-stead of being weaker, all the elements in favor of agitation are stronger now than they were in 1835, when it first commenced, while all the elements of influence on the part of the South are weaker. Un-less something decisive is done, I again ask what is to stop this agi-tation, before the great and final object at which it aims—the abo-lition of slavery in the States—is consummated? Is it, then, not certain, that if something is not done to arrest it, the South will be forced to choose between abolition and secession? Indeed, as events are now moving, it will not require the South to secede, in order to dissolve the Union. Agitation will of itself effect it, of which its past history furnishes abundant proof—as I shall next proceed to show.

28.   It is a great mistake to suppose that disunion can be effected by a single blow. The cords which bound these States together in one common Union, are far too numerous and powerful for that. Dis-union must be the work of time. It is only through a long process, and successively, that the cords can be snapped, until the whole fab-ric falls asunder. Already the agitation of the slavery question has snapped some of the most important, and has greatly weakened all the others, as I shall proceed to show.

29.   The cords that bind the States together are not only many, but vari-ous in character. Some are spiritual or ecclesiastical; some political; others social. Some appertain to the benefit conferred by the Union, and others to the feeling of duty and obligation.

30.   The strongest of those of a spiritual and ecclesiastical nature, con-sisted in the unity of the great religious denominations; all of which originally embraced the whole Union.

31.   The first of these cords which snapped, under its explosive force, was that of the powerful Methodist Episcopal Church. . . .

32.   The next cord that snapped was that of the Baptists. . . .

33.   The strongest cord, of a political character, consists of the many and powerful ties that have held together the two great parties. . . .

34. If the agitation goes on, the same force, acting with increased intensity, as has been shown, will finally snap every cord, when nothing will be left to hold the States together except force. But, surely, that can, with no propriety of language, be called a Union, when the only means by which the weaker is held connected with the stronger portion is force. It may, indeed, keep them connected; but the connection will partake much more of the character of subjugation, on the part of the weaker to the stronger, than the union of free, independent, and sovereign States, in one confederation, as they stood in the early stages of the Government, and which only is worthy of the sacred name of Union.

The second half of paragraph twenty is clearly transitional; it does not, however, set up the argument that is to follow, but only introduces the first element of it. The reason for this obliquity is apparent if one looks, again, for the skeleton of the argument.

The first paragraph of the section, paragraph twenty-one, really sets up the term, "northern opposition to slavery," although this is somewhat obscured by Calhoun's posture as indifferent judge. It should be noted that the positions set up by Calhoun are not comparable; the North protests that slavery is immoral, the South answers that it is necessary. A good deal of the pained windings and turnings in the speech are due to this disparity. Human beings are not very happy responding to a moral argument with a pragmatic one.

Paragraph twenty-two appears, on first inspection, to be a second major element in the argument, particularly since it is supported by four more paragraphs. But the section cannot be read in such terms. This paragraph has to be paraphrased as, "stimulated by northern preponderance." It thus must modify the first term, "northern opposition to slavery," and not be another term.

A second term is added in paragraph twenty-seven, which asserts that the said opposition to slavery will lead to disunion or abolition.

The third term is introduced, rather oddly, at the end of the same paragraph, beginning with "Indeed, as events are now moving. . . ." This term might be paraphrased as, "because (such antagonism to slavery) destroys mutual social and political institutions."

The full enthymeme would then be, "Northern antagonism to slavery, aroused by northern power, will lead to secession (or abolition, but this is not really considered as a possibility in the speech), because that antagonism destroys mutual social and political institutions." The implied major premise, "Anything that destroys mutual social and political institutions will lead to secession," is paraphrased, after a fashion, in the conclusion of the section, paragraph thirty-four, which asserts, "that can, with no propriety of language be called a Union, when the only means by which the weaker is held connected with the stronger portion is force."

The materials that clothe this skeleton are in part obvious and in part worth attention. The antagonism of the North to slavery (¶ 21) is asserted and elaborated on by a division of that antagonism into several classes, but no proof is offered. It was presumably unnecessary. The growth of abolitionist sentiment, because of the failure of politicians to control it, is elaborated through three paragraphs, twenty-three to twenty-six, interrupted by a reassertion of Calhoun's own position in regard to the whole controversy, the position of disinterested analyst. This interruption functions to break up what is otherwise a rather long piece of *narratio,* and it usefully reminds the reader of Calhoun's chosen role at a point when it is important to the effect of the speech that it be remembered. It should be noted that Calhoun also emphasizes an element that is not a term in his enthymeme, the dependence of northern agitation on the growth of northern power.

The demise of the Union, forecast in paragraph twenty-seven, is argued for by a disguised "if-then" argument, "If slavery agitation has been more and more successful to this point, then it will be ultimately successful."

The last element of the enthymeme, "because such antagonism to slavery destroys mutual social and political institutions," is introduced in a very odd fashion at the end of paragraph twenty-seven. The point itself is almost slipped in (perhaps because Calhoun sensed its weakness), and then we get very elaborate evidence, paragraphs twenty-eight through thirty-three, indicating that domestic institutions are splitting up as a result of the issue of slavery. It is apparent to any reader, a century later, that Calhoun did, indeed, have evidence that domestic institutions were breaking up, but he has not really established the fact that northern, and not southern, behavior was responsible for this. Calhoun himself was aware, on some level, of this discrepancy, and hence the peculiar handling.[2]

These two major sections, together with the subsection to the last, constitute Calhoun's essential argument, and hence it will be worthwhile at this point to see just what it is. We have up to this point been presented with two structural syllogisms. Formulated as thesis statements, they are roughly as follows:

1. The loss of equilibrium between the states has occasioned southern discontent, because it has been unnaturally achieved.
2. Northern opposition to slavery, stimulated by northern power, will lead to disunion, because it destroys the mutual institutions which are the basis for union.

The structural problems in the essay as a whole, manifesting themselves particularly in paragraph twenty, originate in the peculiar relationship that these enthymemes bear to each other. One would expect sequential arguments to be logically related to each other —to constitute, in fact, a sorites. But these enthymemes do not have that relationship. They have in common only the fact that they are both concerned in some way with the preponderance of the North, and in the second enthymeme this is not even a major term. Hence paragraph twenty, which should have served to connect the two pieces of a single argument, necessarily functions to conceal the fact that they are not fundamentally connected.

This structural deficiency is not the result of incompetence. Calhoun had urged for years two different theses concerning the Union. One was that the Union could only be saved by giving some

---

[2] It is perhaps worth pointing out that defects in an argument are almost invariably signalled in some way. The writer, in a kind of subliminal distress, will either obscure the move he is making by passing over it hastily, as in the above passage, or he will attempt to fill a gap in his logic with flag-waving rhetoric to distract the reader or listener from the problem. It is a part of sophistication in reading that we become aware of these responses; the problems that they attempt to conceal are often the most interesting parts of the essay or speech.

sort of veto power over federal action to the individual states. The second was that abolitionist agitation had to be silenced. In this final speech of his career he merely attempts to provide a theoretical justification for both positions. The structural problem occurs because these two positions are not logically related to each other.

The rest of the speech is reasonably straightforward. It will be observed that, with the argument completed, Calhoun is free to assume his real relationship to the conflict, that of an outspoken defender of the southern cause.

35.   Having now, Senators, explained what it is that endangers the Union, and traced it to its cause, and explained its nature and character, the question again recurs, How can the Union be saved? To this I answer, There is but one way by which it can be, and that is, by adopting such measures as will satisfy the States belonging to the Southern section, that they can remain in the Union consistently with their honor and their safety. There is, again, only one way by which this can be effected, and that is by removing the causes by which the belief has been produced. Do this, and discontent will cease, harmony and kind feelings between the sections be restored, and every apprehension of danger to the Union removed. The question, then, is, How can this be done? But, before I undertake to answer this question, I propose to show by what the Union cannot be saved.

36.   It cannot, then, be saved by eulogies on the Union, however splendid or numerous. The cry of "Union, Union, the glorious Union!" can no more prevent disunion than the cry of "Health, health, glorious health!" on the part of the physician, can save a patient lying dangerously ill. So long as the Union, instead of being regarded as a protector, is regarded in the opposite character, by not much less than a majority of the States, it will be in vain to attempt to conciliate them by pronouncing eulogies on it.

37.   Besides this cry of Union comes commonly from those whom we cannot believe to be sincere. It usually comes from our assailants. But we cannot believe them to be sincere; for, if they loved the Union, they would necessarily be devoted to the constitution. It made the Union, and to destroy the constitution would be to destroy the Union. But the only reliable and certain evidence of devotion to the constitution is, to abstain, on the one hand, from violating it, and to repel, on the other, all attempts to violate it. It is only by

faithfully performing these high duties that the constitution can be preserved, and with it the Union.

38. But how stands the profession of devotion to the Union by our assailants, when brought to this test? Have they abstained from violating the constitution? Let the many Acts passed by the Northern States to set aside and annul the clause of the Constitution providing for the delivery up of fugitive slaves answer. I cite this, not that it is the only instance (for there are many others), but because the violation in this particular is too notorious and palpable to be denied. Again, have they stood forth faithfully to repel violations of the constitution? Let their course in reference to the agitation of the slavery question, which was commenced and has been carried on for fifteen years, avowedly for the purpose of abolishing slavery in the States—an object all acknowledged to be unconstitutional—answer. Let them show a single instance, during this long period, in which they have denounced the agitators or their attempts to effect what is admitted to be unconstitutional, or a single measure which they have brought forward for that purpose. How can we, with all these facts before us, believe that they are sincere in their profession of devotion to the Union, or avoid believing their profession is but intended to increase the vigor of their assaults and to weaken the force of our resistance?

39. Nor can we regard the profession of devotion to the Union, on the part of those who are not our assailants, as sincere, when they pronounce eulogies upon the Union, evidently with the intent of charging us with disunion, without uttering one word of denunciation against our assailants. If friends of the Union, their course should be to unite with us in repelling these assaults, and denouncing the authors as enemies of the Union. Why they avoid this, and pursue the course they do, it is for them to explain.

40. Nor can the Union be saved by invoking the name of the illustrious Southerner whose mortal remains repose on the western bank of the Potomac. He was one of us—a slave-holder and a planter. We have studied his history, and find nothing in it to justify submission to wrong. On the contrary, his great fame rests on the solid foundation, that, while he was careful to avoid doing wrong to others, he was prompt and decided in repelling wrong. I trust that, in this respect, we profited by his example.

41. Nor can we find any thing in his history to deter us from seceding from the Union, should it fail to fulfill the objects for which it was instituted, by being permanently and hopelessly converted into the means of oppressing instead of protecting us. On the contrary, we

find much in his example to encourage us, should we be forced to the extremity of deciding between submission and disunion. . . .

42. Having now shown what cannot save the Union, I return to the question with which I commenced. How can the Union be saved? There is but one way by which it can with any certainty; and that is, by a full and final settlement, on the principle of justice, of all the questions at issue between the two sections. The South asks for justice, simple justice, and less she ought not to take. She has no compromise to offer, but the Constitution; and no concession or surrender to make. She has already surrendered so much that she has little left to surrender. Such a settlement would go to the root of the evil, and remove all cause of discontent, by satisfying the South, that she could remain honorably and safely in the Union, and thereby restore the harmony and fraternal feeling between the sections, which existed anterior to the Missouri agitation. Nothing else can, with any certainty, finally and for ever settle the questions at issue, terminate agitation, and save the Union.

43. But can this be done? Yes, easily; not by the weaker party, for it can of itself do nothing, not even protect itself, but by the stronger. The North has only to will it to accomplish it, to do justice by conceding to the South an equal right in the acquired territory, and to do her duty by causing the stipulations relative to fugitive slaves to be faithfully fulfilled, to cease the agitation of the slave question, and to provide for the insertion of a provision in the Constitution, by an amendment, which will restore to the South, in substance, the power she possessed of protecting herself, before the equilibrium between the sections was destroyed by the action of this Government. There will be no difficulty in devising such a provision, one that will protect the South, and which, at the same time, will improve and strengthen the Government, instead of impairing and weakening it.

44. But will the North agree to this? It is for her to answer the question. But, I will say, she cannot refuse, if she has half the love of the Union which she professes to have, or without justly exposing herself to the charge that her love of power and aggrandizement is far greater than her love of the Union. At all events, the responsibility of saving the Union rests on the North, and not on the South. The South cannot save it by any act of hers, and the North may save it without any sacrifice whatever, unless to do justice, and to perform her duties under the Constitution, should be regarded by her as a sacrifice.

45. It is time, Senators, that there should be an open and manly avowal on all sides, as to what is intended to be done. If the question is not

now settled, it is uncertain whether it ever can hereafter be; and we, the representatives of the States of this Union, regarded as governments, should come to a distinct understanding as to our respective views, in order to ascertain whether the great questions at issue can be settled or not. If you, who represent the stronger portion, cannot agree to settle them on the broad principle of justice and duty, say so; and let the States we both represent agree to separate and part in peace. If you are unwilling we should part in peace, tell us so; and we shall know what to do, when you reduce the question to submission or resistance. If you remain silent, you will compel us to infer by your acts what you intend. In that case, California will become the test question. If you admit her, under all the difficulties that oppose her admission, you compel us to infer that you intend to exclude us from the whole of the acquired territories, with the intention of destroying, irretrievably, the equilibrium between the two sections. We would be blind not to perceive in that case, that your real objects are power and aggrandizement, and infatuated not to act accordingly.

46. I have now, Senators, done my duty in expressing my opinions fully, freely, and candidly, on this solemn occasion. In doing so, I have been governed by the motives which have governed me in all the stages of the agitation of the slavery question since its commencement. I have exerted myself, during the whole period, to arrest it, with the intention of saving the Union, if it could be done; and if it could not, save the section where it has pleased Providence to cast my lot, and which I sincerely believe has justice and the Constitution on its side. Having faithfully done my duty to the best of my ability, both to the Union and my section, throughout this agitation, I shall have the consolation, let what will come, that I am free from all responsibility.

The structure of this section is straightforward. After an introductory paragraph, Calhoun sets up, not an argument, but a *praeteritio* (see the Glossary): The Union cannot be saved by eulogies, it cannot be saved by invoking the name of George Washington, it can be saved only by "a full and final settlement." This long *praeteritio* in itself, without the marked change in tone of the speech, would be sufficient to signal the end of the really argumentative section. It actually constitutes a long and elaborate conclusion, although a second conclusion is added in paragraphs forty-five and forty-six.

Within this structure several interesting moves are made.

There is a minor argument in the last sentence of paragraph thirty-six. Paragraphs thirty-seven through thirty-nine set up a *paralipsis*, because what they say is not really germane to the argument. If eulogies are in vain, then the motives of eulogizers are irrelevant. But the *paralipsis* is also an argument, in fact a sorites, as follows:

All lovers of the Union are devoted to anything that maintains it.
The Constitution maintains the Union.
Therefore, lovers of the Union are devoted to the Constitution.
But, to be devoted to the Constitution is to refrain from violating it, and to repel violators.
The North does not refrain from violating it and does not repel violators.
Therefore, the North is not devoted to the Constitution.

It follows, of course, that the North did not love the Union either, which was the point Calhoun proposed to make.

The *praeteritio* is an effective rhetorical device with which to introduce this third section because it gives the impression of a practical man sweeping away false possibilities to make way for the true and necessary solution to the problem. Its effectiveness depends, of course, on the prior establishment of a position by argumentation from which he can draw the conclusion he wishes. This conclusion, in paragraphs forty-two to forty-four, is not really argued; it is set up largely by *antitheses* (see the Glossary): not the South but the North, justice and not less, and so forth.

To understand the articulation of any argumentative speech or essay as a whole, it is useful to think of it as a series of strategies enabling the speaker or writer to say something with the greatest possible effect. One begins by wanting to show one's audience that "X is better than Y." This would be the conclusion of the speech, and what precedes it is simply a series of strategic moves permitting one to so declare as persuasively as possible. In practice, of course, the writer will frequently blur his general strategy somewhat with secondary intentions. But he must always keep moving toward the realization of his chief intention or the speech or essay will collapse into incoherence.

This point of view is obviously applicable to the speech just analyzed, with only minor modifications. The ostensible conclusion, paragraphs forty-five and forty-six, is really a kind of formal rounding-off, chiefly functioning to restore the ethos established in the beginning and abandoned in section three. In fact, the whole of section three, the lengthy *praeteritio,* constitutes the real conclusion, which is brought to its point in paragraphs forty-two and following. And what Calhoun says is simple enough; if the Union is to be saved, the North must meet the conditions demanded by the South (specifically, by Calhoun), and not the other way around. He feels that he need not argue this point, but merely assert it, because of the position that he established prior to this conclusion. Having established the South as the victim of northern machinations and having convicted the North of being the destructive aggressor in the matter of the Union itself, the rest follows. The *praeteritio* is, consequently, a part of the whole proof structure even though it is not itself an argument.

Yet there remains a kind of ambiguity about the speech, which is really an ambiguity about Calhoun's intentions. And the question is: to whom is it addressed? To answer, "to the Senate and beyond that to the country as a whole," is not sufficient. The significant audiences for a speaker or writer are defined by their attitudes toward himself. It is useful to think of three potential audiences for each speech or essay: one's own party, one's opponents, and a middle party that might go either way. Every speaker, of course, would like to address all three audiences with equal effect; in practice a speaker must choose, because the grounds that might move one audience are apt to leave the others unimpressed.

Ideally, Calhoun's strategy in this speech would have been (1) to clear the South of blame for any subsequent disagreeableness, (2) to put northern spokesmen on the defensive, and (3) to win sympathy from neutral observers. And the ambiguity of the speech arises because, although Calhoun's original ethos of the indifferent observer seems to be directed to (2) and, indirectly, to (3), in his long *praeteritio* he suddenly shifts to an ethos that is only appropriate to (1).

Did Calhoun suddenly alter his intention at the very conclusion of his speech? Surely not. Rather, Calhoun's ostensible audience, his northern opponents, was never his real audience. If Calhoun had been interested in communicating with the North, as he seems to be, he would have attempted to find arguments whose major premises the North might have accepted, or at least ones they might have been troubled by. But the premises behind this speech are southern ones from the very beginning. Calhoun's real object in this speech was to frame a theoretical justification for secession.

Given this intention, the break in ethos that marks the third section was precisely right. Having established his ground for secession in the guise of an indifferent observer of the scene, he stepped forward in his own character to rally the troops.

Conclusion

It might, perhaps, have been preferable to introduce the subject of essay and speech structure with a simpler example. But simplicity in these matters is hard to find. And the Calhoun speech is a typical, even better than typical, example of the way argument, in practice, works most of the time. It is a straightforward structure leading to a conclusion in a reasonable sort of way. The complexity of the speech lies not in its structure but in the intention behind the structure. Calhoun had not one, but two objectives in this speech. In the first place, he wanted to provide a justification for southern secession. And he did this. But in the second place, he did not want the onus of doing it. So the justification is enveloped in, and somewhat blurred by, an apparently conciliatory intention, to define the possibilities for conciliation. Calhoun's speech is not exceptional in this respect; human beings are seldom single-minded, and human situations are seldom simple.

Part II

Textual Rhetoric

As was pointed out earlier, classical rhetoricians (at least as they are represented by surviving texts) were generally preoccupied with the problems inherent in structural rhetoric—with the finding and classifying of arguments, with their effective arrangement, and so forth. But this was not the essence of rhetoric in the popular mind. One of the many ironies in the history of rhetoric is that rhetoric was generally regarded not as the organization of parts of discourse, but as the manipulation of language to doubtful ends. The charge against rhetoric was—and is—that it had as its objective inducing conviction where the mere facts did not warrant conviction. This was of course largely accomplished by textual rhetoric, by the manipulation of words and sentences.

Any discussion of the proper uses of rhetoric must begin by a consideration of this traditional charge, and a passage from a late Platonic dialogue, the *Theaetetus,* provides a useful text:

All is probability with you, and yet surely you and Theodorus had better reflect whether you are disposed to admit of probability and *figures of speech* in matters of such importance. He or any other mathematician who argued from probabilities and likelihoods in geometry would not be worth an ace.[1]

The implicit comparison in this passage is between "probability and figures of speech" on the one hand and certainty and "factual" speech on the other. More precisely, it is a comparison between rhetoric and logic. This comparison was responsible for the bad name that rhetoric bore from the beginning, and which it still bears. If dialectic was the art of the true, rhetoric could only be the art of the probable, or even worse, of the seeming-true.[2]

But what is involved in this claim for logic as a way to the real truth of things, to reality? Obviously, to propose a method for reaching truth is to assume that truth necessarily is in a form that makes this method particularly appropriate. The nineteenth-century assumption that mathematics would disclose the ultimate nature of reality presupposed a reality that was, itself, mathematical. The same assumption was implicit in the classical regard for logic, that reality itself was logical or dialectical in character.

This assumption can be illustrated by a reconsideration of the syllogism quoted earlier:

> All men are mortal.
> Socrates is a man.
> Therefore, Socrates is mortal.

[1] *Plato's Theaetetus,* trans. Benjamin Jowett, Library of Liberal Arts, No. 13 (Indianapolis: Bobbs-Merrill, 1949), p. 25. Italics added. The remark is attributed to Protagoras, but the context makes it clear that the principle is accepted by Socrates and the other interlocutors.

[2] The student should not misconstrue this section as an assault on philosophy; the individual who has not engaged in the two-thousand-year-old dialogue that is philosophy will have missed much. But the fact remains that at least a great many philosophers have denied that they were engaged in dialogue, because they assumed that they were pursuing with some success an ultimate truth of things. The point that I would make is that rhetoric has been misunderstood, and denigrated, because these philosophers have encouraged us to believe in a possibility that is no possibility. In fact, a philosophical text lends itself to rhetorical analysis as readily as any other kind; philosophers write persuasive prose, some of it of a very high order.

As was pointed out before, in its essence the syllogism always does the same thing: it relates two terms—"Socrates" and "mortal" in this case—by means of a third term, "man."

If one looks closely at such a transaction it becomes very peculiar indeed. In large measure, this peculiarity lies in the form of "to be" which is inevitably the connection between the terms. At times it is a definitional relationship, an equivalence: "To act nobly is to be a man." But when used in a syllogism, "is" more often proposes a class relationship. It either asserts that "Socrates was short," in which the subject is put in a miscellaneous collection of objects having the predicate in common only, or it asserts that "Socrates was a man," thereby putting one substance, or one kind of substance (i.e., "men," in "Men are mortal") into a larger class of substances.

To regard the syllogism as an approach to reality is to assume for its categorizing terms some sort of ultimate status in the universe. Reality itself, whatever *that* is, would have to be composed of classes and equivalences. It would have to be a large hierarchy of classes and subclasses, and subclasses of subclasses, until every individual thing was included. And these classes would have to be real in some unimaginable way, not matters of convenience.

But this syllogistic world would have another characteristic implicit in the verb "to be." "To be" is not a verb as other verbs— "to run," for instance—because it excludes action. It proposes a state of things beyond the flux of experience. If the syllogism is taken seriously as a truth-telling device, then ultimate reality must be a static world of mysteriously connected classes of objects—a world, in fact, very much like those ideal forms of Plato.

These observations on the nature of the syllogism are not made because any large number of people in the twentieth century cherish the classical hopes for syllogistic logic as a means to truth. But centuries of faith in the syllogism have left their mark on twentieth-century thought, particularly in a common attitude toward language. We still believe that words can be divided into objective and subjective components (denotation and connotation), and we still believe there is something especially manly about the former. (For instance, consider merely the great effort of the social sciences to elaborate a terminology that will eliminate subjectivity.) We expect this objective language to refer to real units of things as they are in a clear and unequivocal way, exactly as the terms of the syllogism seem to do. Finally, we are suspicious of complicated sentences as being, somehow, engaged in falsifying and distorting the truth (which is thereby presumed to be simple in nature). All of these expectations about language are apparent in most twentieth-century writing making large truth claims, and they all derive, and obviously so, from the ancient search for truth by means of the syllogism.[3]

Plato, at least, knew what he was about; he hoped that by logic, or mathematics, man might find a position in the universe that would be absolutely independent of *this* time, *this* experience, *this* physiological constitution, even of *this* mind. Certainty was, and is, possible in no other way. All of the qualities and capacities that make up the human being must be put aside; an absolute judgment can be made only from a point of view that is itself absolute. In the twentieth century we have formally renounced the possibility of absolute objectivity, but our attitudes toward language are still shaped by that possibility. Our attitudes toward language reflect the conditions of a search that we have abandoned.

Of course we frequently use syllogistic formulas in our ordinary language, which would be the poorer without them. But we must recognize that they do not express perceptions; they are abstractions. In our *experience* with Socrates, we do not experience shortness or manness, just as we do not experience a white ball as something round, white, and solid. We experience entities, not qualities. It is convenient to be able to describe objects by relating them to abstract qualities, but we accomplish this relating by an abstractive mental operation, after the experience of the fact. Such statements cannot have any particular status as a higher order of truth.

In short, the classical world was hostile to textual rhetoric because it misunderstood, not merely the nature of language, but

[3] The real function of such language, of course, is to establish an ethos. We assure our hearers that we are delivering God's truth by trying to sound as scientific as possible. Jacques Barzun has handsomely assaulted the practice in Chapter IX of his *The House of Intellect* (New York: Harper and Brothers, 1959), pp. 216–249.

the nature of the reality available to human beings. And at some level this misunderstanding persists today. Language is not a means of declaring truths about an objectively perceived world, because as human beings we cannot perceive the world objectively. It cannot be a means of pointing to this or that object, because we have no way of knowing objects in themselves.

To put it another way: an act of perception is a kind of transaction, in that it necessarily includes the observer as well as the observed. It is obvious enough that I cannot see a physical object in its entirety at any one time; from any position that I assume, that physical object will have a backside invisible to me. But this limitation is multiplied a hundred- or a thousand-fold when human activity is under consideration. As a perceiver I am not merely limited by my spatial relationship to that activity; I am limited by the experience I bring to the perception, by my intelligence, by my estimate of what I ought to perceive—in short, I am limited by myself. Any account of complicated human behavior, for instance, is necessarily an act of self-revelation as well as a statement about what has been observed.

Nor do human beings really perceive objects. We do not perceive white balls or mothers or psychologists; we perceive contexts in which these happen to be found. An accurate description of human perception would not speak of objects, but of object-relationships. These object-relationships vary with the slightest shifts in context and perspective, and they are in some measure created by the past experience each observer brings to them. Human beings share a world, but it is necessarily different for each one. It is not even fixed for a single individual over any length of time.

Such are the characteristics of our human world, and we speak truly about it when we are faithful to our perception of it. Truth in speech is not merely a matter of immediate and direct reports of our perceptions as opposed to the larger generalizations about human experience, although it should be self-evident that the former are necessarily closer to experience than the latter. To speak truly is to accept our human perspective at all levels of discourse, to recognize that abstractions about "man" or "learning," for instance, are rooted in our own perceptions and are as ultimately subjective as a lyric by Emily Dickinson. The writer's job at every level of abstraction is to report his conclusions as accurately as he can, as his conclusions; the major enemy of such accuracy is an artificial language designed to deny the subjectivity of the experience by the creation of a "scientific" ethos.

Human languages (or at least the languages of the Western world) are extraordinarily well-adapted to the job of accurate communication, primarily because, considered word by word and sentence by sentence, they are so very imprecise. The miracle of human communication is possible because these imprecise counters respond so sensitively to their context. For instance, "Leaves fall in the garden" and "The garden is full of leaves" mean very different things because "leaves" and "garden" have been mutually altered in the process of being reversed and by having the verbal element changed. The meaning of both words would inevitably be altered further if more sentences were added to these two. It is the imprecision of language in its raw state that makes this alteration—toward greater precision of meaning, it should be noticed—possible. It is by relating these amorphous counters to each other that we achieve the individual experience, the individual point of view, the individual judgment.

But this language will not work for us if we confine ourselves to simple sentences and dictionary meanings. Language must be forced to yield an approximation of the individual's view of the world by an habitual violence on the part of the writer. Words must be warped into new meanings. Sentences must double back upon themselves. We must repeat and compare and catalog.

Textual rhetoric is simply a classification of the common alterations in language that enable us to escape the limitations of dictionaries and even grammars to say what we mean. It is not, as Socrates assumed in the *Gorgias,* a technique for deceit; it is a technique for getting at the truth, the human truth. Of course, rhetoricians, like other people, deceive, and they may use their art to this end. The use of rhetoric for deception must be considered in its place. But the way rhetoric works in truth-telling must be our first consideration.

Chapter IV

The Function
of Textual Rhetoric

We have defined textual rhetoric as the classification of the various kinds of distortions introduced into language in the endeavor to make it yield human truth. These distortions can, of course, be used to another end, to misrepresentation. But the precision of communication that we now take for granted would be impossible if the distortions of language described by textual rhetoric were not available to us.

To speak of the distortion of language implies the existence of a condition of non-distortedness, of norms, against which particular distortions can be measured. Textual rhetoric indeed presupposes the existence, in the reader's mind, of standard, normative patterns of discourse. In the matter of word order, for instance, the normal English pattern is subject-verb-object, with modifiers as close as possible to the words they modify.[1] In other languages, in German

---

[1] There is a minor theoretical difficulty in such a position, since in most texts (the present one, for instance) non-normal sentences will be found to outnumber the so-called normal ones. The distinction is a matter of ear; surely most people would feel that such a sentence as, "When I went home, I found Archibald there," a modification of, "I found Archibald there when I went home." The present discussion would not be invalidated if the student should prefer to recognize, with linguists, the existence of several basic sentence structures of coordinate significance.

or Latin for instance, different norms prevail. What norm prevails in a particular instance is of little consequence. It is merely necessary that there be normative structures in terms of which rhetorical variations can be assessed.

Below the level of grammatical structures, at the level of word meanings, the function of textual rhetoric needs to be distinguished from considerations of diction. We are in the presence of rhetoric when we sense a violated norm of word usage.

Of course, any alteration in diction is important to meaning. It has been pointed out that no word retains quite the same meaning when it is shifted to a new context; the meaning may not hold steady even when it is displaced in a sentence. To take a most elementary example: a logician, in reducing the sentence, "The wicked alone are happy," to a logical proposition, came up with the statement, "All happy individuals are wicked." But these two sentences do not say the same thing. The first statement is an indictment of the world; the second is an indictment of happiness. The same example shows the importance of grammatical form to meaning. In part, these sentences mean different things because "wicked" has become "the wicked," and the noun is more concrete (which usually means something like "more experiential") than the adjective.

Hence even small variations in context and form effect meaning. But it is also true that words tend to carry with them a normative context. "Salt" implies one context and "sodium chloride" another, and in each case the usual context carries over, to some degree, into a new context. On the other hand, when the normative context of diction is mutually reinforced—that is, when the words of a piece of discourse are drawn roughly from the same context— we have so-called usage levels, formal, colloquial, and so forth.

These characteristics of diction are important and useful; writers play with them habitually. But they are not really accessible to analysis because no violated terms are implied. "The wicked alone are happy" and "All happy individuals are wicked" mean different things, but one cannot say that one is normal and the other not. We can characterize diction (as formal or whatever) but we have no means of moving beyond such gross classification. And the normative context that most words carry is too weak to permit analysis.

Alterations in diction become rhetorical—become, in fact, tropes—when there is a sharp tension between the particular use and some perceived normative use. A paradigmatic trope attempts to get at the character of *A* by relating it to something else, to *B*. Of course, there are other kinds of tensions between the particular and normative that are usefully classed as tropes, as the Glossary makes clear. The word "normative" poses at least a theoretical problem here, but perhaps we can simply say that a word is used normally when we feel that it points directly to our experience of something.

Tropes are signaled by a tension between a word and its context. If the context makes it clear that the word "catsup," for instance, refers to a thin, red paste made from tomatoes, the word is being used normally. But in some contexts it might be clear that the word "catsup" referred to a fluid more commonly called "blood." In this instance, "catsup" would be a trope.

But it would not be merely a substitute for "blood"; it would significantly alter the account of the experience thus reported. Tropes are always worth our attention, because they are perhaps the chief means available to the writer to get at the experience itself rather than a statement about experience. It seems paradoxical that experienced reality must be approached in such an indirect fashion, but it is a paradox that anyone who has responded even to Joyce Kilmer's "Trees" can confirm.

What, precisely, do the distortions of textual rhetoric, in diction and grammar, accomplish? No classification can claim to be exhaustive; rhetoric can do whatever it does. But most rhetorical figures will be found to be performing one of the following functions: emphasis, division, comparison, and definition or redefinition. In addition, textual rhetoric is indispensable to the establishment of the position, or stance, of the writer toward his subject, to the definition of his attitude toward that subject. Finally, both rhetorical and logical devices are necessary to the change in levels of abstraction upon which all argumentative discourse depends.

Some figures ordinarily perform one specific job no matter what the context. The *comparatio,* for instance, sets up a comparison. But even the function of the *comparatio* can never be taken for granted. All figures are capable of performing a variety of functions; one figure may perform several functions at the same time. The balance of this chapter will discuss, briefly, these possible functions of textual rhetoric.

Emphasis

The writer of direct discourse must habitually contend with the problem of keeping the reader aware of the relative importance of his terms. How much weight and consideration a reader will give to a particular conception will depend to a surprising extent on the simple matter of the space it gets and the time it requires for understanding. But from the writer's point of view, there is no necessary correlation between the importance of a conception and its complexity. The subject of his thesis, for instance, will invariably be of more importance to his argument than a qualification of that subject; at the same time, the qualification may be much more complicated, and therefore require much more space for simple understanding. Simply to state, for each conception or term, what is necessary for clarity in such an instance would grossly falsify the relative importance of the two conceptions, and the reader would be very apt to misunderstand the whole argument as a consequence. Since the complexity of the qualification defies reduction, the writer has no choice but to amplify and emphasize the simple, but unfortunately important, subject of his thesis. He will have recourse to *emphasis*.

This function of rhetoric is omnipresent in both poetry and prose. It can be performed by almost any figure, but *accumulation* is perhaps the most common emphasizing device. Quintilian's example of this figure illustrates a common kind of emphasis:

> What was that sword of yours doing, Tubero, the sword you drew on the field of Pharsalus? Against whose body did you aim its point? What meant those arms you bore?
>
> (*Institute* VIII. 4. 27)

We have a series of figures—three rhetorical questions—a *repetitio* of the word "sword" and the accumulation itself, in that the three questions all mean roughly the same thing. The function of this accumulation is simply to lend force to the point.

The above quotation is very dramatic, but emphasis is by no means confined to such situations. The following passage is at least as obviously directed to this function, although it is drawn from a soberly scientific article:

> In sleep and dream, man's activity in the outer world is suspended, especially his motor activity. Attention and perception are withdrawn from outer reality. The necessity to cope with the environment is interrupted for the duration of sleep. The stringent rules of logic and reason subside,—rules which during waking life are geared to useful, rational, adaptive, behavior and thought. The psyche receives leave, for the period of conventional control of sleep, from the demands of active life in society. As Freud expresses it, endopsychic censorship is reduced.[2]

This passage is a very long accumulation. The conception is stated in the first sentence; it is applied specifically through three more; and the thought of the first sentence is repeated again in the last two sentences. Such accumulation is a measure of the importance of the conception—a simple one—to the writer's thesis.

But emphasis can have another function, illustrated by the following sentences:

> At first sight we might imagine that knowledge could be defined as "true belief." When what we believe is true, it might be supposed that we had achieved a knowledge of what we believe.[3]

Now, both of these sentences say the same thing; the figure is an accumulation. But Mr. Russell is not merely lending weight to what is being said; he is also helping the reader. What he has to say is at first sight confusing. To enable the reader to follow him, he offers first the general idea, and then he says the same thing in

[2] Ernest G. Schachtel, "On Memory," *A Study of Interpersonal Relations,* ed. Patrick Mullahy (New York: Hermitage, 1949), p. 32.

[3] Bertrand Russell, *The Problems of Philosophy* (New York: Galaxy, 1959), p. 131.

a more complicated, and more accurate, way. The accumulation is thus a help to the reader as well as a rhetorical move.

A chronic confusion about the nature of direct discourse has frequently led to a mistaken condemnation of emphatic figures, particularly in freshman handbooks. A typical passage would go something like this:

> Do not repeat yourself. If what you have to say is said clearly in the first place, it is not necessary to say it again.

The badness of the advice is evident in the fact that it can hardly be given without recourse to the supposed vice it cautions against.

Virtually every rhetorical figure makes the passage in which it occurs more prominent, and hence emphasis is omnipresent in discourse. Some Renaissance rhetoricians, consequently, argued that the chief function of all rhetorical figures was to emphasize. This is a gross exaggeration of a significant truth.

Division

A second important function of rhetoric is the separation of conceptions or objects ordinarily lumped together. Sometimes one wishes to separate consequences of an activity. Sometimes one wishes to divide a concept. A classical instance of the latter activity, accomplished by a *structural distributio,* will be found in the Glossary. A somewhat different use of the *structural distributio* is seen in the second paragraph of Matthew Arnold's "Sweetness and Light":

> I have before now pointed out that we English do not, like the foreigners, use this word [curiosity] in a good sense as well as in a bad sense. With us the word is always used in a somewhat disapproving sense. A liberal and intelligent eagerness about things of the mind may be meant by a foreigner when he speaks of curiosity, but with us the word always conveys a certain notion of frivolous and unedifying activity.[4]

[4] Matthew Arnold, *Culture and Anarchy,* ed. J. Dover Wilson (Cambridge: Cambridge University Press, 1932), p. 43.

Here Arnold takes a word, curiosity, with a customary usage that he does not like, and creates, by means of accumulation and antithesis, a new and more desirable meaning. He thus builds a *structural distributio* by claiming a new sense for the word in question.

Division can function less obviously, as in the following example:

> . . . However, all scientific statements and laws have one characteristic in common: they are "true or false" (adequate or inadequate). Roughly speaking, our reaction to them is "yes" or "no."
>
> The scientific way of thinking has a further characteristic. The concepts which it uses to build up its coherent systems are not expressing emotions. For the scientist, there is only "being," but no wishing, no valuing, no good, no evil; no goal. As long as we remain within the realm of science proper, we can never meet with a sentence of the type: "Thou shalt not lie." . . .
>
> From this it might seem as if logical thinking were irrelevant for ethics. Scientific statements of facts and relations, indeed, cannot produce ethical directives. However, ethical directives can be made rational and coherent by logical thinking and empirical knowledge. . . .[5]

The function of the passage is obviously to establish a role for science in the matter of ethics. But Einstein approaches the problem indirectly; only after he has carefully established what science cannot do (largely by accumulation, it will be noticed) does he propose a positive function. By the distinction he implicitly divides ethics into principles and elaborations, the latter being susceptible to scientific treatment.

Many figures can be used to make divisions of concepts. Most figures involving two clauses can function to set up a division, as can comparisons and, on occasion, tropes.

Definition and Redefinition

It is obvious that the writer must specify what he is talking about, must define. But this necessity is not to be taken for granted;

[5] Albert Einstein, "The Laws of Science and the Laws of Ethics," in *Essays: An Analytic Reader,* ed. Ralph W. Rader and Sheldon Sacks (Boston and Toronto: Little, Brown, 1964), p. 106.

its definitions are central to every argument. The way reality looks is in part determined by the position from which one regards it, and a definition necessarily reflects that position. Dictionary definitions are, as a consequence, seldom useful to the writer of argument. He must propose his own, as he needs them, and they will be an essential part of the argument itself.

Very often, and particularly at the beginning of an argument, these definitions will be undisguised. In the third paragraph of his book, *The Lonely Crowd,* for instance, David Riesman defines the subject of his argument:

"Social character" is that part of "character" which is shared among significant social groups and which, as most contemporary social scientists define it, is the product of the experience of these groups.[6]

These initial definitions are a part of the "given" of an argument; they cannot really be supported by argumentative means without getting involved in another argument. The reader must accept them at least as hypotheses or reject the whole book without reading it.

But definitions are not always so easy to spot. About one page later, Riesman has a definition of a different sort:

What is the relation between social character and society? How is it that every society seems to get, more or less, the social character it "needs"? Erik H. Erikson writes, in a study of the social character of the Yurok Indians, that ". . . systems of child training . . . represent unconscious attempts at creating out of human raw material that configuration of attitudes which is (or once was) the optimum under the tribe's particular natural conditions and economic-historic necessities."[7]

The first two sentences raise a question to which definition would seem inappropriate; what is it that relates character and society? One would expect an argument of one kind or another. But what one gets is a definition of the ends of child training, although this

[6] David Riesman, with Nathan Glazer and Reuel Denney, *The Lonely Crowd* (Garden City, N.Y.: Doubleday, 1950), p. 18.

[7] *Ibid.,* p. 19.

character is hardly clear on first sight. Moreover, it is not a neutral definition; most anthropologists would probably deny the relationship between culture and economics that this passage implies. The definition functions to establish a connection that is indispensable to Riesman's whole book, without involving him in what might otherwise be a protracted discussion. The reader might feel, of course, that some discussion of so important a connection would have been useful.

Redefinition very often looks and functions much like definition; the writer more or less openly considers a definition he does not like and modifies it to suit his own purposes. But redefinition can work much more subtly; a term can be transformed in what seems at first sight casual accumulation. In the passage quoted above, for instance, the first sentence asks "What is the relationship between social character and society," the second, "What is the necessary and determinative relationship." The second sentence does not simply amplify the first; it redefines the connection Riesman will inevitably discover thereafter.

This kind of movement is very common in direct discourse. A psychologist writing of different kinds of thinking asserts, "They are all activities—behavior patterns which are either overt and publicly observable or else covert yet capable of being objectified under certain favorable conditions."[8] These terms, "activities" and "behavior patterns," are not synonyms in the vocabularies of many of us, nor does the text provide any warrant for believing that they should be so regarded. Actually, the first term functions as a bridge, a neutral description which would be generally accepted, from which the writer can advance to the definition that he wants, which is not at all neutral. As with the Riesman quotation, this redefinition enables the writer to get to his own argumentative ground as economically as possible.

Given the fact that an argument proceeds by connecting terms one to another, and the further fact that these terms are almost always defined *ad hoc,* for the specific purpose the writer has in mind, it follows that definitions and redefinitions will be omni-

---

[8] Robert Thomson, *The Psychology of Thinking* (Baltimore: Penguin Books, 1959), p. 18.

present in argumentative discourse. The writer is entitled to make his definitions to suit his own point of view. But the reader is not obliged to accept these definitions if they seem unwarranted. He should know when something is being defined, and should decide whether or not the definitions bear an illuminating relationship to his own perceived reality.

Comparison

Writers ordinarily put one object by another for one of .two reasons. In the first place, comparison is virtually indispensable to any writer who would get at a thing or an experience in itself. It is thus very nearly the basic strategy of the writer of imaginative discourse, the poet or the novelist. Comparisons at least analogous to those of poetry are found also in argument. Paul Valery, for instance, in attempting to get at the relationship between the creation of literature and its appreciation, writes:

There are many effects—and among them the most powerful— which require the absence of any direct correspondence between the two activities concerned. A certain work, for example, is the fruit of long labor; it combines a large number of trials, repetitions, rejections, and choices. It has taken months, even years of reflection, and it may also presuppose the experience and attainments of a whole lifetime. Now, the effect of this work may take no more than a few moments to declare itself. A glance will suffice to appreciate a considerable monument, to feel its shock. In two hours all the calculations of the tragic poet, all the labor he has spent in ordering the effects of his play, shaping every line of it one by one; or again, all the harmonic and orchestral combinations contrived by the composer; or all the meditations of the philosopher, the long years he has put into curbing, controlling, withholding his thought until he could perceive and accept its definitive order, all these acts of faith, all these acts of choice, all these mental transactions finally reach the stage of the finished work, to strike, astonish, dazzle or disconcert the mind of the *Other,* who is suddenly subjected to the excitement of this enormous charge of intellectual labor. All this makes a *disproportionate* act.

One may (very roughly, of course) compare this effect to the fall, in a few seconds, of a mass which had been carried up, piece by piece, to the top of a tower without regard to the time or the number of trips.[9]

This is a standard kind of comparison; to explain a complex relationship, the writer simply invites the reader to imagine its physical equivalent.

At times one senses a more important function for this kind of illuminative comparison. In the introduction to *Patriotic Gore,* Edmund Wilson writes:

I think that it is a serious deficiency on the part of historians and political writers that they so rarely interest themselves in biological and zoological phenomena. In a recent Walt Disney film showing life at the bottom of the sea, a primitive organism called a sea slug is seen gobbling up smaller organisms through a large orifice at one end of its body; confronted with another sea slug of an only slightly lesser size, it ingurgitates that, too. Now, the wars fought by human beings are stimulated as a rule primarily by the same instincts as the voracity of the sea slug.[10]

This comparison is too vivid simply to illuminate its subject; the reader feels that in some sense it controls it. The sea slug and human history have come together in Mr. Wilson's mind in a way that is too intimate for one to be simply illuminating the other.

The second reason for using comparisons, although usually not such extended ones, is that they function as a kind of quick proof. Freud, defending psychoanalysis, wrote:

Whereas the psychology of consciousness never went beyond this broken sequence of events which was obviously dependent upon something else, the other view [psychoanalysis], which held that what is mental is in itself unconscious, enabled psychology to take its place as a natural science like any other. The processes with which it is concerned are in themselves just as unknowable as those dealt with by the other sci-

---

[9] Paul Valery, "A Course in Poetics: First Lesson," trans. Jackson Mathews, *The Southern Review,* V, No. 3 (Winter 1940), 406.

[10] Edmund Wilson, *Patriotic Gore* (New York: Oxford University Press, 1962), p. xi.

ences, by chemistry or physics, for example; but it is possible to establish the laws which those processes obey. . . .[11]

In the same passage, speaking of psychological hypotheses, he says of them:

> We can claim for them the same value as approximations as belongs to the corresponding intellectual scaffolding found in the other natural sciences.

In both quotations, the function of the references to the natural sciences is not to illuminate, it is to support psychoanalysis by allying it to a more prestigious study. Such argumentative comparisons are of course very common in psychological and sociological writing, where so much depends on the prestige of the study. The behaviorist Eysenck, defending intelligence tests, writes:

> To analyse out "intelligence" from the whole background of a person's emotional needs, experiences, and motivations is said to be "atomistic" and fallacious. But surely we do the same, with good success, in the physical sciences? We might say that in measuring the length of a bar of metal we are surely "handicapping" the bar by measuring it during a cold spell; it would be much longer in the heat of summer. This is perfectly true; "length" and "temperature" are not independent variables. . . . Similarly, it is quite possible that anxiety and intelligence interact.[12]

Comparisons of one sort or another are inescapable; they help the writer to get over awkward hiatuses as well as to define the things he wishes to talk about. But in every case what is brought forward as the basis for a comparison has some degree of further function besides simple contrast. Mr. Wilson's sea slug, for instance, was not the only available activity to illuminate human history. The selection of the sea slug is a part of the definition Mr. Wilson finally proposes, and not merely a convenient foil for that definition.

[11] Sigmund Freud, *An Outline of Psychoanalysis* (New York: W. W. Norton, 1949), pp. 35–36.

[12] H. J. Eysenck, *Uses and Abuses of Psychology* (Baltimore: Penguin Books, 1953), p. 27.

Position

A writer of argumentation must, whether he likes it or not, indicate his own relationship, or stance, toward the subject he is writing about. As has been argued earlier, he has no option in the matter; being there, he must define himself. The worst stance of all is that which pretends that it is no stance, that the writer, like a peculiar sort of mirror, simply reflects the existence of things in their inevitable relationships.

In most argumentative prose, position is not a particular problem for the reader (although it is always one for the writer). The writer defines himself and his relationship to his subject in his introduction and he maintains those definitions thereafter in large part by consistency of tone. At times the writer feels obliged to interrupt his argument to reestablish himself and his relationship to his subject, as does C. S. Lewis in the essay analyzed in Chapter VI; and at times the writer's strategy dictates some sort of radical redefinition, as was seen in the Calhoun speech previously analyzed. But these tactics are not common.

The three lengthy examples of introductions analyzed in Chapter II, together with the introduction analyzed in Chapter VI, indicate the range of positions or stances ordinarily found in argumentative prose. But there are occasions when the writer's position is more complicated. The following passage from *The Education of Henry Adams* is a useful illustration:

Had he been born in Jerusalem under the shadow of the Temple and circumcised in the Synagogue by his uncle the high priest, under the name of Israel Cohen, he would scarcely have been more distinctly branded, and not much more heavily handicapped in the races of the coming century, in running for such stakes as the century was to offer; but, on the other hand, the ordinary traveller, who does not enter the field of racing, finds advantage in being, so to speak, ticketed through life, with the safeguards of an old, established traffic. Safeguards are often irksome, but sometimes convenient, and if one needs them at all, one is apt to need them badly. A hundred years earlier, such safeguards as his would have secured any young man's success; and although in 1838 their value was not very great compared with what they would have had in

1738, yet the mere accident of starting a twentieth-century career from a nest of associations so colonial—so troglodytic—as the First Church, the Boston State House, Beacon Hill, John Hancock and John Adams, Mount Vernon Street and Quincy, all crowding on ten pounds of unconscious babyhood, was so queer as to offer a subject of curious speculation to the baby long after he had witnessed the solution.[13]

The Education is, among other things, an attempt to understand the relationship of the last half of the nineteenth century to preceding ages. But Adams' own attitude toward this relationship cannot be a simple one. On the one hand, he wrote at a time when belief in inevitable improvement, in progress, was very strong, and he himself could never utterly reject it. On the other hand, he obviously preferred the past. What position toward this relationship of past and present, then, could he assume? Almost inevitably, he assumed an *ironic* position or stance. Adams did not resolve these contradictory attitudes; he simply combined them into one complex stance by describing the past as simultaneously attractive and "troglodytic." Something like love for the past and a kind of contempt for it coexist for the moment.

Generalization and Particularization

Every example of discourse is pitched at a particular level of abstraction, someplace between the concreteness of the individual thing and a very inclusive class concept. Discourse about human beings, for instance, can range from the individual "Sam" through "Kentucky Mountain Man" to "American" to the most general concept, "man" or "animal." The level of abstraction is a part of the character of a particular piece of discourse, and together with the author's stance toward the subject, goes a long way toward the definition of its particular style.

But such a level of abstraction will ordinarily constitute only a kind of norm or median for the writer. His major strategy usually involves working to another level of abstraction, because something

[13] Henry Adams, *The Education of Henry Adams,* intro. D. W. Brogan (Boston: Houghton Mifflin, 1961), pp. 3–4.

has meaning for us, we "understand" it, precisely as we perceive it in relationship to another abstractive level. The writer concerned with Sam, for instance, can only make him meaningful to the reader by relating him to some general conception of human behavior—some higher level of abstraction.

This higher level of abstraction, however, probably has this possibility of making the concrete meaningful precisely because it can be related to our own experience—a lower level of abstraction. The writer must often establish this experiential connection in the course of his argument—must relate his median level to a lower level of abstraction. In poetry or fiction these shifts between levels of abstraction may be implicit. But it is the mark of argumentation that these shifts be ordinarily explicit.

In short, the writer of argumentation will be found to move frequently from his median level of abstraction to others, higher or lower. The shift to a higher level of abstraction can be called, for convenience, "generalization"; to a lower level, "particularization." These two kinds of movement obviously parallel induction and deduction, and indeed, these logical procedures are indispensable to argumentation precisely because they are such convenient devices for shifting levels of abstractions. But other rhetorical structures can accomplish the same ends.

Generalization is particularly characteristic of creative writing. The novelist or the poet ordinarily begins with the more or less concrete, and somehow he must extend this concreteness, must make it stand for more than itself merely. No one is interested in what happened to a group of Russians in 1812 or to a poet in 1600, unless what happened can be extended in some fashion so as to become relevant to the reader at a later time. In imaginative discourse, however, this extension is often merely implicit. It is likely that the chief value of tropes to poetry, for instance, is that they establish an implicit relationship between levels of abstraction.

It is obvious that in argumentation the chief devices for generalization will be logical, perhaps not so obvious that they will be inductive. But when the argumentative writer has recourse to specific instances, his object is to persuade the reader to generalize from those instances to the level of abstraction in which the writer is interested. Whether a particular device generalizes or particularizes must depend on the level of abstraction the writer wants to end up with.

Other rhetorical devices can be used to generalize. For instance, the behaviorist must somehow move from the activities of a specific group of animals (or sophomores) in a specific situation to some much larger generalization in which he is ultimately interested. He cannot do this by induction, however; his samples are too small and too selective. He will ordinarily do it, rather, by implicit or explicit redefinition. At some point in his argument, the observation that he proposes to report—"these animals did so and so," for instance—will become a statement about "learning."[14]

Particularization is more common to argument than generalization; this is sufficiently proven by its characteristically deductive structure. The writer of an argument must assume the existence of a body of generalizations agreed upon by himself and his audience. The introduction of a "reason" into his discourse is actually an appeal to a higher level of generalization.[15] For instance, if one were to argue that "Rudolph necessarily misunderstands the nature of language because he is a logical positivist," the implied major premise, "All logical positivists misunderstand the nature of language," is pitched at a higher level of abstraction than the proposed conclusion about Rudolph. The writer would be particularizing from an abstraction already given.

Nonlogical means of moving from one level of abstraction to another are also available for particularizing. Irwin Edman writes, for instance:

The fact is, however, that this theory of art as escape fails to take into account much that is true of aesthetic experience, and is an insult to

[14] In fact, he will Platonize; he will posit the existence of something in the universe called "learning," of which his particular study is only an instance. His generalizing move is hence of a most extreme kind.

[15] The deductive structure appealing to a class concept that is coincident with one of the concepts being related should be regarded as a kind of redefinition. For instance, if I should attempt to establish that "Andrew is rational" by appealing to the fact that "All men are rational" as a major premise (and it is also assumed that "Only men are rational," so that on the circle diagram the circle "men" coincides with the circle "rational"), I am simply substituting the term "rational" for the term "man."

the more rich and positive aspects of aesthetic enjoyment and production. It abstracts the Aesthetic Man much as the early nineteenth century abstracted the Economic Man. No one is ever, or ever for long, an
aesthetic observer, and part of aesthetic enjoyment is the rendition, vivid
and revealing, of the world we know and the nature we are. The eye of
the beholder is the eye of a human being. . . .[16]

The general function of this passage is obviously emphatic; it is a
series of accumulations. But the last sentence is also a kind of
sententia; it is in fact an appeal to a higher order of truth to support the relative particularity of the judgment the writer wants to
enforce. Argumentative prose is necessarily full of such particularizing moves.

At first sight this variety of function to be found within even
a simple-looking essay is bewildering, and its consideration may
seem to introduce a degree of complexity into the business of reading not to be justified by its utility. But this is not the case. The
student who would learn to read argumentation intelligently must
abandon the naïve conception of an argument as a series of terms
or conceptions straightforwardly connected in some sort of sequence
in time, as a common-sense consideration of practical problems in a
practical light. This no argument can be.

Although every argument must establish for itself a level of
generality, a particular distance from the concrete activity it wishes,
ultimately, to bring about, it will never maintain this level. It will
move up to generalizations of a higher level of abstractions, or down
toward particularity more or less constantly. If one could draw the
line an apparently simple argument is strung upon, it would look
like the fever chart of a very sick patient.

But if we were to improve upon this image, we would have to
see this line as strung with beads of various sizes, where the writer
stops and enlarges upon an important point. We would have to
visualize little lines running off the main one, where conceptions
are developed to be rejected in favor of the one in which the writer
is interested. We would have to see some beads deliberately strung
and then, as deliberately, removed for other beads similar at first
glance but really quite different. Any argument, in short, is an

[16] Irwin Edman, *Arts and the Man* (New York: W. W. Norton,
1939), p. 24.

extremely complicated structure, and if we are unable to grasp that structure, we will not understand the argument as we should. The consideration of textual rhetoric that follows in the next two chapters has been designed as a guide to an understanding of that structure in its details.

Chapter V

The Glossary[1]

The following glossary is unlike the classical glossaries from which
it has been drawn chiefly by reason of its intent. Classical rhetoric
from the beginning to the end was concerned with the art of speaking and writing, and classical glossaries of terms reflect this orientation. The present glossary is concerned primarily with reading.
Our intention has been to provide a reasonably brief critical vocabulary that will enable students and teachers to talk about
literature of all kinds in a more precise way than contemporary
critical language permits. We believe, further, that this vocabulary
permits a disciplined close reading of texts, minimizing the hazards of free association implicit in close reading at the present time.

Hence what follows is not an attempt to reproduce classical

[1] This glossary is the product of six years of experimentation and
thought by myself and Professor Leonard Nathan (who must thereby
assume joint responsibility for it). It is not designed for the analysis of
argumentation only; we have concluded that the ordinary student of
rhetoric would profit most by a glossary of terms applicable to any form
of English discourse. (This same glossary, except as it might be modified
by further experience, will be a part of a forthcoming volume by Professor Nathan and myself entitled *The Rhetoric of Poetry*.) The student
who is only interested in argumentation might simplify his labors by
simply learning to recognize tropes without attempting to distinguish
among the different kinds.

glossaries—an unproductive enterprise, even if their lack of consistency did not make it impossible. Rather, it is an attempt to provide a reasonably brief vocabulary that classifies the shapes habitually imposed on language in an attempt to make it reflect as accurately as possible the intentions of the writer.

This objective has, in the first place, provided a principle of selection. It was inevitable, given its ambiguous objectives, that classical rhetoric would aim at a description of all the shapes that language might take, and by the end of the sixteenth century the Renaissance successors of classical rhetoricians had detected and given names to some two hundred such shapes. But much of this terminology was engaged in isolating nonfunctional differences. For instance, the *Ad Herennium* distinguished four kinds of repetition, the *repetitio,* the *complexio,* the *conversio,* and the *traductio,* according to the place of the repeated word in the sentence or clause. But, while repetition can profoundly affect meaning, the place of a repeated word is not of great consequence.

In the present glossary the number of figures has been sharply reduced by two means. First, figures not clearly functional have been simply omitted. Second, and rather more often, this glossary represents a conflation of classical terms. In the instance noted above, for example, the glossary proposes one term, *repetitio,* to cover all instances of repetition, regardless of place in the clause or sentence.

Our concern to present textual rhetoric as a way of reading has, in the second place, led to great freedom of definition. We have stayed as close to classical usage as possible, but where the usual definitions of a particular figure seemed to blur rather than accentuate function, we have not scrupled to propose definitions having no classical warrant. As an instance, we have separated terms that were equivalent in classical rhetorics, *metaphor* and *translatio,* to identify a difference in usage not previously recognized.

At the same time, of course, we have tried to indicate our departures from classical definitions by indicating what those definitions were. Also, in deference to contemporary usage, we have retained several figures simply because they are reasonably well known—*synecdoche* and *simile,* for example. A *synecdoche* is merely a variety of a larger figure, *metonymy,* as a *simile* is (ordinarily) merely a *translatio* or *metaphor* preceded by "like" or "as." These distinctions are not very important. But we have retained the terms because they are already current.

We have tried to emphasize, frequently, that any classification of language must be after the fact. Writers do not write figures of speech. They establish complex verbal relationships in order to embody some particular intention. The rhetorician follows after and proposes a classification for the kinds of distortion of normal syntax and diction he observes. It is important to keep this in mind because language will always be more subtle than the definitions which rhetoricians propose for its elements, and the student who is uncomfortable with less than one-to-one relationships between definitions and instances would do well to avoid the subject of rhetoric altogether. Rhetoric cannot be an exact and inclusive science. The authors have spent years experimenting with rhetorical glossaries, and the present one is the most useful that they have been able to devise. But in instance after instance the student will find that a particular arrangement of language can reasonably be classified as either of two figures, as they are defined by the glossary. "Is this a *distributio* or simply an antithesis?" Over and over there will be room for debate, and the student must learn to be comfortable with the fact that there can be no definitive answer. If the debate calls attention to the text in a new way, it doesn't make any difference whether the particular figure is a *distributio* or not.

A word must be said about the terminology of this glossary. Neatness would have dictated that it be derived from one language, Latin, Greek, or English, and not a polyglot mixture of all three. But usage dictated the other course. The traditional terms are, by and large, Latin, and it would have been obfuscatory to propose Greek equivalents. At the same time, some of the best known rhetorical terms—*metaphor* and *synecdoche,* for example—are Greek, and it would have been pedantic to sacrifice what the student already knows to neatness.

The authors rely heavily upon two sources, Quintilian's *Institutes* and the *Ad Herennium.* These two documents constitute the mainstream of western rhetorical tradition, especially as regards figures, and there seemed to be no point in departing sharply from them. Some breadth of interest is gained in that the *Ad Herennium* in its stylistic interest is sophistic, while the *Institutes* embodies a serious, philosophical attempt to deal with rhetoric and oratory.

As for the arrangement of the present glossary, there is no obvious and natural way to group all the figures of speech that make up textual rhetoric. But there are three natural groups within the whole, so far as function is concerned: the argumentative figures, the tropes, and the stance figures. These groups are recognized in the following list. What remains is frankly miscellaneous, since any attempt to further discriminate classes ultimately ends in confusion.

The student must not be misled by the classification of a particular figure as a trope, a stance figure, or an argumentative one. Most figures, we believe, function generally according to their classification. But language does what the writer wants it to; the rhetorician does not prescribe.

It should, finally, be pointed out that a glossary such as the present one is best learned through use in rhetorical analysis. There is no point in learning figures in abstraction, even for those rare students who are able to learn in this fashion. A figure becomes significant and memorable when we see it at work in discourse.

Argumentative Figures

Most rhetorical figures function by setting up some kind of a relationship between concepts or terms. The peculiar mark of argumentative figures is that they establish such relationships by appealing to other terms. However, we have included in this category certain figures that have a peculiar argumentative force without such an appeal (e.g., the *exemplum*) or that are generally found in support of more explicitly argumentative figures (e.g., the *distributio*).

Enthymeme. This term should carry its normal, logical meaning, as proposed in Chapter I.[2] Briefly, it is a syllogism with a premise

---

[2] Classical rhetoricians attempted to set up a rhetorical enthymeme to rival the logical one, with indescribable confusion as the result. Quin-

omitted; in most instances, it is the major premise that is merely implicit.

Whenever a writer gives a reason for something in an argument, he uses an enthymeme. On a very simple level, the statement, "Everyone ought to learn how to swim, because swimming is good for one's health," is an enthymeme; the first clause is a conclusion, the second, a minor premise supporting that conclusion. The student should try to become acutely aware of such enthymemes, in argumentation and elsewhere, because they can otherwise carry him along by an apparent plausibility that does not stand up to inspection. There are many hazards in the logical move implied by the enthymeme (see Chapter VIII, pp. 206–217), but perhaps the most common is an appeal to an implicit major premise with which we would not agree if we thought about it. The major premise of the above enthymeme, for instance, is, "Everyone ought to learn whatever is good for one's health"—clearly a nonsense proposition.

It will be noticed in the above instance that the writer or speaker attempts to make one statement credible by relating it to a statement that is actually a higher order of generalization, in that "whatever is good for one's health" is a larger class of activities than "swim."[3] This does not mean that there is a particular class of major-premise statements that support enthymemes; rather there is a potential hierarchy of statements, arranged in order of their degree of abstraction. The enthymeme merely attempts to support a statement at one level of abstraction by relating it to a higher level. One could, for instance, turn the major premise of the previous enthymeme, "Everyone ought to learn whatever is good for

---

tilian apparently would have preferred to use the term to designate some kind of conclusion *(sententia)* drawn from contraries *(Institutes* VIII. 5. 9). And there was an attempt to distinguish between the enthymeme, thus defined, and the *epicheireme,* in which all three elements of the syllogism were explicit, with or without arguments for each, and aimed at probability rather than proof *(Institutes* V. 14. 5–25), and *apodeixis,* a clear proof *(evidens probatio—Institutes* V. 11. 7). It seems better to confine oneself to the basic term, enthymeme.

[3] See the discussion of "Generalization and Particularization" in the previous chapter.

one's health," into a conclusion by devising a new "because clause" —"because health is a necessary prerequisite to pleasure."[4]

An enthymeme is usually signaled by one of a number of subordinating conjunctions (see p. 37), but sometimes a conjunction will be merely implied by the relationship of two clauses or sentences. For instance, if one should say, "Everyone ought to love children; they are the trustees of the future," the second clause is clearly a reason for the first, and a subordinating conjunction is implied.

The enthymeme needs to be distinguished from the *counter-statement* and the *explanatory statement*. The *counter-statement* simply contradicts what has gone before. For instance, if one should say, "The sky is not blue; it is black," the second clause merely refutes the first. In the usual terminology, no reason has been given. However, the distinction between an enthymeme and a counter-statement may not always be so easy to draw, particularly since counter-statements may also be formulated with subordinating conjunctions. For instance, the statement, "Julie did not attack Pinkie; she was in the washroom at the time," is clearly a counter-statement. But it could readily be reformulated in this fashion: "Julie could not have attacked Pinkie because she was in the washroom at the time." No end is served by attempting to distinguish between the two sentence forms; both are counter-statements.

An *explanatory* statement gives a reason for another statement, but it does not, in its relationship to the statement being explained, propose a classification of experience in which the latter is by its nature included. An example might be, "Carol was late because she had a flat tire." The second clause explains the first, but it does not appeal to a more inclusive principle to do it, even though it uses a subordinating conjunction characteristic of the enthymeme.[5]

Perhaps the best test of the enthymeme is that proposed earlier,

---

[4] It has been pointed out above (p. 114) that where the middle term coincides with one of the other terms ("All men are rational" and "Only men are rational"), the "because clause" actually proposes a redefinition.

[5] Any time an explanatory clause introduces a third term, some kind of enthymeme can be deduced. But in the case of an explanatory statement or a counter-statement, the major premise to be deduced will either be silly or manifestly not true—"Anyone who has a flat tire will be late" is simply a false statement.

that it appeals to a higher level of abstraction to substantiate a more concrete statement. Both the counter-statement and the explanatory statement remain on the same level of abstraction as the assertion they support.

Ratiocinatio.   An author using this argumentative figure advances toward his conclusion by a series of arguments. The *Ad Herennium* (IV. 16. 23) defines the *ratiocinatio* as a series of questions and answers having this relationship, and it offers the following example:

> When our ancestors condemned a women for one crime, they considered that by this single judgment she was convicted of many transgressions. How so? [introductory sentence] Judged unchaste, she was also deemed guilty of poisoning. Why? Because, having sold her body to the basest passion, she had to live in fear of many persons. Who are these? Her husband, her parents, and the others involved, as she sees, in the infamy of her dishonour. And what then? Those whom she fears so much she would inevitably wish to destroy. Why inevitably? Because no honourable motive can restrain a woman who is terrified by the enormity of her crime, emboldened by her lawlessness, and made heedless by the nature of her sex.

There is clearly a kind of progression in this passage, from adultery, to fear of relatives, to wish to destroy, to poisoning. It is less clear that a sorites (see p. 31) of sorts lingers behind the passage, but this is the case. Actually, the passage is a deplorable example of argumentative rhetoric, and one trusts that no lady ever suffered on account of such specious reasoning. The writer has in fact put together a very dubious sort of sorites and a *gradatio* (see p. 163), which is not even an argumentative figure.

The definition of the *ratiocinatio* in the *Ad Herennium* specifies that it be in the form of questions and answers. This requirement is unnecessarily limiting, although the figure frequently takes this form. Its essential characteristic, an argumentative movement from conclusion to conclusion, is seen in the following passage from Paine's *The Rights of Man*, even though questions are not asked (he is arguing that a government based on inheritance depends upon ignorance):

As the exercise of government requires talents and abilities, and as talents and abilities cannot have hereditary descent, it is evident that hereditary succession requires a belief from man, to which his reason cannot subscribe, and which can only be established upon his ignorance; and the more ignorant any country is, the better it is fitted for this species of government.[6]

Another characteristic example of the *ratiocinatio* is seen in the letter that Lincoln wrote to Conklin, August 26, 1863:

You dislike the Emancipation Proclamation, and perhaps would have it retracted. You say it is unconstitutional. I think differently. [introductory] I think the Constitution invests its commander-in-chief with the law of war in time of war. The most that can be said—if so much—is that slaves are property. Is there, has there ever been, any question that, by the law of war, property, both of enemies and friends, may be taken when needed? And is it not needed whenever taking it helps us or hurts the enemy?[7]

This is clearly a *ratiocinatio,* although the last elements are rhetorical questions. It is a *ratiocinatio* because it is an argument moving from position to position to conclusion.

The *ratiocinatio* is obviously an argumentative figure; it is, in fact, an extended enthymeme although it is often complicated by nonlogical elements and structural distortions. It is perhaps found most often in passages rebutting some position, where its speed is an advantage.

The *ratiocinatio* needs to be distinguished from the *gradatio,* which attempts to create a climactic structure like the *ratiocinatio* but which is not logical in its movement. The two figures are frequently confused, as in the example proposed by the *Ad Herennium.*

Sententia.   The *Ad Herennium* and Quintilian roughly agree in defining this figure as a concise and weighty saying; the English word "sententious" in its better sense retains a large part of the

[6] *The Rights of Man,* in *Life and Writings of Thomas Paine,* ed. Daniel E. Wheeler (New York: Vincent Parke, 1908), IV, 189.

[7] Abraham Lincoln, *Speeches and Letters* (New York: E. P. Dutton, 1949), p. 209.

connotation of the Latin. Ideally, it is a statement that has only to be heard or read to command assent, as Paris' "The previous gifts that the Gods lavish on a man are not to be despised" (*Iliad*, III, 65). Because of its conciseness and assurance, there is a suggestion of folk wisdom about the *sententia;* it professes to be the wisdom, not of an individual, but of mankind. In the Homeric poems, it was almost the only method used to argue a point, and it was still a potent argumentative method in the sixteenth century. Today it is regarded with a good deal of suspicion.

The *sententia* has three functions. First, it is an argumentative figure; as Quintilian pointed out, it can function very well as the first premise of a syllogism. (Today, it is more apt to turn up as the implied first premise of an enthymeme.) However, it is probably a bad figure upon which to base an argument explicitly. Once it has been said, there is not much to do with it except to catalog instances in a sort of laundry list. It is most effective in argumentation when it is used to support a position that has been established by other means.

As described above, the *sententia* is used to support in some way a statement of a lower order of abstraction; it is introduced to argue for, or at least give weight to, a particular application of the more general truth proposed by the *sententia* itself. But its second function is the opposite of this; it can be used to generalize a particular truth. This function is especially common in poetry and fiction:

> It is not growing like a tree
> In bulk, doth make man better be;
> Or standing long an oak, three hundred year,
> To fall a log at last, dry, bald, and sere:
>> A lily of a day
>> Is fairer far in May,
> Although it fall and die that night;
> It was the plant and flower of light.
> In small proportions we just beauties see;
> And in short measures life may perfect be.
> (BEN JONSON, "Oak and Lily")

The last two lines are two *sententias*. But they have no argumentative function; they generalize the statements made earlier (which are already highly generalized) into universal claims.

The third common function of the *sententia* is illustrated by the following quotation:

> Here, again, we must be careful. We shall ruin mathematical education if we use it merely to impress general truths. The general ideas are the means of connecting particular results. After all, it is the concrete special cases which are important. Thus in the handling of mathematics in your results you cannot be too concrete, and in your methods you cannot be too general. The essential course of reasoning is to generalise what is particular, and then to particularise what is general. Without generality there is no reasoning, without concreteness there is no importance.[8]

This paragraph, incidentally, illustrates very well the disparity that is possible between the importance of what is being said and the time it takes to say it. Everything is said, virtually, in the first three sentences, but if they were allowed to stand by themselves (in the context of the whole essay) they would not have the weight they require. The rest of the paragraph is amplification by *distributio* and accumulation.

But a paragraph is not a collection of sentences about a particular subject; any sensitive writer knows that a good paragraph has an appropriate shape. Particularly, the function of many paragraphs requires that they have some sort of light emphasis in their tails to indicate climax and conclusion. The last sentence in the above paragraph was framed as a *sententia* to permit it to function in that fashion. Hence we have an example of a *sententia* used primarily as a structural figure.

Exemplum. The *Ad Herennium* defines this figure, usefully, as "the citing of something done or said in the past, along with the definite naming of the doer or author" (IV. 49. 62). It is thus a quotation, or an opinion, attributable to a specific authority: Saint Paul says, "Wives submit yourselves unto your own husbands, as unto the Lord." (It might also be, "Saint Paul says that wives ought to submit to their husbands.")

The *exemplum* is clearly an argumentative figure, even though

---

[8] Alfred North Whitehead, *The Aims of Education* (New York: Mentor Books, 1953), p. 63.

its appeal is to authority rather than to evidence or principle. Its value in an argument varies from time to time; it is perhaps less used in this century than it has been in the past, since we generally distrust arguments from authority. But it is perhaps a useful support for an argument already made; it reassures the reader by pointing out that other people have arrived at the same conclusion being urged upon him.

Example.   Classical writers did not recognize this as a figure, but it clearly falls within their definitions of figurative language nonetheless. It has two functions. In the first place, the *example* can be simply explanatory. The numerous and necessary "for instances" that are to be found in this chapter, for instance, ordinarily introduce examples that clarify the preceding definitions, or at least were intended to do so.

But the *example* can also be argumentative since, as has been said (p. 46), it is the form that induction takes in argumentation. Several examples that are inductive in function are illustrated in Chapter I. Another would be:

> But what if we are unable to find by this method a common thread binding philosophical undertakings together? Viewed with their intentions in mind, philosophies and philosophers differ as much as Aristotle differs from Hume, or the mystic Jacob Boehme from the positivist Carnap. In fact, few experts agree that philosophy is a single-minded undertaking. Bertrand Russell thinks that the whole tradition initiated by Socrates was a regrettable mistake. Benedetto Croce held that nearly all that goes under the name of philosophy is in the nature of a support to theological interests entirely extraneous to philosophy as he understood it. Wittgenstein seems to hold that the whole of the philosophical venture is a sort of mental aberration resulting from misuse of language. Marx and his followers view other philosophers as dupes of capitalist usurpers.[9]

In this paragraph we have a question, a sort of topic sentence, amplified by a *correctio,* and thereafter a series of examples that function largely as evidence for the position proposed in the topic sentence.

[9] Arturo B. Fallico, *Art and Existentialism* (Englewood Cliffs, N. J.: Prentice-Hall, 1962), p. 9.

It is important to distinguish the illustrative example from the argumentative (persuasive) example, but it must also be recognized that the two functions cannot be sharply distinct. That example which clarifies a concept cannot help having some persuasive function, and the converse is surely true also. At times it may be impossible to say that one function or the other is primary, as in the following example:

> For two hundred years, these ideas [of science] have been applied to technical needs; and they have made our world anew, triumphantly, from top to toe. Our shoes are tanned and stitched, our clothes are spun and dyed and woven, we are lighted and carried and doctored by means which were unknown to neat Mr. Pope at Twickenham in 1740.[10]

The second sentence is probably illustrative, but it surely carries also a substantial persuasive function.

Analogy (Similitudo).   The enthymeme argues for its proposition by appealing to some larger principle which presumably includes the proposition; the example cites one or more specific instances which are presumably included in the proposition. The *analogy,* on the other hand, seeks to support its proposition by finding some parallel instance, some likeness to the proposition under consideration in a similar proposition.

The usual definition of an analogy goes something like this: If two objects, or situations or whatever, have several things in common, and one of them has some further, related characteristic, then it can be argued that the other has it also. Or, as a logician might say, if both X and Y have certain characteristics $a, b,$ and c in common, and Y also has a further characteristic $d,$ then it can be argued that X must also have this further characteristic $d.$

Analogies in argumentation, however, are seldom so extended. More common is the form found so frequently in Plato: if a man who has learned the art of building is a builder; a man who has learned the art of music a musician; of medicine, a doctor; then a

---

[10] J. Bronowski, *The Common Sense of Science* (London: William Heinemann Ltd., 1951), p. 146.

man who has learned justice is a just man.[11] In other words, the analogy may set up a series of relationships between terms having, obviously, something in common and then extend the relationship to other terms where the relationship is not obvious.

Perhaps even more common is the simple one-term analogy. For example, Sartre writes:

Has anyone ever asked, "What painting ought he [the artist] to make?" It is clearly understood that there is no definite painting to be made, that the artist is engaged in the making of his painting, and that the painting to be made is precisely the painting he will have made. It is clearly understood that there are no *a priori* aesthetic values, but that there are values which appear subsequently in the coherence of the painting, in the correspondence between what the artist intended and the result. . . . Painting can be judged only after it has once been made. What connection does that have with ethics? We are in the same creative situation.[12]

In actual practice most analogies do not label themselves so clearly as either of these examples do. Woodrow Wilson in his well-known Pueblo speech on behalf of the League of Nations, asserted:

I had a couple of friends who were in the habit of losing their tempers, and when they lost their tempers they were in the habit of using very unparliamentary language. Some of their friends induced them to make a promise that they never would swear inside the town limits. When the impulse next came upon them, they took a street car to go out of town to swear, and by the time they got out of town they did not want to swear . . . Now, illustrating the great by the small, that is true of the passions of nations.[13]

The argument, paraphrased, goes like this: Nations are like men, and wanting to swear is like wanting to go to war, and hence, since

[11] Plato, *Gorgias,* trans. W. C. Helmbold, Library of Liberal Arts, No. 20 (Indianapolis: Bobbs-Merrill, 1952), pp. 19–20.

[12] Jean-Paul Sartre, *Existentialism and Human Emotions* (New York: Philosophical Library, 1957), pp. 42–43.

[13] Woodrow Wilson, "Address at Pueblo, Colorado, September 25, 1919," *The Messages and Papers of Woodrow Wilson* (New York: The Review of Reviews Corporation, 1924), II, 1129.

an enforced delay in the case of men eliminates the desire to swear, it will eliminate the desire to go to war in the case of nations.

The analogy is perhaps indispensable to argumentation (it is at least omnipresent in the prose of every period), but it is hard to see how it might ever be a decisive argument and it can be quite misleading. The essence of the figure, or strategy, is to place a relatively unknown concept (or whatever) against a better known one, and deduce qualities of the former from the latter. But the relationship between the two concepts is necessarily ambiguous because one is unknown in part.

The analogy is most readily confused with the comparison. The difference between the figures is functional; the analogy is an argumentative figure, the comparison an explanatory one. Such a difference cannot be absolute, since any clarification of a concept is apt to add to its persuasiveness. But in general the distinction is easy enough to draw, and worth drawing.

Because the analogy is such a questionable logical instrument it is generally called an extrapolation by scientists.

Contrarium. The *contrarium* can be understood as a variation of the analogy. Like the analogy it argues from a kind of parallelism, but it introduces the conception of more probable–less probable. Briefly defined, its argument is that if something that seems more likely is actually not true, then something else that is less likely is also not true. It is thus also a brief a fortiori argument (see Aristotle's *Rhetoric* II. 23. 1397b). An example, paraphrased from Aristotle, would be, "If even the gods are not omniscient, then certainly human beings are not." The *contrarium* can, of course, be positive: "If even human beings are able to anticipate events, then certainly the gods can." The examples quoted by the *Ad Herennium* (IV. 18. 25) are all questions: "Now how should you expect one who has ever been hostile to his own interests to be friendly to another's?" Essentially, the figure argues that something is more or less probable than something else to which it is parallel.

Expeditio. This argumentative figure works by elimination; one sets up all possible alternatives, in action or explanation, and eliminates all but one. The *Ad Herennium* gives as an example a law case about a piece of land, in which it is argued that the land must have been taken by force, since it could not have been inherited, nor purchased, nor gotten by prescription, nor occupied as vacant (IV. 29. 40). In logic this argumentative figure is called a disjunctive syllogism.

The *expeditio* can of course work negatively; we can argue that such and such a thing cannot be, or be true, by exhaustively listing the possibilities for such being and showing that such and such a thing does not belong to any of them. Thus Lucretius (who habitually argues in this fashion) attempts to prove that the universe could not have a third sort of thing, besides atoms and the void, by arguing that everything could either be touched or it could not. But everything that could be touched was made up of atoms; everything that could not was void. Ergo. It will be observed that in this instance it is really an argument from definition.

In its complicated forms the *expeditio* needs to be distinguished from the *ratiocinatio.* The *ratiocinatio,* however, is a progressive figure; it establishes a position, by question and answer, and then moves to another. The *expeditio* is static; it argues by exhausting all possibilities, or all but one.

Rhetorical Question (Interrogatio).   A *rhetorical question* is one to which there is only one correct answer, implied in the question itself. It is most often argumentative, because it is a way of calling attention to an axiom of some sort, to a proposition that is so obvious, in the context, that it cannot even be argued for by the usual means. Mill, attacking the doctrine of a substance underlying appearances, wrote, "If there be such a *substratum,* suppose it at this instant miraculously annihilated, and let the sensations continue to occur in the same order, and how would the *substratum* be missed?" This is a rhetorical question because it presumes the answer, "in no way," and it treats that answer as self-evident.

The usage of the rhetorical question may vary somewhat from this norm. Thus, Sir Thomas Wyatt, defending himself against some trumped-up charges, wrote, "Come on now, my Lorde of London [Bishop Bonner], what is my abhominable and vicioue livinge? Do ye know yt or have ye harde yt?" Used in this fashion, the rhetorical question is a kind of challenge to which there is presumably no response. But it can also be strategic, designed to put an opponent at a severe disadvantage, as when Cicero opened his "First Oration against Cataline" with the rhetorical questions, "How much further, Cataline, will you carry your abuse of our forebearance? How much longer will your reckless temper baffle our restraint?" Cataline cannot very well answer, "Not much longer." The question is loaded. The rhetorical question can also be defensive, as when Emerson wrote, "Is it so bad, then, to be misunderstood?" This is to accept an accusation and then deny its importance.

The last quotation illustrates the hazard of rhetorical questions. Emerson is surely using his to carry the reader past a difficulty. But one does not have to answer, "no," and if one does not, Emerson's argument is in ruins.

Definition. This is not, of course, technically a figure at all; it is much more apt to be a sequence of figures working to a particular end. But it requires notice because arguments habitually depend on definitions, and they are not always good ones. A definition is a way of classifying experience, and important definitions are always *ad hoc*—formulated for the specific purpose the writer has in mind.

This *ad hoc* character is not always apparent because we are accustomed to think of definitions as ways of isolating classes of things already existent in nature. The word "tree," for instance, ought to be defined so as to include all of the objects in nature that are already, in some sense, trees, and no other objects.

But this will not do. Even the concept "trees" will be found to be very fuzzy on its margins; there must always be something a little arbitrary about our distinction between trees and bushes. This being the case, concepts that have no objective referent at all, such as truth or justice, can never be defined otherwise than in terms of the particular purpose of the writer. Every such term could be defined in many different ways, each of which could be valid and useful in a particular context.

To point out the *ad hoc* character of definitions is not to say that every definition is a good one. A definition ought to be regarded as a kind of generalization not unlike that of the example.

It is an invitation to see whether or not the category proposed for certain of our experiences organizes them into a meaningful class—to see whether or not, in other words, the category is useful not only for the writer's purposes but for our own. Furthermore, the criterion of usefulness needs to be emphasized. Since no large concept—not "man," nor "truth," nor "learning"—can be defined as some sort of superessential essence including or refuting other definitions, then the value of the definition for some particular end bulks proportionately larger.

It would be supererogatory to illustrate definitions in a chapter devoted to them, but it should be noted that defining is not limited to formal definitions. Since communication can do nothing other than propose relationships between concepts, the definition of those concepts will, in one way or another, constitute the bulk of most written discourse.

Distributio.   This figure is closely related to the definition; it is, in fact, a way of redefining. It has two forms. The most common one, described by classical rhetoricians, consists of some sort of division of a concept, or action, and an apportioning of its parts. One can distribute duties, as in the speech quoted in the *Ad Herennium:* "The duty of the prosecutor is to bring charges; that of the counsel for the defense to explain them away or rebut them; that of the witness to say what he knows or has heard," and so forth (IV. 35. 47). Demosthenes, speaking against an opponent who was a naturalized citizen of Athens, similarly distributed his citizenship: "I assign him to that class which entitles him to the greatest respect, though I deny his right to acquire illegally privileges not enjoyed by us who are citizens by birthright" (*Against Aristocrates* 24).

This form of the *distributio* is sometimes difficult to distinguish from the antithesis (see below). The antithesis distinguishes: not this, but this. The *distributio* distinguishes but in addition apportions in some fashion. It is this apportioning that gives the *distributio* its argumentative force.

The second form of the *distributio* is far more important because it is frequently at the very center of an argument; it can usefully be distinguished as a *structural distributio*. One of the great examples of this *structural distributio* is found at the beginning of Burke's *Reflections*. The justification of the Revolution was, of course, the extension of human liberty. To this Burke replied:

> I flatter myself that I love a manly, moral, regulated liberty as well as any gentleman of that society [The Revolution Society] be he who he will. . . . But I cannot stand forward and give praise or blame to anything which relates to human actions, and human concerns, on a simple view of the object, as it stands stripped of every relation, in all the nakedness and solitude of metaphysical abstraction.[14]

In this passage Burke takes a fundamental concept, liberty, and divides it, into "regulated liberty" on the one hand, and abstract, metaphysical liberty on the other. He then distributes the divided concept, the first part to himself, the second to his opponents. (The *distributio* must do both things; it must divide, and it must apportion.) With this figure, he sets up the fundamental argument of his whole treatise, reiterated thereafter in antithesis after antithesis: the choice between specified, guaranteed liberties, and a general, abstract liberty.

Tom Paine, in his reply to Burke, inevitably set up his own *distributio:*

> Every country in Europe considers the cause of the French people as identical with the cause of its own people. . . . But those who rule those countries do not entertain quite the same opinion. . . . The people are not to be confounded with their government; and this is especially the case when the relation of the English government to its people is considered.[15]

Paine's *distributio* is not of a concept; it is of nations. A nation is composed of a government and the people, and by implication Paine distributes them: Burke is a government man.

The importance of the *structural distributio* is easy to understand. No one is willing to oppose liberty or virtue or patriotism.

[14] Edmund Burke, *Reflections on the Revolution in France,* Part I, ch. i, Library of Liberal Arts, No. 46 (Indianapolis: Bobbs-Merrill, 1955), p. 8.
[15] Preface to the French edition of *The Rights of Man,* in *Life and Writings of Thomas Paine,* ed. Daniel E. Wheeler (New York: Vincent Parke, 1908), IV, xxi.

When one of these broad, generally accepted concepts comes up, the writer who would get to any specific problem must divide the concept and apportion its parts.

It should perhaps also be pointed out that the *structural distributio* can have an important function in narrative literature, particularly in drama. In the first scene of *Antony and Cleopatra,* Antony says:

> Let Rome in Tiber melt and the wide arch
> Of the ranged empire fall: Here is my space,
> Kingdoms are clay; our dungy earth alike
> Feeds beast as man. The nobleness of life
> Is to do thus [Hugs Cleopatra, surely].

Here Shakespeare in effect sets up a *structural distributio.* The goodness of life is apportioned between empire on the one hand and Cleopatra on the other; this choice, reiterated dozens of times in comparable *distributios* and antitheses, sets up a fundamental issue of the play (although one cannot conclude that this issue is "what the play is all about").

The Tropes

Most figures of speech are really special arrangements of syntax; we balance words against each other and so forth. Tropes, however, are semantic rather than syntactic; they are alterations in word meanings. Briefly, we have a trope when there is a fundamental syntactic discontinuity between two words (one of which may be implicit), and at the same time there is a basic connection. Both conditions must be present for there to be a trope. If there is no discontinuity, we have normal word usage. If there is no basic connection, we have nonsense. To put it another way, a trope is created by a semantic discontinuity in which the discontinuous words or concepts coalesce meaningfully. It can be seen from this definition that it is the especial mark of the trope that, used freshly, it creates a new meaning.

For instance, the expression, "hard surface," is not a trope, because the conception "hard" is felt to be a natural and direct modification of "surface"; there is no discontinuity between the two words. However, "hard sound" would generally be regarded as a trope because there is a discontinuity between the two words ("hard" is a quality which we perceive by touch), and, in addition, the average reader would recognize a meaningful connection between the two words. The first time the expression, "hard sound," was used, a new concept, a new perception, came into being.

Discontinuity and connectedness are the mark of the trope. But different kinds of tropes can be distinguished if we look more closely at particular examples. Every trope, for instance, involves at least two concepts. "Hard sound," although it is a single concept, is engaged in isolating a certain kind of aural experience from the general class of "sounds." "Sound" can hence be called the *base term* or *base concept;* "hard" can be called a *figurative term* or *figurative concept.* These would seem to be the only terms involved in this trope. But in a trope such as "pearly teeth," the base term, "teeth," is very clearly connected to the figurative term by a third term, "white." This can be called a *linking term* or *linking concept.* The implicit presence of this third term makes "pearly teeth" a different kind of trope from "hard sound," in which there was no such term.

But another sort of complexity in tropes needs to be recognized. "Pearly" and "hard" in the above examples function grammatically as modifiers. Most tropes are *modified tropes* because they depend on this relationship. But we need not speak of "pearly teeth" on all occasions; in the proper context it would be sufficient to speak of "those pearls." In this instance, the figurative term has simply been substituted for the base term. Both base and linking terms are still present in our understanding of the figure, but they have become implicit. Such a trope can be described as *substituted.*

The division of the genus "trope" into classes, into metaphors, *translatios,* and so forth, is worth doing because the various tropes work very differently, and the kind of tropes that regularly prevail in the work of a certain writer, or even of a certain period, can tell us a good deal about that writer or period. But in specific instances, particularly when the base term is implicit, it may be difficult to decide just what figure of speech a particular trope happens to be. The difficulty is seldom very important. There is considerable value in distinguishing the *translatio* from the *abusio* and the metaphor, for instance, insofar as numbers of these figures will give a particular character to a piece of discourse. But if the distinction is not clear in a particular instance, it is not worth wasting time trying to decide which figure it is.

A further difficulty—again, a minor one—appears when we are studying the discourse of an era other than our own. The discontinuity between base and figurative concepts is in part a matter of usage, and what is initially a trope can in time become ordinary language. For instance, the first writer to alter the concept "day" by calling it "sweet day" invented a trope; "sweet" is a taste word miles from any experience with "day." But "sweet" was very widely applied early in the history of the language, so that many people would not feel any particular discontinuity between the two terms today. No discontinuity, no trope. Of course, this problem is really one of standard usage, and is by no means peculiar to rhetorical analysis.

One further caution. It is necessary to speak of tropes as incorporating a relationship between terms. But we perceive them thus only after an act of abstraction and analysis. We experience a trope as a unified concept, as something given to the mind as a whole. Although the abstractive character of definition requires us to speak of them otherwise, as if they had parts, this should not be allowed to obscure our initial response to them. A good trope is a kind of perceptual act.

Translatio.   The word *translatio* is the Latin equivalent of the Greek word *metaphor;* for classical rhetoricians they meant the same thing. But modern rhetoric very badly needs to make a distinction among tropes where ancient rhetoric made none, and hence it is useful to separate the words and apply them to two different figures of speech.

A *translatio* is, simply, a linked trope, as this was defined earlier. It is a base term modified by a figurative one, in which some sort of linking term is implicit. "Stony-hearted" is a *translatio* because "heart" is not ordinarily thought of as "stony"; however, the two words together make sense because the reader senses a third, implicit term, "hard," which makes the connection. ("Hard heart" is of course a dead *abusio;* see below.)

A *translatio* need not be an obvious adjective-noun phrase; this figure lends itself readily to substitution. Spenser, for instance, sets up a series of *translatios* as noun equivalents:

> If sapphires, lo! her eyes be sapphires plain;
> If rubies, lo! her lips be rubies sound,
> If pearls, her teeth be pearls, both pure and round. . . .
> *(Amoretti,* No. XV)

The development of these *substituted translatios* is clear enough: for instance, "sapphire," the figurative concept simply replaces the base concept, "eyes," and the linking term is "green." Both the base and linking concepts are implicit in our understanding of the figure.[16]

It should be noted that the linking term of a *translatio* is always relatively simple. In the example from Spenser this simplicity is apparent, but it may not be apparent on first inspection in more elaborately worked examples of the figure, as in the following:

> Thou dirge
> Of the dying year, to which this closing night
> Will be the dome of a vast sepulchre,
> Vaulted with all thy congregated might
> Of vapours, from whose solid atmosphere
> Black rain, and fire, and hail will burst. . . .
> (SHELLEY, "Ode to the West Wind," 11. 23–28)

The complexity here lies only in the supporting syntax and the extension of the figure. The *translatio* is made up of the base term, "night," and the figurative term, "dome of a vast sepulchre"; they are clearly linked by "space enclosure." The other materials—particularly the "closing" and "vast" of the figure itself, and the subsequent elaboration introduced by "vaulted"—is hung onto this primary equivalence in an effort to give it richness and movement. The elaboration should not obscure the fact that this is a *translatio*

---

[16] It is obvious that secondary linking terms will ordinarily be present also in a *translatio*. In the Spenser catalog, "preciousness" and perhaps "gleaming" are also implicit in the base-figurative relationship. But the colors clearly predominate.

at bottom, functioning exactly as Spenser's *translatios* function, to heighten and vivify some quality of an object or an abstraction—in Spenser, the brilliance and value of a woman's features; in Shelley, the funereal sense of the closing night of winter.

Most of the trite descriptive efforts of bad poetry and popular music are *translatios;* they can be invented for any occasion without any special insight into one's subject. However, the figure can be very effective at times, especially when it is combined with other figures. Shakespeare's "That time of year thou mayst in me behold,/ When yellow leaves, or none, or few, do hang," is basically a *translatio.* The base term, "That time of year," is linked to the figurative one, "yellow leaves," by the linking concept of "winter." But "That time of year" is also a *paraphrasis* for old age—see below.

The *translatio* is most readily confused with the *abusio;* a useful way of making the distinction will be found at the end of the discussion of that figure.

Abusio (Catachresis).   An *abusio* is like a *translatio* in that it involves a base term and a figurative one; the two are distinguishable because the *abusio* does not have a readily identified linking concept. This is, of course, a matter of degree; the fact that one senses the appropriateness of the base-figurative conjunction implies some sort of connection. But one cannot readily specify this connection for the *abusio.* In the phrase, "long on brawn, short on brains," for instance, the connection is some perception of quantity, but no single term answers to that perception. The *Ad Herennium* gives several examples of this sort: "The powers of man are short," "small stature," and "the long wisdom of man," among others; in each instance words that are ordinarily applied to one kind of measurement are applied to another. "Short" is substituted for "brief" or "limited," and so forth. The figurative terms in each instance, "short," "small" and so forth, are connected to their base terms by an analogous rather than a linking relationship, since one kind of quantifying word has been substituted for another. The same kind of *abusio,* less mechanical than those from *Ad Herennium,* is seen in Florizel's comment in *The Winter's Tale:* "She is as forward of her breeding [bringing up] as/ She is i' the rear o' her birth" (IV, iii, 583–84). "Forward" and "rear" are connected to their base terms by the connecting conceptions of "distinguished" and "undistinguished." Sharply quantitative distinctions have been substituted for qualitative conceptions very far from them in ordinary usage.

Abusios of quality work exactly the same way and are very common. Donne speaks of "sour prentices," meaning something like "joyless prentices" ("The Sun Rising," 1.6); Ulysses in *Troilus and Cressida* declares that he has "a young conception in my brain" (I, iii, 311), meaning a conception he has just arrived at. In both instances a quality is being applied to a base term to which it would ordinarily be inappropriate.

But the forms that the *abusio* can take do not lend themselves readily to classification. Dylan Thomas' "Once below a time" is an *abusio* in which the mediation is one of opposition; the figurative "below" is simply substituted for the base, "upon." A substitution of a less violent kind is found in Donne's "But since my soul, whose child love is" ("Raire and Angeles," 1.7); "child" stands for a relationship not readily subsumed in a linking concept. "A stupid calme" ("A Calme," 1.2) by the same poet defies specification even more. Verbs can be substituted *abusios,* as in Gloucester's remark in *King Lear:* "Do you smell a fault?" (I, i, 16). The base term is "detect"; the figure is an *abusio* because a verb from a different experiential order is substituted for it.

One other rather odd use of language is best categorized as an *abusio;* it is well illustrated by a phrase from William Morris' "Defence of Guenevere": "looking on the tenderly darkened fingers." Out of the context of the whole phrase, "tenderly darkened" would be nonsense rather than a figure. But poets know, if other people do not, that the laws of grammar are rough approximations of our experience of language, that a modifier need not relate primarily to the word dictated by grammatical structure. In this quotation "tenderly" glances off the term it ostensibly modifies because it doesn't make sense there, but it attaches itself to both "looking" and "fingers."

In summary, the distinction between the *abusio* and the *translatio* is determined by whether or not one senses the presence or absence of a specific linking term. When the figure is substituted, or a verb, no other test is possible. However, when it is an adjective-noun phrase, a ready test is available. The *translatio* joins two nouns by turning one of them into an adjective—"stony-hearted," for example. But the figurative term of the *abusio* is already an adjective; a trope results from the disjunction in meaning between the two.

Quintilian would have liked to limit the *abusio* to word substitutions where the "right" word did not exist (*Institutes* VIII. v. 34–36). But he observed that even in his time poets did not observe this rule, and used *abusios* where "right" words were available. An example of an *abusio* according to Quintilian's strict definition might be Emily Dickinson's "Pain has an element of blank" (in a poem generally referred to by this first line), in which "blank" conveys a powerful kind of meaning in the context, even though it is obviously misused, and where there isn't any "right" word available.

Metaphor.[17]   The *metaphor* is perhaps best described as a trope in which the figurative term is superimposed on the base term and is so appropriate that a kind of fusion results. The mark of the metaphor, consequently, is a relationship between figurative and base terms so extensive as to be unparaphrasable. It goes without saying, of course, that this relationship will be too immediate to permit a linking term.

A useful example of the metaphor is found in Shakespeare's sonnet, the first few lines of which are quoted above. The whole first stanza reads as follows:

> That time of year thou may'st in me behold
> When yellow leaves, or none, or few, do hang
> Upon these boughs which shake against the cold,
> Bare ruin'd choirs, where late the sweet birds sang.
> (Sonnet 73)

The first two lines, as was pointed out, set up a *translatio,* albeit a complicated one. The fourth line, on the other hand, is a metaphor. Old age is no longer like a tree; the skeletal, ruinlike character of

---

[17] The student perhaps needs to be reminded that the following discussion of the metaphor is our own. Although metaphors, as we define them, are to be found in Greek literature, rhetorical focus on oratory prevented the recognition of this use of language.

the tree, qualified by the sense of loss and by silence, is superimposed on the idea of old age. In the first two lines the figure brings a quality to old age; in the last line the figure has become a characterization of it. (The third line is probably someplace between *translatio* and metaphor; the line between the two figures is not an absolute one.)

Another example of a metaphor at work is seen in Dylan Thomas' line, "And I must enter again the round zion of the water bead" ("Refusal to Mourn the Death, by Fire, of a Child in London"), the "round zion of the water bead" clearly means, in the context of the poem, "the earth." But it is the earth sanctified somehow, and it is also the whole process of life and death. The line is actually unparaphrasable. If someone were to ask for an explanation, beyond the most obvious one, all that one could do would be to repeat the line again. A metaphor proposes a resemblance that is multiple and unique; behind it lies the mystic's vision of the unity of all creation.

The distinction between metaphor and *translatio* is between a kind of substitution and a qualification; this is not a distinction between good and bad. The opening lines of Edgar Lee Masters' epitaph for Ann Rutledge set up a metaphor that is less effective than a great many *translatios:*

> Out of me unworthy and unknown
> The vibrations of deathless music:
> "With malice toward none, with charity for all."

"Deathless music" obviously proposes to make a multifaceted connection with the Lincoln quotation. But, equally obviously, it is not a particularly effective figure.

Nevertheless, it is true that the metaphor and *translatio,* while superficially resembling each other, actually represent entirely different ways of seeing the world. The metaphor is after some sort of unity underlying disparity; it is a figure characteristic of, and almost limited to, poetry. It functions to communicate human experience from the inside. The metaphor, thus defined, was unknown to classical rhetoricians because it is foreign to the spirit of argument. A genuine metaphor in an argument would violate the presumptions of this kind of discourse and violate its ends, which are necessarily abstract conclusions.

The *translatio,* on the other hand, is useful to all kinds of writing. It stays on the outside of an experience, acting to heighten and vivify it. It is very useful in making abstract conceptions concrete, but it does not arrest the movement of thought, as the metaphor tends to do.

The implications of this distinction have not been investigated, although they are very interesting. Metaphor is characteristic of certain times and certain poets, and not of others. It is so rare in Middle English poetry, for instance, that one can regard it as accidental when it occurs. But metaphor is the mark of sixteenth-century English poetry. (In the last few years certain poets seem bent on getting rid of it again.) But, among sixteenth-century English poets, one, Edmund Spenser, is as bare of metaphor as any medieval writer.

Modern readers are apt to regard metaphor as the mark of poetry, and to reject as verse the work of those in whom it is not found. This is, of course, a personal value judgment. It is more important to recognize that the metaphorical vision of reality is not given to everyone at all times.

Metonymy (Denominatio, Hypallage).   This well-known figure is traditionally described as a particular kind of substitution: the abstract for the concrete, the container for the thing contained, the cause for the effect, and so forth, with the reverse substitution a possibility in each instance. This definition will usually permit us to recognize the figure, but if it is applied rigorously it proves to be unnecessarily limiting.

For instance, "He has a good head" would seem at first sight to fit the definition proposed; "head," the figurative term, has been substituted for "brain," the base term, as the container for the thing contained. But this is not really what we mean by the expression; the implicit base term is really "intelligence." And this term is harder to reduce to the definition. Similarly, there is a very common kind of metonymy in Puttenham's "Thy hands they made thee rich, thy palate made thee poor"; "hands" is obviously a substitution for "work," "palate" for "appetite." But under what class of substitution does it belong? Finally, specifiable class connections are obviously impossible if the figure is to include examples like Yeats's characterization of a woman revolutionary as one who would teach men to "hurl small streets against the great." Here characteristic details of two ways of life have been substituted for the people living thusly, the rich and the poor.

The only kind of class term under which all of these examples might be subsumed is the dichotomy of abstract and concrete; in each instance quoted above the figurative term is more concrete, more sensuously apprehensible, than the base term. However, this concrete to the abstract relationship does not link the term. The link, in every case, comes out of our own experience. When Donne writes, "For God's sake hold your tongue" ("The Canonization," 1. 1), the linking concept between the figurative term "tongue" and the implicit base concept "talk" is our habitual experience of their connectedness. One could perhaps describe this linkage by paired opposition (the instrument for the action in this case), but an attempt to express all the oppositions possible in this sort of figure would be tedious, and there would be small profit in the enterprise.

We can, hence, define a metonymy briefly as a trope in which a figurative term is substituted for a base term; these terms are linked by our experience of their close connectedness. In general, they are related as the concrete to the abstract.

This sort of metonymy is chiefly a vivifying figure; it often brings a kind of immediacy and vitality to discourse. However, it is ordinarily simple in its effect. The metaphor particularly, but also the *translatio* and the *abusio,* tend to complicate a line of thought. The figurative terms necessarily lie somewhat apart from the base terms they modify or replace. Discourse is opened up and slowed by them. The metonymy, on the other hand, lies directly on the line of discourse in which the base term functions; it merely brings concreteness to that discourse. Thus, it is peculiarly suited to heroic poetry. (Homer and the later Yeats abound in metonymies!)

However, one must note an exception of some importance to these general remarks. Classical rhetoricians noted that a metonymy could run from the abstract to the concrete, or from the concrete to the abstract. This is indeed the case and it makes some difference in the effect achieved. When King Lear says that he is going "To shake all cares and business from our age,/ Conferring them on younger strengths" (I, i, 41–42), he is very decidedly moving from the concrete to the less concrete. The base term, for which "age" stands, is his aged self, while "strengths" stands for stronger people. This figure can usefully be described as a *reverse* metonymy, because it not only moves in exactly the opposite direction than that of the usual metonymy, from the concrete to the more abstract rather than the other way round, but also because it functions quite differently. It is one of the figures by which human beings depersonalize themselves, in poetry, drama, argumentation, and real life, in situations in which personal relations would be awkward. Any court, or courtly, scene, in fictive or real life, will be found to be stuffed with metonymies of this reversed sort ("His excellency," etc.).

Synecdoche (Intellectio).   This is a variety of metonymy; it is the substitution of a part for the whole, or less commonly, the whole for a part. "It was a navy of a thousand sail" is a very simple synecdoche in which a part, "sail," is substituted for the whole, "ships." It thus answers to the same sort of description as the metonymy; it is a substituted trope in which the linking term is experience.

Classical rhetoricians perhaps separated synecdoche from metonymy because of its special vividness. When Hamlet says of the dead Polonius, "I'll lug the guts into the neighbor room" (*Hamlet,* III, iv, 212), by the part that he chooses to stand for the whole he very economically expresses his opinion of the counsellor. The same sort of economy is seen in Yeats's reference to the consequences of the engendering of Helen in "Leda and the Swan": "The broken wall, the burning roof and tower/ And Agamemnon dead."

Epithet (Antonomasia, Pronominatio, Appositum).   An *epithet* is a noun, qualified by one or more adjectives, that presumably characterizes someone or something to which it is applied; it may be used in apposition or it may substitute for its object. Homer offers innumerable examples:

> But when he found himself alone he prayed fervently to King Apollo, *Son of Leto of the Lovely Locks.* "Hear me, *god of the Silver Bow, Protector of Chryse and holy Cilla,* and *Lord Supreme of Tenedos!"*

All of the italicized phrases are epithets. Quintilian would make a difference between a noun phrase in apposition and the same phrase substituted for the original noun, calling one an epithet and the other *antonomasia* (*Institutes* VIII. 6. 29–30, 40–44), but there is no functional difference between the figures. Epithets can be used, as in the example above, to elevate an action; Homer's incessant use of them is in part responsible for the power and weight of the *Iliad*.

It should be noted that many epithets are really specialized tropes; "the Golden-haired," for Aphrodite, is a synecdoche, for instance. The distinguishing marks of the epithet are that it has an apposition-like quality, and that it is not really used to convey information.

Also, it is perhaps useful to recognize an extension of the epithet, which might be called the allegorical epithet. Examples would be Henry IV's description of Hotspur as "Mars in swaddling clothes" (*I Henry IV*, III, ii, 132), or Sidney's description of Stella's kiss: "A double key which opens to the heart." The relationship of such figures to allegory is obvious; they imply a whole landscape. And while they superficially resemble epithets, their effect is quite different. The allegorical epithet, unlike the Homeric one, is a slow and diffuse figure; it arrests the movement of thought as Homer's epithets do not. The first book of the *Iliad*, for instance, would be transformed if even half of the heroic epithets were replaced by allegorical ones.

Pun (Amphibolia, Paranomasia, Adnominatio).   This figure was recognized by classical rhetoricians (see *Institutes* VI. 3. 47), but it did not become important until the Renaissance. It presumes a realization of the ambiguous relationship between language and experience that is generally a Renaissance phenomenon. A *pun* is, of course, a play on words, either words sounding alike, or one word with different meanings. When Falstaff says, "By the Lord I'll be a brave judge," and Prince Hal answers, "Thou judgest false already," he is punning (*I Henry IV*, I, ii, 66–67).

If such classification were important, the pun would probably have to be classed as a mediated trope, with the figurative meaning and base one held in the same term.

Although poets have used the pun with some success in serious poetry, it is most often a stance figure. When it is not merely a conversational tic, it functions to control discourse indirectly. Shakespeare's Cressida (in the first two acts of *Troilus and Cressida*) used it as a device to keep the conversation on her favorite subjects, Troilus and sex, without really committing herself to either, and Falstaff also used it to control the conversation. It can function to stop a conversation entirely. When Cicero answered *sero* (meaning either "very late" or "too late") to the repeated question "When did Clodius die?" he thoroughly deflated the prosecutor by destroying the tone of the discourse.

Simile (Imago).   This is, again, a figure that is preserved among figures of speech only because it is widely known. Although variously defined, the *simile* has always been regarded as a *translatio* (*metaphor* in classical terminology; see Aristotle's *Rhetoric* III. 4. 1406b) preceded by "like" or "as." "Leapt on the foe as a lion" is the same thing as "The lion [that is, Achilles] leapt." When a simile meets this definition there is little point in identifying it as something other than a *translatio*. The explicit sign-words, "like" or "as," merely weaken the trope, if anything.

These sign-words, however, do not always indicate a simile; "like" or "as" may also introduce *comparisons* (see p. 163). Briefly, the difference between a *translatio* and a comparison is that the former uses a figurative term to modify the meaning of the base one; the latter either attempts to find a general parallelism between the two terms, or it is quantitative. These are two very different sorts of function which the term simile readily confuses.

The heroic simile is a special case, named after the type of poetry in which it is usually found. The heroic simile builds up an elaborate and extended background of *translatios* against which an action is presented. Its function is to create a sense of magnitude and elevation against which heroic actions may seem credible.

Transgressio.   In classical rhetoric, this is the same figure as the *hyperbaton* (see p. 166); it is here disjoined, arbitrarily, to serve as the name of an important poetic figure. A *transgressio* can be defined as the use of a word in a new grammatical function—a noun for a verb, an adjective for a noun, and so forth. In popular idiom, the *transgressio* appears in phrases like "to dog it" or "to dog someone's heels." (If such phrases are used a sufficient number of times, of course, "dog" makes its appearance in the dictionary as a verb and the *transgressio* disappears.) Literary examples are Milton's "vast abrupt" and Shakespeare's "The hearts/ That spaniel'd me at heels. . . ." The figure is omnipresent in Shakespeare's language and, among modern poets, Dylan Thomas uses it almost as frequently as did Shakespeare.

The *transgressio* seems to be chiefly an attempt to break up the formulary character of language. It is a characteristic of Western European languages, at least, that they tend to move toward abstraction; hundreds of phrases that once were quite concrete have become abstract. "He followed me around like a dog" does not have a specific referent; "dog" is a pseudo-referent in this context because the reader instantly interprets it to mean "abjectly," without ever thinking "dog." The poet, by his use of *transgressio,* recovers concreteness. The distorted grammatical relationships send the reader back to the thing itself.

(A new term has seemed advisable for this figure since it really falls under onomatopoeia according to Quintilian (VIII. 6. 31–33), and it seems unkind to attempt to extend the definition of a figure known to every sixth-grade student of Edgar Allan Poe.)

Paradox.   A *paradox* is a statement containing a patent self-contradiction that is yet true or at least is proposed as truth. In prose, the paradox is almost always a witty figure, ranging from the mechanical upside-down witticisms of Oscar Wilde to the serious paradoxes of Bernard Shaw. The essence of this sort of paradox is an assault on the conventional meaning of a word. When Dick Bludgeon says to the pastor's wife in *The Devil's Disciple,* "I'm sorry to see by your expression that you're a good woman," he implies that the conventional good woman is actually bad.

A paradox is ordinarily a more serious figure in poetry because it is apt to be pointing out some discontinuity in the nature of things. The paradoxes found in Donne's *Holy Sonnets,* for instance, are used to get at the alogical character of religious conversion:

for I
Except you' enthrall mee, never shall be free,
Nor ever chast, except you ravish me.

(No. XIV)

This paradox does not hinge upon the meaning of a phrase but upon some alogical character that the poet has found in his experience of reality.

The classical view limited this figure to the surprise *(inopinatus)* caused by something trivial being advanced where something serious was expected, or unorthodox opinions expressed for their witty, ingenious, or flippant effect *(Institutes* IX. 2. 23–24).

The *oxymoron* should perhaps be mentioned here; it is a fairly well-known figure although it is of limited importance. It is a kind of paradox in which contradictory substantives are linked as adjective-noun phrases, as in Sidney's "lovely hate" *(Astrophel and Stella,* LX) or "dumb eloquence" (LXI). As the two illustrations suggest, the oxymoron has the same range of seriousness as the paradox, from shallow witticism to real perception. The opposition need not be so stark as the above examples suggest; A. E. Housman's "lovely muck," in "Terence, This is Stupid Stuff," probably ought to be called an oxymoron.[18]

Personification (Conformatio, Prosopopoeia).   There seems to be some advantage in distinguishing two related uses of this figure. In the first, *personification* takes place when human attributes, such as will, choice, intelligence, or even a human personality, are attributed to dumb or inanimate things. Since this kind of attribution is so common in the language (the courageous lion), it is best to limit the figure to those instances in which the attribution is deliberate. A famous instance of this sort of personification is found

---

[18] It should perhaps be pointed out that much poetry is centrally concerned with adjusting terms that are essentially oxymoronic to each other. Much traditional love poetry, for instance, revolves around a paradoxical relationship between lover and mistress. But the sophisticated poet will ordinarily avoid the flat juxtaposition of paradoxical terms that is the oxymoron.

in the speech opening *I Henry IV:* "No more the thirsty entrance of this soil/ Shall daub her lips with her own children's blood." In these lines, the personality of a mother is attributed to England. A more common kind is found in Virgil's *Tenth Eclogue:*

> For him even the laurel, even the tamarisks, wept,
> For him lying under a solitary rock even the pine-clad
> Maenalus wept, and the stones of ice-cold crags.
>
> (LL. 13–14)

The way personification works is obvious in both quotations; it intensifies an emotion by a kind of hyperbolic generalizing. The disadvantage of the figure is that it can very easily become merely pretty. (The pathetic fallacy, pointed out by Ruskin, is a corruption of the personification; the writer takes his own figure seriously and becomes hopelessly sentimental.)

The second type of *personification,* which has no warrant in classical rhetoric, can be defined as the attribution of personality to human traits or to human states. The best example of the latter is the personification of death and love, so common in European literature ("Death be not proud. . ."). A good example of the personification of human personality traits is seen in one of Drayton's sonnets:

> Now at the last gasp of love's latest breath.
> When, his pulse failing, passion speechless lies,
> When faith is kneeling by his bed of death
> And innocence is closing up his eyes. . . .

Here a human condition, love, is represented as attended by human personality traits. As this last quotation suggests, this type of personification lends itself to allegory, and further examples are given under that entry.

Allegory (Inverso, Permutatio, Illusio).   An *allegory* sets up a figurative line of action to express a literal, and usually abstract, thought. The connection between the two is only implicit. Thus, "The ship [of state] sails dangerous coasts" dramatizes a literal and abstract statement, "The nation is in peril," by setting up a visual and active situation that has no necessary connection to nations in trouble. A spectacular example of allegory of this sort is seen in the first eight lines of Keats's "On First Looking into Chapman's Homer":

> Much have I travell'd in the realms of gold,
>   And many goodly states and kingdoms seen;
>   Round many western islands have I been
> Which bards in fealty to Apollo hold.
> Oft of one wide expanse had I been told
>   That deep-browed Homer rules as his demesne;
>   Yet never did I breathe its pure serene
> Till I heard Chapman speak out loud and bold.

Here Keats has vivified the experience with literature by equating literature to strange lands. Allegory has sometimes been described as extended simile; as this example shows, it is at least more commonly extended *abusio*. "Other lands" is an apt point of reference for "literature," but it is not a mediated trope.

Vivification is also the object in extended allegories like *The Faerie Queene;* the writer attempts to present directly human experience that cannot be directly observed. But the technique has been considerably enlarged by the addition of personification, and it might be well to distinguish between *allegory* and *personified allegory*. The difference is that in allegory, the object is to present the experience of a unified consciousness (as in the Keats poem); in personified allegory, the consciousness itself is fragmented and subjected to allegorization. The allegorical landscape becomes peopled with characters like holiness, justice, and so forth, perhaps presented under very thin disguises, and these characters are manipulated to present, directly and concretely, some human conflict. In this effort personified allegory is perhaps attempting what cannot be done, and it is surely not literary as that word has been understood since the Renaissance.[19] In a play like *King Lear,* for instance, the mental states of the characters are of supreme importance, but they are approached indirectly. The play is actually a mass of clues

---

[19] Such a remark is, of course, intended to be descriptive, not evaluative.

inviting us to recreate for ourselves the mental states of its characters. This is the literary way of proceeding, and it presumes an immensely dynamic creative effort on the part of the audience.

Personified allegory attempts to avoid the ambiguities of the
literary method by personifying the mental states in which it is
interested and making them the actors in a drama. But mental
states can seldom be actors. In *The Faerie Queene,* for instance, the
Red-Cross Knight represents holiness, and the action begins with
his being ensnared by false appearance. But holiness, a mental
state, is not subject to deception, although holy men are perhaps
readily deceived. Allegory, when it is personified, must continually
move from abstractions to thin human beings in order to have any
plot.

Other uses of allegory must be noticed. It has frequently been
a pedagogical device, a futile attempt to clothe the dull but profitable in an interesting fable. *The Faerie Queene* suffers, in part,
from this intention. Allegory has also been the main device of coterie literature at times. It takes an audience "in on" the game to
match literal and figurative meanings when these are arbitrarily
linked, especially when the linking is ironic or intentionally inap-
posite (this form is called *illusio*), and it is fun to be an insider in
anything. A large part of the charm of the *Romance of the Rose* in
its own day must have been found in the status that knowledge of it
conferred.

Lastly, allegory is used in discursive or argumentative literature. Thus Edmund Burke, discussing the proper response of the
French people to their misfortunes, rather surprisingly set up a
castle allegory:

Your constitution, it is true, whilst you were out of possession, suffered waste and delapidation; but you possessed in some parts the walls,
and in all the foundations of a noble and venerable castle. You might
have repaired those walls; you might have built on those old foundations.[20]

[20] Edmund Burke, *Reflections on the Revolution in France,* Part I,
ch. iii, Library of Liberal Arts, No. 46 (Indianapolis: Bobbs-Merrill,
1955), p. 40.

Why did Burke violate the sobriety of his argument with this odd image? The reason is apparent if one looks at the passage in the context of Burke's whole argument. It is precisely in respect of the applicability of his political theory to contemporary France that Burke's argument is very weak; France did not have the constitutional kind of government Burke advocated. Hence, his allegory is a kind of pulling-off from the facts, a bridge over a hiatus. He surely did not resort to allegory consciously in order to conceal a weakness in his thesis, but the allegory developed as a response to a feeling of uneasiness with which most writers are familiar.

Stance Figures

All discourse reflects, and depends on, a particular attitude toward its subject, a stance, and very often it involves some sort of definition of the writer as well. Stance and definition do not depend on this figure or that; they pervade the whole discourse. But there are certain figures that are particularly stance figures, and it is useful to isolate these as the third category of figures of speech. All of the figures below most commonly function to define stance, but it should be pointed out that one cannot specify the function of any figure in advance of its use. Any of these figures might be found in a particular passage to serve some other end than that of stance.

Apostrophe (Aversus). This figure, as its original meaning suggests, requires some kind of turning away from whomever the discourse is aimed at, very often to the gods or a personification. Or it may be a prosecutor turning from the jury to address directly the defendant. Ordinarily the *apostrophe* functions to emphasize, and classical writers associated it with appeals to emotion. The author of the *Ad Herennium* treats it under the heading of *exclamatio* (IV. 15. 22), and describes it as a figure expressing grief or indignation. It is thus a dangerous figure, since if the audience is not ready to follow the speaker to the emotional heights demanded by it, they are lost to him forever.

The apostrophe can also function as a diversionary device. Demosthenes, in his oration, "On the Crown," uses the figure constantly: turning away from the "men of Athens," his proper audience, to attack directly his opponent, Aeschines. His object was to distract attention from the technical issue of the trial (because he was technically guilty) to the character of his accuser. He was then able to contrast his own public character with that of Aeschines.

The speaker using the apostrophe represents himself as being overpowered by emotion. In dramatic literature, particularly, it can be used to indicate to an audience the profound feelings of a character. Thus Lear interrupts an angry argument with his daughters with the following apostrophe:

> You heavens, give me that patience, patience I need!
> You see me here, you gods, a poor old man,
> As full of grief as age; wretched in both.
> (II, iv, 274–276)

The scene is profoundly moving because we are already deeply involved with Lear. In the later heroic drama writers tended, unsuccessfully, to use the apostrophe to create emotion in the first place. (See also *Institutes* IX. 2. 38.)

Correctio. This is a figure in which what has just been said is improved upon with a more fitting, usually a more emphatic, expression, as in "It was good; no, it was marvelous." The Bible is full of *correctios,* as in Psalm 7: "Let the enemy persecute my soul, and take it; yes, let him tread down my life upon the earth, and lay mine honour in the dust." A mark of the figure is, obviously, a sense of climax (*Ad Herennium* IV. 26. 36). With this traditional figure ought to be included a figure which Quintilian calls an *aposiopesis* (otherwise called *obticentia, reticentia,* or *interruptio*), in which the speaker interrupts himself with some indication of the inadequacy of what has been said or ought to be said. Thus Demosthenes, flaring out at his opponent in an apostrophe, leaves his statement unfinished: "Why you—I know not what name you deserve!— When you saw me . . ." ("On the Crown"). In both kinds of figure, the effect is ordinarily dramatic emphasis, and indicates the inadequacy of the first expression. Iago gets the same effect, in answer to Brabantio's "Thou art a villain," when he answers, "You are—a senator" (*Othello*, I, i, 119). So it might as well be called a *correctio*.

The *correctio* can also be a stance figure when the movement is anticlimactic. A writer or speaker who says, "He is a reckless driver, or, at least in this instance, a careless one," is informing the audience that he is very careful about what he says and is thence to be trusted. Since the effect was probably calculated, the inference that the speaker wants the audience to make is unwarranted. But at least they know the light in which he wants to be regarded.

Exclamation (Exclamatio). A figure in which strong emotion is shown, as when Cicero in "The Second Philippic" exclaims, "Oh! what outrageous indecency! What intolerable impudence and wickedness and licence!" It is frequently found conjoined with the apostrophe, by which the speaker turns away from his audience to someone else.

The exclamation is probably a natural human response to strong emotion, and in dramatic works it is used to represent such emotion. When it is used in speeches, essays, or poetry it is of course calculated, and it becomes an appeal to pity, indignation, and so forth. Like the apostrophe, the exclamation is a dangerous figure, to be used very sparingly. It breaks the flow of discourse, and can alienate the reader or hearer by asking for an emotional response he is not prepared to make. It is only useful when the audience already feels the emotion to be demanded, and hence is ordinarily found in conclusions.

Hyperbole (Superlatio). Quintilian defines *hyperbole* as "an elegant straining of the truth," either to exaggerate or to minimize, and the *Ad Herennium* proposes a similar definition (*Institutes* VIII. 6. 67–76; *Ad Herennium* IV. 33. 44). Since this involves the difficult business of determining what the truth is before you know whether you have a figure or not, it seems desirable to narrow the definition.

In general, hyperbole can profitably be defined as intentional exaggeration that is meant to be understood as exaggeration. Such hyperbole functions either as a device for humor or to indicate the mental state of the speaker, who finds words inadequate to the expression of his amazement or chagrin.

But it needs to be noted that poetry uses hyperbole quite differently. It is often used in foil material to sharpen the contrast in which the poet is interested. In "To his Coy Mistress," Marvel deliberately uses hyperbole ("And my vegetable love will grow,/ Vaster than empires, and more slow") to create an unreal state of things against which reality can be measured.

As we see perhaps particularly in the Pindaric odes, poetry has been traditionally concerned with wonders—with things or events which are seen as lying outside natural or human possibilities. Poetry is still concerned with wonders, although Achilles and the gods have been rather generally abandoned, and wonders require the use of hyperbole. When Shakespeare begins a sonnet (55) with "Not marble, nor the gilded monuments/ Of princes, shall outlive this powerful rhyme," the reader understands this as hyperbole, but understands also that such hyperbole is the dramatization of a wonder—the power of poetry—which cannot be approached directly.

Irony.   Two of the world's greatest ironists, Socrates and Lucian, were Greeks, but in general irony did not become a widely popular figure until the Renaissance, and hence it is best to consider the term as it came to be defined in modern times.

One needs to distinguish three kinds of irony. *Dramatic irony,* found only in dramatic narratives, is not a figure but a kind of strategy; it establishes some important disparity between what the audience knows and what one or more characters in the narrative know. The classic example of dramatic irony is *Oedipus Rex,* in which the hero, Oedipus, determinedly pursues information which the audience knows will be fatal to himself. *Othello* and *Macbeth* are also full of dramatic irony. This strategy tends to dignify the hero, and make action awesome, because it pits the hero against the universe itself. It also raises questions about the disparity between appearance and reality—very disturbing questions to human beings.

Socratic irony (for want of a better term) is related to dramatic irony in that it is again a strategy and not a figure. The disparity in this case is between a person's real and assumed character. Socrates habitually represented himself to his interlocutors as a kindly, fuzzy-minded, disinterested, and thoroughly amiable old man. The attentive reader knows that he was far from being this sort of person, and his interlocutors guessed it, and were frequently frustrated by it. Chaucer discovered this sort of irony for himself, and it was also brilliantly managed by Swift, particularly in *The Tale of a Tub*. For Socrates it was an argumentative strategy (of a kind Plato should have deplored!) which made it possible for him to explore the position of an opponent with a minimum of exposure of his own position. Will Rogers is the best-known representative of an American variant in which the writer sets himself up as just a plain man of the people, talking "common sense." Chaucer and Swift used it as a deflationary strategy; the uncontrolled and inept enthusiasms of the pseudo-Chaucer of *The Canterbury Tales* is the best possible commentary on the pretensions of Chaucer's other characters.

Verbal irony (the most important from a modern point of view) is a figure; its essence is a disparity between what is said, and what is intended, or really thought. We are aware of the disparity either by reason of what we already know of the speaker or by the context. Clough's "The Latest Decalogue" is a series of ironies ("Thou shalt not covet, but tradition/ Approves all forms of competition"), which we recognize as such because we know that no educated man would say such things seriously, and the skill of the verse tells us that Clough is both educated and intelligent. It is verbal irony because Clough does not create a role for himself.

The essence of verbal irony is ambiguity. When one is ironic about a subject, one refuses to assent to the usual view of it, and at the same time one does not flatly condemn the usual view. We do not know, exactly, *where* the ironist stands. It is thus very useful. Since there are many things in the world to which a rational human being can neither assent nor flatly dissent, irony permits a complexity of stance which the complexity of the world demands. It can also, of course, be a vice, a way of not taking a stand on anything. (See Yvor Winters' discussion of *romantic irony* in his discussion of modern literature, *In Defense of Reason* [Denver: Alan Swallow, 1947], pp. 65–74.)

Irony needs to be distinguished from sarcasm, particularly. Sarcasm is a low-powered figure of speech designed to emphasize what is meant by saying the opposite; irony is not so obvious. (For a discussion of the classical use of the term, see *Institutes* IX. 2. 40–44.)

Litotes (Lítotes).   This figure is defined in the *Ad Herennium* as a kind of understatement, as when a notably gifted general says, "By labor and diligence I have contrived to be no laggard in the mastery of military science." The *litotes* is thus a stance figure, designed to maintain a sympathetic relationship between the speaker (or writer) and his audience; it accomplishes this by implying that the speaker does not think himself better than anyone else. (The reader is at liberty to judge the sincerity of the speaker's professed view of himself.)

It is, however, a tricky device. A sensitive listener will be offended by the litotes when it is used by a politician pursuing high public office with all his might. Also, the writer (usually) who uses this figure when it is not absolutely necessary is actually using it as a device to interject his own person into a discussion where it does not belong. T. S. Eliot does this frequently in his prose, and in the end his use of the litotes antagonizes at least some readers.

But there is another use of the litotes that is characteristic especially of heroic poetry, although it is also found elsewhere. When Agamemnon, at the beginning of the *Iliad,* says to Chryses, "Now go, anger me not, that you may go the safer," the last clause is clearly understatement. But here its function is not to ingratiate; it is to terrorize. Part of the grandeur of the heroes in primitive literature is due to their frequent use of this figure, which suggests, first, a passion very difficult to check, and second, a degree of terror greater than any specific threat could call up. The heroic litotes does not threaten; it menaces.

Related to the heroic litotes, and perhaps most common of all, is the litotes that understates to imply magnitude—"It was no little task," "Not a few came," and so forth. In this usage, the litotes is the first half of an antithesis, with the big end simply implicit.

Paralipsis (Occultatio).   A *paralipsis* is an interruption in the logical structure of an argument by the introduction of materials irrelevant to the ostensible subject of the discourse. Thus Demosthenes, in his oration *Against Aristocrates* (213), says in a series of instances designed to discredit the counsels of Athens:

That whereas the Euboea, dealing with this very Charidemus, whose mother belongs to their city,—I will not mention who his father is or where he comes from, for it is not worth while to make unnecessary inquiries about the man . . . (etc.)—will you, men of Athens. . . .

The information about Charidemus' father is irrelevant to the question at issue, as Demosthenes recognizes, but he introduced it in the very act of saying that he would not.

The paralipsis reflects a double intention. Writing or speaking is coherent when it has a single, definite end; the rational line of development characteristic of good writing is made possible because such writing has a single end in view. But very often a writer or speaker will feel some sort of ambiguity about his end, or he will in fact have two ends in view. For instance, the ostensible end of a political oration may be to prove that the speaker has not engaged in any shady financial dealings. This ostensible end will determine the shape of his speech. But the speaker will probably not be terribly concerned about shady financial dealings per se; he will be really concerned to make people think well of him. A whole lot of material—the speaker's war record, his domestic concord, his dog—can contribute to this second end although it is irrelevant to the question of financial responsibility. This other material will ordinarily be introduced into the speech by a paralipsis or two.

The paralipsis can work to legitimate ends—the whole, marvelous praise of Athens in Pericles' "Funeral Oration" is actually a paralipsis—but the figure is most often misused. If there is any sort of debate going on, the paralipsis puts one's opponent at a severe, and unfair, disadvantage. If he responds to the paralipsis, the whole issue under consideration is apt to dissolve in an exchange of irrelevancies.

Other Figures

The classification of rhetorical figures proposed in the previous three sections was in some sense natural; at least all of the figures in each group bore a functional resemblance. That is not true of the remainder. Various subgroups might be isolated—i.e., one-term figures—but these subgroups would not be functional, and furthermore any system of subgroups would exclude some important figures. Consequently, we have thought it best simply to list the balance of the figures of speech alphabetically.

Accumulation (Congeries).   This term is most useful if it is confined to structures in which two or more sentences, or occasionally clauses, say essentially the same things. Thus Cassirer wrote,

> Tylor's *Primitive Culture* propounded an anthropological theory based upon general biological principles. He was one of the first to apply the principles of Darwin to the cultural world. The maxim *Natura non facit saltum* [nature does nothing by leaps] admits of no exception. It holds just as much for the world of human civilization as for the organic world.[21]

The second sentence says very much the same thing as the first, and the fourth repeats the substance of the third; it would be no trick at all to combine the sentences of each pair and considerably reduce the number of words used. But this sort of elaboration is functional. Cassirer is giving weight to what is being said here; the repetition of the thought in a somewhat different form makes it more important than it would otherwise be. Accumulation also contributes to clarity, of course, but its major function is to apportion more importance to a thought than simply saying it would demand. The importance of an idea is not necessarily directly proportionate to the number of words required to say it, and every skilled writer attempts to redress imbalances. The reader ought to be aware of these attempts.

The usual structure of an accumulation is reflected in the quotation; first there is a general statement of the point; then it is restated in greater detail or with a more specific application to the subject.

Antithesis (Contentio, Contrapositum).   This figure, about which there was little agreement among classical writers, can be described

---

[21] Ernst Cassirer, *The Myth of the State* (Garden City, N. Y.: Doubleday, 1955), p. 18. My observations are, strictly speaking, about the language of the translator, Professor Charles W. Hendel, of course. The translation in brackets is mine.

as the setting of parts of a discourse in opposition to each other, with the opposition ordinarily contained in some sort of periodic sentence structure. The elements of an antithesis can be words, phrases, clauses, or ideas. "To be or not to be" is a simple antithesis; "Little and big,/ Short and tall,/ Young and old,/ One and all," is a series of antitheses functioning to dramatize the idea of inclusiveness. For a more complex kind of antithesis see Brutus' defense of his part in Caesar's assassination: "Not that I loved Caesar less, but that I loved Rome more. Had you rather Caesar were living, and die all slaves, than that Caesar were dead, to live all freemen?" (III, ii, 22–5). It is important to notice that an antithesis does *not* require that the elements opposed to each other be literally antithetical in meaning; they need merely constitute some sort of opposition in the particular context. Antony's "I come to bury Caesar, not to praise him" (III, ii, 81) is an antithesis, even though "bury" and "praise" are not antithetical outside this context. It should also be noted that the *commutatio* (see below) is a special kind of antithesis, worth distinguishing from the more general term.

The usual form of the antithesis is negative in that it puts concepts in opposition to each other: "not love, but war." But it may also be additive. "We must not only win the war but secure the peace" should be regarded as an antithesis because it has the same range of functions as the negative form.

The obvious function of the antithesis, negative or additive, is to emphasize by some sort of contrast. But perhaps it always does more, in that it contributes to the definition of the concept. What I define a concept in terms of, even if those terms are negative, is an important element in my attitude toward that concept. When I say, "not this, but that," I am not merely emphasizing a difference, I am setting up a class within which a distinction is being made, and hence I am significantly contributing to the concept by the alternative I reject. The additive antithesis is obviously definitional.

The antithesis is related to the *distributio* in its functioning, as in the Brutus quotation above, since it defines not merely a way of looking at a course of action, or a choice, but the limits of choice and action to be considered. It differs from the *distributio* in that it does not apportion what has been distinguished or divided. In arguments (or plays) one sometimes finds antitheses used over and over to remind the reader of some fundamental *distributio* set up earlier.

Asyndeton (Dissolutio or Dissolutum).   The *Ad Herennium* (IV. 30. 41) defines this figure as the presentation of separate parts, as follows: "Indulge your father, obey your relatives, gratify your friends, submit to the laws." It offers another example, "Enter into a complete defence, make no objection, give your slaves to be examined, be eager to find the truth." It is thus a kind of quick catalog. Both the *Ad Herennium* and Quintilian see the especial mark of the figure as the omission of connective particles between the things listed, but this is of small consequence in English (an "and" after "friends" in the first example would make some difference, but not very much), and hence it seems sensible to use the term asyndeton to describe any rapid list, connected or not. The *Ad Herennium* distinguishes the asyndeton from the *articulus*—described as a figure in which single words are "set apart by pauses in staccato speech"—but again this is a distinction that is not very useful in English. An example would be from Donne's "Sonnet XIV": ". . . for you/ As yet but knocke, breathe, shine, and seek to mend." But even in these lines there is an "and" prohibited by the classical definition. It seems best to lump all these list figures together under the name, asyndeton.

The asyndeton is apt to have one of two very sharply different uses. It can be simply a means of passing rapidly over details that are necessary to continuity but do not require any elaboration: "The murderer then opened the window, stepped onto the ledge and slid down the drainpipe." Perhaps more commonly, the asyndeton lends a terseness to the material that actually functions to accentuate and dramatize, as in Caesar's "I came, I saw, I conquered," or the well-known World War II report of a pilot who radioed, "Sighted sub, sank same." It should be noted that the asyndeton also lends itself to a comic effect, particularly when its elements are not parallel in importance.

Commutatio.   This is an antithetical figure, with the key words so reversed that one sentence or (more often) one clause is put in opposition to the other. The classical chestnut illustrating this figure is,

"You must eat to live, not live to eat" *(Ad Herennium* IV. 28. 39). The best-known modern example is the late President Kennedy's "Ask not what your country can do for you: Ask what you can do for your country." The figure is mainly used for paradoxical wit, and it is no surprise to find Oscar Wilde a master of the *commutatio:* "No crime is vulgar, but all vulgarity is crime." (Notice that the *form* of key words can be altered.)

When the *commutatio* is used for purposes other than witticism, it needs to be used sparingly because it is followed by too great a period. If it is used at all frequently, it makes for jerkiness. (The late President Kennedy's speeches were marred by this fault.) Shakespeare uses it occasionally to end decisively a scene. (See *Antony and Cleopatra,* I, iii, 103–104).

Comparison (Similitudo).   The *Ad Herennium* quotes, as an example of the comparison, the following:

> In maintaining a friendship, as in a footrace, you must train yourself not only so that you succeed in running as far as is required, but so that . . . you easily run beyond that point.
>
> (IV. 47. 60)

As the quotation clearly shows, the comparison makes its point by relating the conception under consideration to a conception similar or parallel to it, and the resemblance that it discovers is not confined to one point but is multiple. It has a kind of linear quality— A is to A_1 as B is to B_1 and so forth.

It is thus related to *analogy* (see above). However, the distinction is worth making. The comparison aims at the elucidation of one term or relationship. The analogy, on the other hand, is an argumentative figure; it aims to deduce some necessary consequence from the relationship that it establishes. The distinction is worth preserving because it behooves us to know when something is being proven.

Since the comparison is frequently introduced by "like" or "as," it must also be distinguished from the *translatio* similarly introduced, traditionally called a simile. The most immediate criterion for differentiation is that, while the comparison at least implies multiple and point-to-point connections between its objects, the simile usually sets up a single connection, and if one senses more than one connection, they are simultaneous and not linear. There is an alogical quality about the simile (and the *translatio* of which it is a variation); it frequently surprises us even while we are struck by its truth. The simile, consequently, is the result of some sort of creative act. The comparison, on the other hand, seldom surprises and frequently seems false and abstract. As writers, we do not need to discover it; we can deduce it logically from our rhetorical necessities of the moment.

The distinction between the comparison and the simile is eminently worth drawing because the figures work quite differently and are appropriate to different circumstances. The simile, as has been said, is a trope, and consequently it generalizes even while it pursues particularity (see Chapter V, p. 147). The user of similes is to some extent after the essential nature of the thing (unless, of course, it is a quantitative simile). The comparison, on the other hand, aims at clarity; it does not generalize particularly.

Donne and the other metaphysical poets used the comparison (and the related argumentative figure, the analogy) with great effectiveness, but ordinarily it plays only an incidental role in poetry. Furthermore, because of a kind of softness about it, it may easily run to mere prettiness. Shakespeare parodies this tendency in the euphuism of his day in Falstaff's famous speech: "For though camomile, the more it is trodden on, the faster it grows, yet youth, the more it is wasted, the sooner it wears" (*I Henry IV,* II, iv, 454–456). It is obvious that the comparison is related to *allegory,* since both depend on a parallel development of figurative and literal (although the literal in allegory is only implied), and they both attempt to explain and clarify by a sort of double linear development.

(The above definition is a simplified version of that of the *Ad Herennium* [IV. 46–48. 59–61]; Quintilian seems to use the term *comparatio* for any figure involving comparison or similarity.)

Descriptio.   As its name suggests, the *descriptio* is a figure in which details are used to give a coherent picture of a thing or an event— in other words, for description. Hence it hardly requires illustration. The value of the term is simply that it calls attention to a particular kind of rhetoric, and where and how description is used is an important part of a writer's strategy and intention.

Classical rhetoricians subdivided *descriptio* and made distinctions that were not functional. The author of the *Ad Herennium* confined the term *descriptio* to an exposition of consequences (IV. 39. 51), distinguishing it from *demonstratio,* a vivid presentation of some event (IV. 54. 68). The same source also introduces the term *notatio* for character delineation and *effictio* for physical description (IV. 49–51. 62–65). There is no point in this proliferation of terminology if one is interested merely in analysis.

Gradatio (Climax).   As its name indicates, this is a progressive figure; a *gradatio* advances from one statement to another until it achieves, finally, some sort of climax. The most famous instance, probably, is found in Demosthenes' *De Corona:*

> I did not say this and then fail to make the motion; I did not make the motion and then fail to act as an ambassador; I did not act as an ambassador and then fail to persuade the Thebans.

Classical rhetoricians tended to make the essence of the figure lie in the successive repetitions (of "motion" and "ambassador" in the quotation). But this limitation would virtually confine its use to formal declamation, or to exercises in verbal ingenuity, as with Rosalind's description in *As You Like It:*

> For your brother and my sister no sooner met but they looked; no sooner looked but they loved; no sooner loved but they sighed; no sooner sighed but they asked one another the reason; no sooner knew the reason than they sought the remedy; and in these degrees have they made a pair of stairs to marriage.
>
> (V, ii, 36–42)

The term should include such passages as that from *Antony and Cleopatra* concerning Lepidus:

> Caesar, having made use of him in the wars 'gainst Pompey, presently denied him rivality, would not let him partake in the glory of the

action; and not resting here, accuses him of letters he had formerly wrote to Pompey; upon his own appeal, seizes him; so the poor third is up till death enlarge his confine.

(III, v, 6–11)

There is in the *Antony and Cleopatra* quotation both a sense of progressive action and a kind of climax. These constitute the most useful criteria for a *gradatio*.

The *gradatio* can perform a variety of functions. In the first quotation it obviously works to make Demosthenes' point more emphatic; in the second it works to make the lovers' courtship a comically headlong rush toward matrimony; in the *Antony* passage it compresses action while preserving a sense of movement. It needs to be distinguished from the *ratiocinatio,* which is an argumentative figure, and the *distributio,* which is always engaged in dividing up something.

Hyperbaton.   A useful modern definition of this term would be, any pronounced distortion of normal syntax for the sake of emphasis, as in the following from *Isaiah:* "Thou hast made of a city an heap; of a defenced city a ruin" (25: 2). Similarly, in the peroration of his First Inaugural Address, Lincoln reversed the sentence order to heighten the effect of his antithesis: "In your hands, my dissatisfied countrymen, and not in mine, is the momentous issue of civil war."

Classical writers defined this figure as a violation of natural word order for the sake of elegance. They recognized two species: the *anastrophe,* in which two words are transposed (*virtute pro vestra* instead of the normal *pro vestra virtute*), and the *hyperbaton* proper (called *transiectio* by the *Ad Herennium*), in which a word or phrase is shifted radically out of its place in the sentence. The relative inflexibility of English syntax makes redefinition desirable (*Ad Herennium* IV. 32. 44; *Institutes* VIII. 6. 62–69).

Paraphrasis.   In classical rhetoric, this word generally meant merely "paraphrase." But Quintilian also recognizes it as a figure (*Institutes* VIII. 6. 59–61). A *paraphrasis* in the classical sense is a kind of substitution, usually the substitution of the elaborated and often abstract for the direct and concrete. Homer uses it constantly as a device for lending weight and dignity to his narrative, as when he says of the Greeks, "But when they had put aside desire for food and drink. . . ."

But the term needs to be extended to a rhetorical practice that has become so common in the last several centuries that it might well be regarded as a modern invention. This is the circumlocution that is designed to soften the impact that more direct speech might have. "To liquidate the opposition" is a modern paraphrasis for execution or murder; its advantage is that it does not call up any image of the consequent corpses. (If it is used often enough, of course, it will, and then it will no longer be paraphrastic, or useful.)

Paraphrasis in this second and modern sense differs from most other figures, of course, in that it is not a particular structure; it is detected only by the difference between the words actually used and those one would expect, and the intention reflected in that difference. Indeed, a paraphrasis may be implicit in another figure: "love-child" is both a kind of metonymy (the cause for the effect) and a paraphrasis ("bastard" being felt to be indelicate in some quarters).

Praeteritio.   This is a figure in which a writer brings up things that he does not really propose to discuss; oftentimes he will bring up and immediately abandon several such points. The *praeteritio* is seen in its simplest form in Cicero's first oration, *Against Verres:* "I will leave unmentioned the shames and disgraces of his younger days, and turn to his quaestorship. . . ." As in the above example, the *praeteritio* may look like a paralipsis; it differs from it in that the material introduced does not lie outside the argumentative structure and hence does not interrupt anything. Cicero, having set up the subject of Verres' life, can properly talk about the sins of his youth. The *praeteritio* is a way of getting them in without boring the audience. In function, of course, it may be very like the paralipsis.

The *praeteritio* has another important function, however; it is one of the most common devices whereby a poet sets up his foil. Shakespeare's Sonnet 130, for instance, sets up a *praeteritio:*

> My mistress' eyes are nothing like the sun;
> Coral is far more red than her lips' red;

> If snow be white, why then her breasts are dun;
> If hairs be wire, black wires grow on her head.
> I have seen roses damask'd, red and white,
> But no such roses see I in her cheeks. . . .

In these lines (and six more) Shakespeare considers one by one the conventional characteristics of a sixteenth-century beauty, and he dismisses them. The poetic *praeteritio* can be phrased in various ways, and a modern poet would probably try to conceal the shape of the figure, but the essence of the figure is that things are considered and then rejected for something better (in this sonnet, for honest praise).

Under this general term ought to be included also the figure called a *deminutio,* by which the poet gets in his contrasting material by professing himself inadequate to do certain things. Thus Horace in his ode *Scriberis Vario* (I. vi) catalogs the things he is not capable of writing about, the doings of Achilles, of Ulysses, and of the person to whom the poem is addressed. The latter was presumably sufficiently flattered by the company he found himself in, so that the proposed epic became unnecessary.

Repetitio (Epanaphora). This figure, which is simply the repetition of a word or phrase (sometimes repeatedly and often within parallel syntactical structures), attracted much attention among classical rhetoricians and was subdivided according to the place in the sentence that the repeated words occupied. Thus, according to the *Ad Herennium* (IV. 13. 19; see *Institutes* IX. 3. 28–47 for a similar division), *repetitio* applied to phrases or clauses beginning with the same word or words in a parallel structure; *conversio* indicated repetitions at the end of phrases or clauses; *complexio* the union of the two; and *traductio* was reserved for instances where the same word was repeatedly introduced into a passage with no particular place in the clause or sentence reserved to it. (It has been thought useful to keep in this glossary another kind of *repetitio,* the *commutatio.*)

The lesson in all of this seems to be that the figure can take such a variety of shapes that one dare not attempt to discriminate among them; otherwise terms will multiply out of all reason. It seems best to retain the general term, *repetitio,* only.

One needs to watch the *repetitio* very carefully, since it can perform a surprising variety of functions. It is in all instances, of course, a figure of emphasis; a word used even twice in a passage picks up a lot of force. But it can also substantially affect the meaning of a passage. In Tennyson's "The woods decay, the woods decay and fall," a large part of the pathos is due to the repetition; without it the passage would lose much of its force. And in Frost's "And miles to go before I sleep,/ And miles to go before I sleep," the simple repetition of the phrase alters its meaning. The first time the phrase is used its meaning is literal; only upon its repetition does it take on the figurative, generalized meaning that is the point of the poem.

Even one-word repetitions can affect meanings, as is seen very clearly in the conclusion of Ruskin's *Munera Pulveris:*

"But nothing of this work will pay?" No; no more than it pays to dust your rooms or wash your doorsteps. It will pay; not at first in currency,—in life; (and in currency richly afterwards). It will pay in that which is more than life,—in light, whose true price has not yet been reckoned in any currency, and into the image, of which all wealth, one way or other, must be cast.

In this passage, the repeated word, "pay," changes its meaning slightly almost every time it is used.

Synonymia. This is, as the name suggests, the use of words or phrases having an identical or near-identical meaning either in sequence or close enough to each other to reinforce the common meaning. It is thus a figure that emphasizes, although, like the *repetitio,* a *synonymia* may affect meaning in important ways.

Zeugma. This is witty use of syntax, in which one word is made to control syntactically two or more dependent words that are not parallel in significance. The classical example is Pope's "She stained her honor and her new brocade," in which he mocks the shallowness of a mind that would equate the two kinds of stains, the effect being all the more devastating by the reversal of the linked nouns from the order one would have expected. The *zeugma* functions in somewhat the same way as the *transgressio,* although it is seldom so effective, because it seldom escapes a sense of contrivance.

Afterword on the Use of the Figures of Rhetoric in the Analysis of Texts

It has been said before, but it is worth repeating: writers write prose or poetry, not rhetoric. This glossary proposes, in sum, a systematic way of analyzing the prose or poetry that the writer writes. In our experience, the knowledge of these figures enables the student—of literature, history, or whatever—to read this prose or poetry with more understanding than they otherwise might. That is the only justification there can possibly be for learning them.

We have presented these figures as though they were particular structures bearing a merely linear or additive relationship to each other. But often this is not the case. Rhetorical complexities are well illustrated in the following passage:

> The scrimmage of politics is for the purpose of determining who shall transact the government's business. If in the struggle the desire to accomplish one's purpose turns into a desire to annihilate one's opponent, the outcome is civil war. Historically, this desire to annihilate finds its support and justification in the Intellect, in ideas, for ideas are clear-cut and divide. Material interests can be compromised, principles cannot. A man who sensibly will not fight his neighbor over depredations in his garden will fight him over being called a liar.[22]

When one looks closely at this apparently spare prose, a great deal of rhetorical complexity becomes apparent. The *translatio* "scrimmage" of the first sentence actually is a kind of contrast to the "civil war" of the second; the sentences, which seem to be progressive and consecutive, might well be called, together, an *antithesis*. The third sentence is an *enthymeme,* the "for" being the equivalent of "because." The fourth sentence amplifies what has been said to this

[22] Jacques Barzun, *The House of Intellect* (New York: Harper and Brothers, 1959), p. 146.

point with an *antithesis*—the only clear-cut and obvious figure in the passage. The last sentence is perhaps best called an *example,* in that it is evidence for what has gone before. But it is an abstract example and its tone is surely *sententious.* The flexible student of rhetoric might do well to choose both possibilities simultaneously by calling it a *sententious example.*

Nor is this passage a rarity, particularly in modern prose. The complexity arises from the fact that Professor Barzun probably never in his life said, "Ah, I need a *distributio* (or whatever) here." A writer begins with a conception, and he distorts the basic language patterns to realize that conception as well as he can. In the course of his wrestling he works out structures that we can profitably classify according to the categories of rhetoric. But we cannot expect that the result—the poetry or prose that has been written to other specifications—will in all cases neatly respond to rhetorical analysis. We need to learn to read carefully and be flexible with our classifications.

Chapter VI

A Textual Analysis

One can readily classify the functions performed by textual rhetoric. But the writer using rhetoric does not think of his activity in terms of functions. He is, rather, trying to realize a particular intention, to convey an insight or a judgment from his head into other heads by means of arbitrary symbols. Consequently, his rhetoric does not fall into predictable patterns of first this and then that. He amplifies, compares, argues as that intention dictates, and sometimes he accomplishes several of these ends at one time. The only way to understand how textual rhetoric functions is to watch it at work in a specific example.

The following essay, "The Abolition of Man" by the late C. S. Lewis, is the first half of a lecture—but it stands by itself well enough, and it argues its thesis persuasively.[1]

> 1. "Man's conquest of Nature" is an expression often used to describe the progress of applied science. "Man has *Nature*⌉   **example**
>   **personification**

[1] C. S. Lewis, *The Abolition of Man* (London: Geoffrey Bles Ltd.; New York: The Macmillan Company, 1962), pp. 39–48. Copyright 1947 by The Macmillan Company. Reprinted by permission of Geoffrey Bles Ltd., and The Macmillan Company.

translatio
whacked" said someone to a friend of mine
not long ago. In their context the words
had a certain tragic beauty, for the speaker
was dying of tuberculosis. "No matter," he
translatio
said, "I know I'm one of the *casualties*. Of
translatio
course there are *casualties on the winning*
translatio
as well as on the losing side. But that
translatio
doesn't alter the fact that it is *winning*."

distributio

I have chosen this story as my point of departure in order to make it clear that I do
not wish to disparage all that is really bene-
ficial in the process described as "Man's
conquest," much less all the real devotion
and self-sacrifice that has gone to make it
possible. But having done so I must proceed to analyze this conception a little
more closely. In what sense is Man the
possessor of increasing power over Nature?

prolepsis

This is what might be called a "some say" introduction; the problem with which the whole essay will be concerned is defined by
setting up a point of view that any sophisticated reader will immediately understand is not Lewis' own. The amplification by
example of the second sentence is almost inevitable in view of the
weight that must be given the idea, "man's conquest of nature." It
should be noted that the first sentence is general; the *example* of
the second sentence sharply lowers the level of abstraction to make
the issue of the essay immediate. This is a common gambit in introductions. But this second sentence does more; the *translatio*
"whacked" sets up five more unobtrusive *translatios* that in sum
define the particular attitude Lewis is to take toward his subject:
the "conquest of nature" is a kind of military assault, an act of war.
This point of view is reinforced over and over again in the body of
the essay.

"I have chosen" begins a *prolepsis* (see p. 50), which, in this
case, performs a double function. One is technical. A "some say"
introduction does not lead easily into the body of an essay; there is

usually a gap between what others say and the beginning of one's own argument. The *prolepsis* functions to bridge, somewhat awkwardly, that gap. The *distributio* makes a traditional disclaimer of irrational hostility while raising the possibility of a serious, and rational, difficulty with the optimistic attitude of the quotation.

But this *prolepsis* has another important function; it defines Mr. Lewis more completely as a person. He has already shown himself in his discussion of his dying friend as a sensitive and sympathetic man capable of seeing "tragic beauty" in a statement with which he will obviously take issue. Now the very bluntness of the *prolepsis* in an introduction tells us that Lewis is also a "no-nonsense" sort of person while what he says assures us that he is reasonable. Informality is implied by the apparent casualness of the diction, although the man dying of tuberculosis prohibits a deterioration to flippancy.

The second paragraph is a good example of the kinds of complexity to be found in a rhetorical function, definition, which might be presumed to be easy and straightforward.

whole paragraph is definition	2. Let us consider three typical examples: the *aeroplane,* the *wireless,* and the *contraceptive.*	examples
antithesis or distributio	In a civilized community, in peacetime, anyone who can pay for them may use these things. But it cannot strictly be said that when he does so he is exercising his own proper or individual power over	enthymeme major— "Anything that can be withheld is not in one's power."
analogy	Nature. If I pay you to carry me, I am not therefore myself a strong man. Any or all of the three things I have mentioned can be withheld from some men by other men —by those who sell, or those who allow the sale, or those who own the sources of production, or those who make the goods.	accumulation
	repetitio What we call Man's *power* is, in reality, repetitio a *power* possessed by some men which they	
enthymeme	may, or may not, allow other men to profit repetitio by. Again, as regards the *powers* manifested in the aeroplane or the wireless, Man is as much the patient or subject as	

enthymeme {

translatio
the possessor, since he is the *target* both for
bombs and for propaganda. And as regards
contraceptives, there is a paradoxical, negative sense in which all possible future gen-
repetitio
erations are the *patients or subjects* of a
repetitio
power wielded by those already alive. By
repetitio
contraception simply, they are denied ex-
repetitio
istence; by *contraception* used as a means
of selective breeding, they are, without
their concurring voice, made to be what
one generation, for its own reasons, may
choose to prefer. From this point of view,
repetitio
what we call Man's *power* over Nature
repetitio
turns out to be a *power* exercised by some
men over other men with Nature as its
instrument.

The previous paragraph has proposed the term with which this one shall be concerned, "man's power over nature." What Lewis must do with it really amounts to a kind of redefinition and, since the success of the essay hangs very much upon this redefinition, he approaches it with great caution. He does not begin with a topic sentence, he begins with three specific *examples* of power over nature. The second sentence is perhaps the most important in the paragraph, because it unobtrusively shifts consideration from "man's power" to "the power of individual men." The *antithesis* completed by the third sentence develops the distinction implicit in the shift of subject; the point is further clarified by a *comparison*. The relationship between the third sentence and the fifth, "Any or all of the three things," is clear enough although the connection is implicit; the latter is really a reason for the former and together they set up an *enthymeme*. Few people would care to argue with the implicit major premise, "Anything that can be withheld from someone cannot be said to be in his power." The subsequent *accumulation* marks the completion of the first stage in the redefinition at which Lewis is aiming.

Lewis embarks on the second stage of his redefinition by introducing a further term, "patient or subject." "Power over nature" has been shown to be a power possessed by some, not by all, men; here the term is further defined to mean the power of some men over all men. But the three examples have been separated. In effect, "contraceptives" has been separated from the other two examples because it involves a further dimension of control, the dimension of time. The implications of this dimension are developed by a *distributio* in which he notices, and dismisses, birth control as a simple means of limiting the population in order to treat it as a kind of selective control. This new dimension of time is dropped, momentarily, but later it will become a central consideration.

One should notice how the subject of the paragraph, "power," is quietly insisted upon by the *repetitios*. The *repetitio* "patient or subject" is really a kind of redefinition of man.

The last sentence is the topic sentence of the paragraph. This structure is unusual. A paragraph usually begins with a declaration of some sort, with the support following. Here Lewis has reversed that procedure, undoubtedly because he felt that readers might resist the declaration if it were proposed first. The unpopular attitude that he advocates makes such strategy necessary.

The next paragraph is perhaps even more complex in the variety of functions that it performs:

Paragraph begins as a prolepsis, but turns into a reprehensio

3. It is, of course, a commonplace to complain that men have hitherto used badly, [antithesis]
repetitio
and against their fellows, the *powers* that science had given them. But that is not the
repetitio
point I am trying to make. *I* am not speaking of particular corruptions and abuses which an increase of moral virtue would [antithesis and accumulation]
translatio
repetitio
cure. I am considering what the thing
repetitio
called "Man's *power* over Nature" must always and essentially be. No doubt, the [expeditio]
translatio
picture could be modified by public own-

> ership of raw materials and factories and
> public control of scientific research. But
> unless we have a world state this will still
> *repetitio*
> mean the *power* of one nation over others.
> And even within the world state or the na-
> *repetitio*
> tion it will mean (in principle) the *power*
> of majorities over minorities, and (in the
> concrete) of a government over the people.
> *repetitio*
> And all long-term exercises of *power,* es-
> *repetitio*
> pecially in breeding, must mean the *power*
> of earlier generations over later ones.

This is ostensibly a *prolepsis* again, as the *repetitio* "I am" indicates, and the very baldness of the intrusion is a guarantee against tricks because it is a reminder that Lewis is a very straight-forward sort of person. At the same time, he restates his position in a general way in two very forthright *antitheses.*

But the real point of the paragraph is probably to be found in the *expeditio* with which it is concluded. This is a *reprehensio* because it anticipates, and blocks off, possible alternatives to the point of view Lewis advocates. In effect, he dismisses questions of particular political arrangements as irrelevant. All control implies power, and power is power over people.

Technically, the essay is at this point mis-paragraphed; as is made clear by what follows, the concluding sentence of the paragraph already quoted functions as a topic sentence for the one to follow. Lewis frequently breaks up his prose in this fashion; it obscures the joints of an essay and makes it seem more like a narrative. But here it also functions to give a *gradatio*-like effect to the *expeditio.*

a kind
of pseudo-
enthymeme

accumu-
lation

4a. The latter point is not always sufficiently emphasized, because those who
write on social matters have not yet
learned to imitate the physicists by always
including Time among the dimensions. In
order to understand fully what Man's

antithesis

> power over Nature, and therefore the
> power of some men over other men, really
> means, we must picture the race extended
> in time from the date of its emergence to
> that of its extinction. Each generation ex-
>
> repetitio
> ercises *power* over its successors; and each,
> in so far as it modifies the environment
> bequeathed to it and rebels against tradi-
>
> repetitio
> tion, resists and limits the *power* of its
>
> translatio
> predecessors. This modifies the *picture*

antithesis

> translatio
> which is sometimes *painted* of a progres-
> sive emancipation from tradition and a
> progressive control of natural processes re-
> sulting in a continual increase of human
>
> repetitio
> *power*. In reality, of course, if any one age
> really attains, by eugenics and scientific ed-
>
> repetitio
> ucation, the *power* to make its descendants
> what it pleases, all men who live after it

accumu-
lation

> repetitio
> are the patients of that *power*. They are
>
> antithesis
> *weaker, not stronger:* for though we may
> have put wonderful machines in their
> hands we have pre-ordained how they are
> to use them.

enthymeme

This paragraph extends the redefinition accomplished earlier; now "man's power over nature" clearly includes man's power over future generations, only briefly touched on earlier in the *distributio* of "contraceptives." The first sentence is a pseudo-*enthymeme* (because it does not imply a major premise) functioning as transition to connect the topic sentence and material of this paragraph. This material does not constitute evidence, properly speaking; the first half of the paragraph consists of two *accumulations*. The point that Lewis wishes to make can hardly be argued; it is a self-evident extension of what he has said before. In such a situation, amplifying figures (of which *accumulation* is the most common) are inescapable if the writer feels his point requires more weight than that provided by a simple statement.

The hypothetical *enthymeme* toward the end of the paragraph beginning "In reality, of course" further extends the definition: *if power over nature is power over succeeding generations, then absolute power over nature is absolute power over succeeding generations.* Another *enthymeme* follows, arguing the same thing more specifically. At this point we have the initial term, "power over nature," redefined, extended in time, and finally, here, made absolute.

But the section above is only the first part of the paragraph, and what follows is curious indeed. Lewis, having extended time forward, now proceeds to extend it backward with the assertion that control over the future will probably be attained by those most emancipated from the past.

enthymeme ⎧ 4b.   And if, as is almost certain, the age
                                                   repetitio
        which had thus attained maximum *power*
        over posterity were also the age most eman-
        cipated from tradition, it would be en-
                                        repetitio
        gaged in reducing the *pow*er of its prede-
        ⎩ cessors almost as drastically as that of its

enthymeme ⎧ successors. And we must also remember
        that, quite apart from this, the later a gen-
                                accumulation
        eration comes—*the nearer it lives to that*
        date at which the species becomes extinct
                 repetitio
        —the less *power* it will have in the forward
        ⎩ direction, because its subjects will be so

enthymeme ⎧ few. There is therefore no question of a ⎫ antithesis
        repetitio
        power vested in the race as a whole stead-
        ily growing as long as the race survives.
        The last men, far from being the heirs of
        repetitio
        power, will be of all men most subject to
          metonymy
        the *dead hand* of the great planners and
        conditioners and will themselves exercise ⎭

enthymeme ⌠   repetitio   trans-
          ⎢ least *power* upon the future. The real *pic-*
          ⎢   latio   personification(?)   ⎤ gradatio
          ⎢ *ture* is that of one dominant *age*—let us
          ⎢ suppose the hundredth century A.D.—
          ⎢ which resists all previous ages most suc-
          ⎢ cessfully and dominates all subsequent
          ⎢ ages most irresistibly, and thus is the real
          ⎣ master of the human species. But even
             within this master generation (itself an in-
             finitesimal minority of the species) the
             repetitio
             power will be exercised by a minority
             smaller still. Man's conquest of Nature, if
             the dreams of some scientific planners are
             realized, means the rule of a few hundreds
             of men over billions upon billions of men.
             There neither is nor can be any simple in- ⎤

paradoxical   repetitio
accumulation ⌠ crease of *power* of Man's side. Each new
             ⎢ repetitio   repetitio
             ⎢ *power* won *by* man is a *power over* man
paradoxical ⎢ as well. Each advance leaves him weaker
accumu-   ⎨ as well as stronger. In every victory, besides ⎤ paradoxical
lation   ⎢   translatio   allegory put
             ⎢ being the *general* who triumphs, he is also   together with
             ⎣   translatio   translatios
                the *prisoner* who follows the triumphal
                car.   ⎦

Why did Lewis introduce at this point the relationship to the past
of those who will finally conquer nature? Later in the essay this
relationship will be of considerable importance, but at this point
it is unnecessary and probably a tactical blunder, since it cannot
be managed adequately. (Freshmen very often get lost at precisely
this point in the essay.) The answer to this question is apparent,
however, when one sees what the real function of the paragraph is:
to establish dramatically the position achieved to this point. Lewis
has succeeded in redefining his major term, "man's conquest over
nature," through a series of steps and he wants to consolidate his
position by presenting the complete redefinition, even though this
involves pulling in material that is, at this point, not merely irrelevant but puzzling.

The fact that the redefinition is complete is also signaled by the sharply increased number of tropes that Lewis permits himself. A *metonymy*, "dead hand" for "power of the past," is followed by a *translatio* and a doubtful *personification*. The *repetitio* Lewis has used throughout the essay to this point, "power," is sharply increased in numbers until it is a kind of insistent hammering at the reader. The redefinition itself is set up in a very forceful *gradatio*, and the paragraph ends with a very daring excursion into *allegory* by means of a couple of *translatios;* the tone of the *allegory* is, furthermore, *sententious.*

Most readers would find this rhetoric successful, but its success depends on the discretion with which Lewis has introduced it. It will be noticed throughout the essay that the most forceful rhetorical figures, particularly the tropes, are virtually confined to summing-up situations, after the point has presumably been established.

That Lewis wishes here to mark a pause in his argument is confirmed by the character of the next paragraph.

whole paragraph is a prolepsis

5. I am not yet considering whether the total result of such ambivalent victories is a good thing or a bad. I am only making

translatio

clear what Man's *conquest* of Nature really means and especially that final stage in the

translatio & repetitio

conquest, which, perhaps, is not far off.

repetitio

The *final stage* is come when Man by eugenics, by pre-natal conditioning, and by an education and propaganda based on a perfect applied psychology, has obtained

accumulation

full control over himself. HUMAN nature

translatio

will be the last part of Nature to *surrender*

translatio

accumulation

to Man. The *battle* will then be won. We

paraphrasis

shall have *"taken the thread of life out of the hand of Clotho"* and be henceforth free to make our species whatever we wish

repetitio

it to be. *The battle will indeed be won.* But who, precisely, will have won it?

antithesis

Technically, this paragraph would have to be described as another *prolepsis;* again Lewis stops the forward movement of the essay to reintroduce himself. But his object was not so much to reestablish ethos as to guard against misunderstanding. The first *antithesis* limits his conclusion to this point, which is then elaborated through sentence after sentence of accumulation. The point made must be thoroughly understood before further progress is possible, and Lewis is willing to stop the movement of his essay completely to be sure that he has been understood to this point. The transitional question with which the paragraph concludes is really a device for indicating that he is about to move on; it has been necessitated by the lengthy and essentially static summation of this paragraph and the preceding one.

The next paragraph can be usefully divided into two paragraphs; most writers would have so divided it: .

repetitio
6a. For the *power* of Man to make himself what he pleases means, as we have
repetitio
seen, the *power* of some men to make other
men what THEY please. In all ages, no
doubt, nurture and instruction have, in
some sense, attempted to exercise this
repetitio
power. But the situation to which we must
look forward will be novel in two respects.
repetitio
In the first place, the *power* will be enor-
distributio ⌠mously increased. Hitherto the plans of
educationalists have achieved very little of
what they attempted and indeed, when we
read them—how Plato would have every⌉   examples
infant "a bastard nursed in a bureau," and   in a
Elyot would have the boy see no men be-   correctio
fore the age of seven and, after that, no
women, and how Locke wants children to
zeugma
have *leaky shoes and no turn for poetry*—⌡
oxymoron   ⌉ gradatio
we may well thank the *beneficent obsti-*
repetitio
nacy of real mothers, *real* nurses, and

> repetitio
> (above all) *real* children for preserving the
> human race in such sanity as it still pos-
>   metonymy   ⎫ enthymeme
> sesses. But the *man-moulders* of the new
>   translatio or
>   abusio(?)   repetitio
> age will be *armed* with the *powers* of an
> omnicompetent state and an irresistible
> scientific technique: we shall get at last a
>   abusio
> race of conditioners who really can *cut out*
> all posterity in what shape they please.

This paragraph begins with three sentences that are, like the previous question, transitional; Lewis restates his conclusion to this point
and then sets up a consideration of what is to come compared to
the past, a consideration having two parts. What follows is a *distributio* rather than a simple *antithesis* because Lewis distinguishes
the new from the old by distributing effective power between them.
The power of the past over subsequent generations is minimized
by the examples, and particularly by the *zeugma,* whose comic discontinuity makes the attempt at control seem absurd. The repetition of the word "real" functions peculiarly; it extends its meaning
from the nouns that the word ostensibly modifies to the past as a
whole, which becomes as a consequence somehow more real than
the present. The second leg of the *distributio* firmly establishes the
omnipotence of the controllers with relationship to the past.

The second section of the paragraph is another *distributio.*
Set up merely as the second novel element in man's new power over
nature, it in fact proposes a new, and a major, element in Lewis'
thesis:

> whole   6b. The second difference is even more
> section is
> distributio   important. In the older systems both the
>   kind of man the teachers wished to pro-
>   duce and their motives for producing him
> accumulation ⎡were prescribed by the Tao—a norm to
>   which the teachers themselves were subject
>   and from which they claimed no liberty to
>   repetitio
>   depart. *They* did not cut men to some pat-⎤ antithesis

accumulation

repetitio
tern they had chosen. *They* handed on
repetitio
what they had received: *they* initiated the
young neophyte into the mystery of hu-
translatio
manity which *over-arched* him and them
alike. It was but old birds teaching young
birds to fly. This will be changed. Values   comparison

accumulation are now mere natural phenomena. Judgements of value are to be produced in the
accumu-   pupil as part of the conditioning. What-
lation
anti-
ever TAO there is will be the *product, not*
thesis
the motive, of education. The conditioners
have been emancipated from all that. It is

accumulation one more part of Nature which they have
translatio
(and may be pun)
conquered. The ultimate *springs* of human action are no longer, for them, some-
repetitio   *translatio*
thing given. *They* have *surrendered*—like

accumu-   *comparison*
lation   *electricity:* it is the function of the Condi-
antithesis   *repetitio*
tioners *to control, not to obey* them. *They*   distributio
know how to PRODUCE conscience and de-
cide what kind of conscience they will pro-
repetitio
duce. *They* themselves are outside, above.

prolepsis For we are assuming the last stage of *Man's*
personification   *translatio*
struggle with Nature. The final *victory* has
trans-
been won. Human nature has been *con-*
latio   *translatio*
quered—and, of course, has *conquered, in*
irony
whatever sense those words may now bear.

Again, the new section begins with a "sign" sentence, warning us in advance of the importance of what is to follow. The structural figure of the paragraph could as easily be called an *antithesis* as a *distributio;* the point of the paragraph is to define an important characteristic of the new age, and this is best done by contrast with the old.

The basic figure, obviously, is *accumulation*, as Lewis describes each situation over and over in different ways; three or four *antitheses* within the overall structure reinforce the contrastive intent. The amount of *accumulation* is in itself indicative of the importance of this point to Lewis' thesis.

But the contrast is reinforced more subtly; the contrast is between human or natural (as Lewis would define it) and nonhuman, and this contrast is proposed by the figures themselves. In the first part Lewis moves carefully, through three sentences of *accumulation*, from "they handed on," to "they initiated the young neophyte," to "It was but old birds teaching young birds to fly." The comparative language, being relatively concrete in its reference, identifies the traditional with the natural. The language in the second half of the contrast is by and large neutral; we find only the *translatio* "springs" (which perhaps refers as well to watch springs in this context) and the *comparison* "like electricity"—both relating man to mechanics. The last three sentences, again, constitute a kind of *prolepsis* as Lewis anticipates a pained response on the part of some readers.

An important element has clearly been added to the argument: the control of human nature implies the control of motives. Why Professor Lewis saw fit to add this element in so devious a manner, as the second of two differences between past and future, is impossible to understand. The gain in continuity is more than offset by possible confusion, if the reader is careless enough to read it as simply what it pretends to be.

This paragraph established what probably constitutes the most significant concept in the whole essay. In the next paragraph, Lewis can immediately draw from this concept the implication that most interests him.

	7. The Conditioners, then, are to choose what kind of artificial Tao they will, *for their own good reasons,* produce in the
accumulation	Human race. They are the motivators, *the creators of motives.* But how are they go-
distributio	ing to be motivated themselves? For a time,

perhaps, by survivals, within their own minds, of the old "natural" TAO. Thus at first they may look upon themselves as servants and guardians of humanity and conceive that they have a "duty" to do a "good." But it is only by confusion that they can remain in this state. They recognize the concept of duty as the result of certain processes which they can now control. Their victory has consisted precisely in emerging from the state in which they were acted upon by those processes to the state in which they use them as tools. One of the things they now have to decide is whether they will, or will not, so condition the rest of us that we can go on having the old idea of duty and the old reactions to it. How can duty help them to decide that? Duty itself is up for trial: it cannot also be the judge. And "good" fares no better. They know quite well how to produce a dozen different conceptions of good in us. The question is which, if any, they should produce. No conception of good can help them to decide. It is absurd to fix on one of the things they are comparing and make it the standard of comparison.

Marginal annotations (left): enthymeme; accumulation; accumulation; personification & enthymeme; another example & enthymeme

Marginal annotations (right): accumulation; rhetorical question; accumulation

Again one observes the care with which Lewis reasserts the position established, with a further *accumulation* and then a transitional question to point up what follows.[2] And again this is followed by a *distributio*. But the management of the *distributio* is worthy of note. The first leg begins with a general statement, that the conditioners may at first be motivated in a traditional fashion. But Lewis then lowers the level of abstraction in an *accumulation* that substitutes the more specific "duty" for the less specific " 'natural'

[2] Since the essay was originally delivered as a lecture, its carefulness can be attributed at least in part to the fact that an oral argument is more difficult to follow than a written one.

Tao." The second leg of the *distributio* is considered on this low, more specific level of abstraction.

The central conception of the paragraph is an *enthymeme* which is climactically asserted in the sentence, "Duty itself is up for trial: it cannot also be the judge." This might be paraphrased as, "Duty cannot be a basis for conditioning because it is a product of it." The major premise, obviously, is that "nothing can be a basis for conditioning which is also a product of it."

It should perhaps be pointed out that this *enthymeme* is felt by many readers to be a weak element in Lewis' argument. It is perhaps the case that one cannot logically assume as an ultimate value an artifact to be made or not made at one's own discretion. But human beings, even those aspiring to be conditioners, are seldom thoroughly logical in fundamental matters.

Lewis' point is that no traditional moral conception can motivate the conditioners, but he has made this point in terms of "duty." He then generalizes it by repeating his *enthymeme* in terms of a single other value word, "good." He can then return to the level of abstraction at which the paragraph began. It functions as a *sententia*, although it is actually the major premise reformulated.

Again Professor Lewis interrupts his argument with a *prolepsis*, and again this is done, at least in part, to slow down the speed of the essay. A great deal has happened in the last two paragraphs, and the reader perhaps needs a little time. One of the facts a student can learn from Lewis is that the speed of an argument is almost as crucial to effectiveness as narrative speed.

all prolepsis	8. To some it will appear that I am inventing a factitious difficulty for my Conditioners. Other, more simple-minded, crit-	antithesis
distributio	ics may ask "Why should you suppose they will be such bad men?" But I am not sup-	
correctio	repetitio repetitio posing them to be bad *men. They* are, repetitio rather, not *men* (in the old sense) at all.	

repetitio   repetitio
They are, if you like, *men* who have sacrificed their own share in traditional humanity in order to devote themselves to the task of deciding what "Humanity"

enthymeme

shall henceforth mean. "Good" and "bad,"
applied to them, are words without content: for it is from them that the content
of these words is henceforward to be de-

reprehensio

Picks up first leg of distributio

rived. Nor is their difficulty factitious. We
might suppose that it was possible to say
"After all, most of us want more or less
the same things—food and drink and sexual intercourse, amusement, art, science,
and the longest possible life for individuals and for the species. Let them simply
say, This is what we happen to like, and go
on to condition men in the way most likely
to produce it. Where's the trouble?" But

not in glossary
—called
antiphrasis by
Quintilian
(ix. 2. 47).

this will not answer. In the first place, it is
false that we all really like the same things.
But even if we did, what motive is to im-

rhetorical
question

anti-
pel the Conditioners *to scorn delights and*
thesis
live laborious days in order that we, and
posterity, may have what we like? *Their
duty?* But that is only the TAO, which they
may decide to impose on us, but which
cannot be valid for them. If they accept it,

antithesis

enthymeme

then they are no longer *the makers of con-*
antithesis
science but still its subjects, and their final
conquest over Nature has not really hap-
rhetorical question
pened. *The preservation of the species?*
rhetorical question
But why should the species be preserved?
One of the questions before them is
whether this feeling for posterity (they
know well how it is produced) shall be
continued or not. However far they may

accumulation

go back, or down, they can find no ground
to stand on. Every motive they try to act on
becomes at once a PETITIO. *It is not that*

implicit
distributio

antithesis
they are bad men. They are not men at all.
Stepping outside the TAO, they have

accumulation

> metonymy
> *stepped into the void.* Nor are their sub-⌉
> jects necessarily unhappy men. *They are*
> antithesis
> *not men at all: they are artifacts.* Man's⌉   paradox
> translatio
> final *conquest* has proved to be the aboli-
> tion of Man.

The *prolepsis* begins by *distributing* the objections, with the second, less difficult, considered first. The objection would only be made by someone who hasn't understood what Lewis has been arguing to this point, and hence he answers it by an unobtrusive *gradatio*-like structure that works through an *antithesis* and a *correctio* to a restatement of his previous *enthymeme*. (His problem is to repeat himself without appearing to do so.)

The second objection is more serious; in effect, it asks why the conditioners cannot go about their business in more or less genial ignorance of the logical difficulty they have gotten into, by simply providing the things everyone wants naturally. Lewis answers in two different ways. In the first place, he asserts that everyone doesn't want the same things. But this would be a difficult point to argue, so he abandons it in a concession which might impress even the casual reader as magnanimous, and he sets up his second response as a rhetorical question. This question simply raises a variant of Lewis' main argument by pointing out the problem of motive raised originally in terms of the conditioned and which applies as well to the conditioners.

This long *prolepsis* is, as was pointed out, a device for slowing down the movement of the essay. But it also reinforces the point made. Lewis is repeating himself, yet most readers would not find the essay to flag seriously. The *antitheses* and the *rhetorical questions* give the paragraph a sense of importance and urgency to which most readers respond.

Lewis would seem to have made his point; the paragraph above concludes with a fine rhetorical rise and the triumphant introduction of the title and presumed subject of the essay. But he has yet another term to introduce before the argument is completed.

9.   Yet the Conditioners will act. When I
said just now that all motives fail them, I   correctio
should have said all motives except one.

antithesis ⎡All motives that claim any validity other
than that of their felt emotional weight at
a given moment have failed them. Every-⎤   accumulation
thing except the SIC VOLO, SIC JUBEO [this
I wish, this I order] has been explained
away. But what never claimed objectivity⎦
cannot be destroyed by subjectivism. The

example ⎡impulse to scratch when I itch or to pull
to pieces when I am inquisitive is immune
from the solvent which is fatal to my justice, or honour, or care for posterity. *When*
                          antithesis
⎣*all that says "it is good" has been de-*

enthymeme ⎡*bunked, what says "I want" remains.* It⎤   a
                 translatio   short
cannot be *exploded* or "seen through" be-   sorites
⎣cause it never had any pretensions. The⎦

enthymeme ⎡Conditioners, therefore, must come to be
                              repe-
⎣motivated simply by their own pleasure. *I*⎦

antithesis ⎡**titio**
as prolepsis *am* not here speaking of the corrupting influence of power nor expressing the fear
that under it our Conditioners will degen-
erate. The very words CORRUPT and DEGEN-⎤   enthymeme
ERATE imply a doctrine of value and are⎦
therefore meaningless in this context. My
point is that those who stand outside all
judgements of value cannot have any
ground for preferring one of their own
impulses to another except the emotional
⎣strength of that impulse. We may legiti-
mately hope that among the impulses
which arise in minds thus emptied of all
"rational" or "spiritual" motives, some
                  repetitio
will be benevolent. *I am* very doubtful
myself whether the benevolent impulses,
stripped of that preference and encourage-
ment which the TAO teaches us to give
them and left to their merely natural
strength and frequency as psychological

antithesis

repetitio · *accumulation*

events, will have much influence. *I am* very doubtful whether history shows us one example of a man who, having stepped outside traditional morality and attained power, has used that power benevolently.

enthymeme

repetitio
I am inclined to think that the Conditioners will hate the conditioned. Though regarding as an illusion the artificial conscience which they produce in us their
repetitio
subjects, *they* will yet perceive that it cre-
repetitio
ates in *us* an illusion of meaning for our lives which compares favourably with the
repetitio
futility of their own: and *they* will envy
repetitio   *comparison*
us as *eunuchs envy men. But I, do not, insist on this, for it is mere conjecture.*

antithesis
enthymeme

What is not conjecture is that our hope even of a "conditioned" happiness rests on what is ordinarily called "chance"—the chance that benevolent impulses may on the whole predominate in our Conditioners. For without the judgement "Benevolence is good"—that is, without re-entering the TAO—they can have no ground for promoting or stabilizing their benevolent impulses rather than any others. By the logic of their position they must just take their impulses as they come, from chance.

accumulation

accumulation

And Chance here means Nature. It is from heredity, digestion, the weather, and the association of ideas, that the motives of the Conditioners will spring. Their extreme
repetitio   *repetitio*
rationalism, by "seeing through" all *"rational"* motives, leaves them creatures of
repetitio
wholly *irrational* behaviour. If you will not obey the TAO, or else commit suicide, obedience to impulse (and therefore, in the long run, to mere "nature") is the only course left open.

paradox

It is important to notice that Lewis, in this entire paragraph, is dealing very cunningly with a thesis-word that can present a good deal of difficulty to a writer, the word "only." As this paragraph makes clear, he wants to assert that "only impulse" can motivate conditioners. To attempt to manage both these thesis-words simultaneously could be extremely awkward, because they really involve two distinct ideas—"impulse will, but nothing else will." The present essay avoids the problem by dealing in effect with the "only" first. Lewis begins by excluding other possibilities as though he were excluding all possibilities. He is then in a position to introduce "impulse" very economically as a simple *correctio*.

The fact that impulse is not eroded by considerations that would destroy a conception like "duty" is self-evident once it has been said; hence, through the first half of the paragraph Lewis is chiefly engaged in amplifying, and he uses the ordinary figures to accomplish it—*accumulation, example, antithesis*. The *enthymemes* are really amplifying figures here, as is shown by their position at the end of the section.

A *prolepsis* follows—"I am not here speaking. . . ." Lewis must use an extraordinary number of these interruptions because his argument is not one that many readers will cherish. In effect, he must stuff up each mousehole as it appears to keep the reader from disappearing into a happier future.

The argument would seem to be complete, and in essence it is. But Lewis has one more surprise in store for the reader. He seems almost to toy with the reader through several sentences of low-pitched speculation about the horrors that await us before he makes his final connection, between "irrational impulse" and "nature." The identification is not proven; it is asserted through two *accumulations* prior to the concluding sentence. The point is not important, but it is shocking, and Lewis can afford to toss it at the reader and, in effect, walk away.

The conclusion is a standard *peroration* for an essay of this sort: a summary.

personification
trans-
10. At the moment, then, of *Man's vic-*
gradatio   latio personification
tory over *Nature,* we find the whole human

translatio
race *subjected* to some individual men,
translatio
and those individuals *subjected* to that in
themselves which is purely "natural"—to
personification
their irrational impulses. *Nature,* untrammelled by values, rules the Conditioners,
personification   commutatio
and, through them, all humanity. *Man's*
translatio personification
conquest of *Nature* turns out, in the mopersonification
ment of its consummation, to be *Nature's*
translatio
          personification   translatio
conquest of *Man.* Every *victory* we seemed
to win has led us, step by step, to this conpersonification   translatio
clusion. All *Nature's* apparent *reverses*

accumulation
                              translatio
have been but *tactical withdrawals.* We
translatio
thought we were *beating her back* when
translatio   accumulation
she was *luring us on.* What looked to us
simile
like hands held up in surrender was really
translatio
the *opening of arms* to enfold us for ever.
If the fully planned and conditioned world
(with its TAO a mere product of the plan-
accumulation   personification
ning) comes into existence, *Nature* will be
irony
troubled no more by the *restive species*
translatio
that *rose in revolt* against her so many
millions of years ago, will be vexed no
irony
longer by its *chatter of truth and mercy
and beauty and happiness.* FERUM VIC-
antithesis   TOREM CEPIT: and if the eugenics are effi-
trans-
cient enough there will be no second *re-
latio   translatio
volt,* but all *sunk* beneath the Conditioners, and the Conditioners beneath her, till
metonymy   metonymy
the *moon falls* or the *sun grows cold.*

Most of this is, obviously, *accumulation,* as Lewis asserts in various ways the point to which the whole essay has been directed, that the ultimate triumph of science will be at the same time the final triumph of nature. The paradoxical character of this thesis is developed in a series of sentences which could well be called *antitheses* ("We thought we were beating her back when she was luring us on").

Lewis' language, and particularly his tropes, are the most notable features of the paragraph. Again, only in the last two sentences, when Lewis has already persuaded those whom he can persuade, does he permit himself *irony* and the two very forceful *metonymies.* A modern audience is particularly apt to take alarm at such language, and Lewis always withholds it until the point has been made.

On the other hand, the paragraph is full of low-level *translatios* reflecting war, subjection, and so forth. These *translatios* come to a kind of climax here in the conclusion, and properly so. Lewis' whole argument requires that we look at conditioning from an unusual point of view. As Lewis' introduction implies, it is usually presented as a part of "man's" increasing control over nature by means of science. It is essential to Lewis' argument that we scrutinize the general noun, that we see that "man" doesn't control anything, that men do. These warfare *translatios* work to that end throughout the first two-thirds of the essay. They are treated climactically here in terms of the *paradox* Lewis has surprised us with, that the control of nature in this respect means the conquest by nature. In effect, he returns to the general noun, "man," but now it is man as loser, not winner.

It is useful, for a moment, to step outside Professor Lewis' organization and try to see the essay as a whole. His structural enthymeme can be roughly paraphrased as follows:

Major premise (implicit): Only that motive which is not the means of control can logically be a basis for control.
Minor premise: Only the natural motive, impulse, remains outside the system of scientific control of human behavior.

Conclusion (and thesis of the essay):   Man's conquest of (human)
nature, properly understood and extended to its logical conclusion (as is only possible through science), will lead to man's
complete subservience to nature.[3]

Lewis begins the essay to be built on this enthymeme by setting up
the subject of its conclusion, "man's conquest of nature." This is
the ordinary procedure, since this element is likely to be also the
subject of the essay, "what it is all about."

Actually, as pointed out, this definition is a redefinition, and a
complicated one. Hence Lewis presents one step in the redefinition
at a time. Paragraphs two and three redefine "man's conquest of
nature" to mean "the control of most men by other men." The
first part of the fourth paragraph extends this redefinition to include the element of time; the last part of this paragraph as well as
the fifth paragraph establish the position so far reached. The first
part of the sixth paragraph, in which Lewis adds his further qualification to the subject, "as is only possible through science," logically should precede the summary which it follows, but the extended redefinition upon which the whole essay depends is very
long and could easily seem static. Hence Lewis makes this further
qualification as though it advanced the argument, when in fact it
does not.

In the second half of this sixth paragraph, we get a further
element of the argument, the first part of the minor premise. But,
as pointed out in the analysis, he does this in a peculiar way. He
points out that "ordinary human motives are the basis of conditioning"; technically, this is the "only" of the premise. Paragraph
seven completes the minor premise in this form—"the usual human
motives cannot act as a basis for the control of human behavior."
The eighth paragraph confirms the premise as established by an-
swering objections.

[3] It should be noticed that this is not a logician's syllogism, although
the relationships are valid. A logician would reinterpret this syllogism
into a sorites consisting of at least three separate syllogistic arguments.
But this is an argumentative syllogism for an argument; the major structural elements of the essay are represented in the logical relationship
that they really bear to one another.

The ninth paragraph can then bring up the exception to the statement as proposed, "impulse"; this exception necessarily transforms the preceding formulation to that proposed in the enthymeme above, "Only the natural motive, impulse, remains outside the system of scientific control of human behavior."

The last element of the enthymeme, the second part of the conclusion ("will lead to man's complete subservience to nature") is then proposed very briefly in the latter part of the ninth paragraph. It is dealt with briefly because it has become self-evident (on the level at which the reader is expected to function). Further elaboration would be anticlimactic.

"The Abolition of Man" well illustrates the observations about the structure of an essay made in the discussion of argumentation. It begins where most essays begin, with the subject of the conclusion of the enthymeme, "Man's conquest of nature." But the essay cannot continue to develop the conclusion of the enthymeme, since to join subject to object of this member would be to conclude the essay. The writer must necessarily, then, turn to the elements of his minor premise.

But one also observes in this essay that all of the skills of the writer are directed to maintaining a sense of progress, of movement. All of the peculiarities of this essay as noted in the analysis (except the climactic structure of the fourth paragraph) have their origin in this necessity for movement—the sequential redefinition of the subject through several paragraphs, the way that the "only" of the enthymeme is handled, the climactic identification of "impulse" with "nature." The essay is a model in that it develops its enthymeme in an argument that never loses its direction and momentum.

But it should also be noted that it is not flawless in its development of the enthymeme from a logical point of view. The term "nature" has not been defined, even though the whole argument hinges upon the distinction between so-called natural human behavior, originating in impulse, and a higher kind of behavior symbolized by such words as "duty." Why did Lewis choose to ignore so obvious a logical requirement?[4]

---

[4] A reason which is irrelevant to the effectiveness of this essay is that he considered it at length in the second half of his lecture.

It is likely that there were two reasons. In the first place, the distinction would have been very difficult to make. But more importantly, the distinction is not necessary to the essay. However "nature" might be defined, the essay points to a difference in human behavior, between impulse and duty, which every reader (not totally hostile on a priori grounds) will accept as a real difference. In argumentation, that is sufficient. An essayist does not prove anything about the real world. He argues for a certain kind of organization of the reader's own experience; his object is to persuade the reader to assent to that reading. If he aimed at proof, every essay would end up in the depths of philosophy.

This is not to say that any argument that wins assent is a good argument. Some arguments, as will be seen in the next part, are bad whether one assents to them or not. The point is that the usual experience of the reader must be, at times, the essayist's criterion of truth.

Part III

Good and
Bad Rhetoric

Rhetoric is the art of persuasion. It would seem to follow that its success could only be measured by its suasory effectiveness, and that defective rhetoric might be simply defined as rhetoric that does not move a specific audience in the way envisaged by the speaker or writer. As bad medicine is medicine that does not heal, so bad rhetoric is rhetoric that does not persuade. Or so the Greeks might have argued, at any rate.

But there are practical difficulties to this practical solution. From this point of view the worst improvisations of the most illiterate, tobacco-chewing, gallus-snapping, backwoods candidate for sheriff would be better rhetoric, if he were elected, than was Lincoln's First Inaugural Address, which didn't impress anyone when it was delivered. From this point of view, President Eisenhower's rhetoric was superior to that of the late Adlai Stevenson. Such judgments deny that there is an art of rhetoric, or at least they eliminate from consideration such elements in writing or speaking as clarity, coherence, and relevance, which are normally considered to be virtues in all human discourse.

On the other hand, one cannot simply presuppose some

ideal form of the art and measure specific examples against that ideal. There is no ideal model for the rhetorician because his art is yet practical, even though practical considerations do not provide in themselves adequate criteria of success.[1]

There is perhaps something arbitrary about any solution to this problem. The critic must assert that there is bad rhetoric just as there is bad poetry, and this badness is not to be measured by any uninformed consensus on the subject. Joyce Kilmer's "Trees" is a bad poem even though it is a very popular bad poem, and even though the critic is unable to point with assurance to any archetypal great poem against which the badness of "Trees" can be measured.

The criteria of good and bad rhetoric must be found in audience response; there is nowhere else to look for it. But not any audience. As with literature, success or failure must be measured against the sensibilities of those with some experience with the kind of discourse in question. At this point in the investigation, we can with some justification regard ourselves as just such an audience. Defective rhetoric, then, is rhetoric that does not accomplish its ends for the readers of this book.

This, of course, limits the kinds of materials worth looking at. There is no point in spending any time on the ineptitudes of ordinary political rhetoric or the inanities of popular opinion magazines. The only rhetoric worth looking at is that aimed at a reasonably well-educated audience.

But an evaluation should be of the art itself and not its point of view. Hence we must concede to the writer or speaker the premises upon which his argument is constructed, since he has very little control of these, and we must concede to him his ends, the purpose to which the rhetoric is directed. The art of rhetoric is, properly speaking, the art of moving from beginning to end, both of which must be conceded by the student to the rhetorician.[2]

It must also be critical. We cannot demand airtight connec-

[1] There have been periods, of course, when the rhetoric of oratory, at any rate, was given over to display, with no other ends in view than the gratification of the audience and self-aggrandizement of the *rhetor*. But this rhetoric is of importance only as a sociological phenomenon.

[2] We make these concessions as students of rhetoric. As readers potentially open to persuasion we would concede nothing of the sort; indeed, we would scrutinize the writer's premises with great care.

tions in the movement from beginning to end. As has been said often enough, rhetoric is not demonstrative, and an inveterately hostile audience can refute any argument whatsoever. Rhetoric presumes at least some degree of sympathetic open-mindedness. The rhetorician aims at probability, and the audience must be open to probable arguments.

In short, for the purposes of this present consideration of rhetoric, rhetorical failure can be defined as the failure to move from premises to conclusion in a way that would convince an audience that is both sympathetic and critical, and that is furthermore reasonably well learned in the art of rhetoric.

The term, "defective rhetoric," it should be noted, is a morally neutral one. Textbooks on logic and writing frequently advise the student to be on the lookout for deception in rhetoric. The assumption is that large numbers of people using rhetoric deliberately propose, in one way or another, to mislead an audience for ulterior ends. That such deception exists is unarguable. But it accounts for only a minor part of the defective rhetoric that one encounters. Aldous Huxley has remarked someplace, "There are no Iagos," and this is as true as such a generalization can be. Men do not ordinarily admit to villainy, even to themselves, and they do not often argue causes that they admit to themselves are bad. As a consequence, immoral rhetoric, which is consciously aimed at deception, is much less common than immoral men, who deceive themselves. It is useful, consequently, to think of defective, rather than deceptive, rhetoric.

Throughout this book, logic (of a sort) has been treated as a branch of rhetoric, and some of the defective rhetoric examined hereafter is of a logical character. But the usual treatments of defective logic are utterly inadequate for argumentation as it has been and is now practiced. Not only do the proposed criteria have comparatively little application, but beyond that, there is a whole range of rhetorical responses to difficulties that such treatments ignore. The present consideration of defective rhetoric will have to consider the ways writers and speakers work around logical difficulties.

The most useful approach to defective rhetoric will be to consider it from the point of view of the writer. This will enable us to see the kind of intellectual problems that lead to rhetorical failures.

Chapter VII

Defective Rhetoric

Anyone who seriously considers modern argumentative rhetoric, in any genre whatsoever, must be astonished at its deficiencies. There are perhaps a dozen bad arguments, measured by the terms proposed in the introduction to this section, for every one that might be regarded as reasonably persuasive.

An explanation, in part, for this habitual failure is that rhetoric and argumentation have not, in modern times, been generally considered arts to be learned. We teach grammar year after dreary year, but the larger communicative structures are ordinarily ignored, even in colleges and universities. Hence, professional essayists and scholars ordinarily write entirely by intuition, and over and over the effort imposes too great a strain on that faculty.

That an educational failure is responsible, at least in part, for the deplorable state of modern argumentation is proved by the one exception to the generalization, legal writing. Law students spend years writing arguments that are judged for their rhetorical success, and as a consequence lawyers, at least within their professional concerns, write argumentation with skill.

But even lawyers fail at times; the writing of argumentation is beset by difficulties that the best of training cannot overcome because they are inherent in the complex relationships existing between the writer and his intention, and the writer and his audience. It has become traditional to talk about the inadequacies of argumentation in terms of Aristotelian logic—in terms of question-begging, circular arguments, and so forth. But these specific deficiencies are almost always manifestations of conceptual problems of far greater import. The nature of these conceptual problems will be apparent if we consider the writing of an argument from the writer's point of view.

The Formulation of an Argument

One must always remember, in reading argumentative essays or listening to argumentative speeches, that every writer begins with his conclusion. This fact is implicit in Aristotle's definition of rhetoric as "the faculty of discovering the possible means of persuasion in reference to any subject whatsoever" (*Art of Rhetoric* I. 2. 2). In other words, the writer does not work from evidence to conclusion, or from major premise through minor premise to conclusion. He begins by knowing "what he wants to say"—his conclusion. He constructs the essay or speech by looking for arguments and evidence to support that conclusion.

This is a peculiar situation, but it is not necessarily scandalous. The thesis that a writer wishes to argue may very well be grounded in his experience. He may formulate his basic argument with great earnestness, trying to understand his real reasons for believing his conclusion to be true, and he may scrutinize very carefully the evidence that seems relevant to those reasons. Undoubtedly writers have proceeded in this fashion, and still do so today. But not very many of them, and not consistently. In many instances it is impossible to write an essay in this way.

In the first place, there is very likely to be some ambiguity in the writer's mind about the conclusion itself. Human beliefs are not all of the same order of importance. Only a very few of our convictions are basic ones, summarizing our experience in a way that seems self-evident, or affirming values that we would be willing to reconsider only in the most desperate circumstances. Most of our convictions are not of this order. They function to support our basic beliefs perhaps, but they are not themselves basic. And these are what we ordinarily argue about.

To take an obvious example: one may believe in the sanctity

of marriage because one believes in God. It would be correct to say that one believes in both propositions. But they would not be believed in to the same degree, or in the same way. The belief in the sanctity of marriage would be a subordinate one, and it might be held in spite of much personal experience that seemed to contradict it. At the same time, the writer would find himself in a position to argue for his attitude toward marriage ten times for every time he argued his primary belief. Consequently, he would continually find himself less than wholehearted in his argument, and he might well end up by writing badly—using arguments that were circular or defective in some other way.

In other words, the writer, like everyone else, ordinarily begins with a very complex mental state. He may think that his beliefs are coherent; they may even be coherent on some ultimate, principled level. But his day-to-day beliefs are not ultimate ones. They derive from ultimate ones, perhaps, but they acquire ambiguities in the process of being derived, and from the application to concrete experience. And these are the beliefs about which we ordinarily argue. As a consequence, one seldom argues from clear and unequivocal grounds.

But there is an even more serious problem that arises from the beliefs that human beings hold and make arguments about. I certainly hold many beliefs because they are consonant with my experience, or because I elect them as good without contradicting my experience. But certainly not all beliefs are of this character. Often in an informal debate about an important question it is very good, if tactless, to ask, "Why do you *want* to believe that?" Preachers through the centuries, for instance, have argued that skeptics refuse to believe in God because of the personal license that such non-belief gives them. In other words, they do not *want* to believe. Skeptics today are perhaps inclined to answer the preachers by asserting that the preachers want to believe in God because they want to be immortal.

There is a better illustration to hand. At any particular time in history there is a dominant *zeitgeist*—a particular stance toward experience which exercises a compelling fascination upon the time. The rationalistic stance in the eighteenth century and the scientific stance of the twentieth are good examples of the phenomenon. In all areas of human concern during such times important hypotheses will be espoused primarily because they permit the individual holding them to relate himself to the desirable zeitgeist. Such hypotheses will be defended by argumentation, even though they have no basis in experience at all. They are hypotheses believed in, after a fashion, because they permit certain kinds of activities.

In short, the writer is seldom working from a clear-cut and unambiguous belief, based on an honest (and that is perhaps too strong a word) evaluation of his experience. At best he is apt to be writing from a position that he believes, experientially, to be true, but that manifests strange and, to him, puzzling deficiencies. At worst he may be defending a position that did not directly arise from his experience at all. These problems in his initial position will almost invariably affect his argument.

But further difficulty in argumentation arises precisely because it is argumentation and hence persuasive in intention. Intention presupposes an audience. Furthermore, an audience needs to be particularized for the writer. He cannot address himself to the universe at large; he must address himself to a particular set of beliefs that he wants to modify.

The problem can be considered concretely. Suppose that I want to persuade more people to support the space program. But what people? Not those who oppose all governmental activity beyond policing; not, probably, confirmed pacifists; not those who are suspicious of all technology. There are people whom it is useless to try to persuade, no matter what the subject. The reason is that argument presupposes the possibility of establishing at least one point of agreement upon which the argument can be constructed. I can argue with somebody only when I can establish a basis from which I can work to the desired conclusion. This basis is, of course, the implicit major premise of my structural syllogism or syllogisms.

But this is not the whole of it. The writer advocating support for the space program would still have a large number of people whom he might persuade. But they would be persuaded for different reasons. An article for a group of scientists, for instance, would be quite different from one addressed to a group of military men, not merely in the kind of technical jargon used, but in the point of departure established. It is easy to imagine a dozen articles proposing the same conclusion—the desirability of the space program—each of which would begin at a different point and consequently develop a different argument, necessarily, because they would be directed to different audiences.

Furthermore, the same writer might well write all of them, and he might write them in good conscience, absolutely convinced of the truth of the conclusion he was urging. But he could not write all of them equally well. If he were a scientist writing for scientists, the chances that the argument would be handled reasonably well would be good. But as his audience departed from that model, his argument would be apt to deteriorate sharply. The reason is that he would be writing increasingly far from his own premises and his own reason.

It is in the nature of argument that the writer will often be addressing an audience with which he shares few premises relevant to the particular subject he has chosen. In such a position he has no choice but to argue from a ground that is not his ground (and may indeed be fallacious in his opinion), and he must make up, not discover, reasons for his conclusion. Few people write really well in such a situation.

To summarize: defective argumentation is not to be understood as a momentary failure, as a defect located in this paragraph or that one. It manifests itself, to be sure, in specific places. But over and over (although not always!) these specific, localized failures can be seen as manifestations of a conceptual difficulty implicit in the whole argument. The part-whole relationship in defective argumentation will be illustrated in the next chapter. Obvious limitations of space make it necessary to discuss failures for the most part in terms of their concrete manifestations. But the student of argumentation should always look to the whole argument to see why the particular failure occurred.

The Logical Failures

It has become traditional for books on argumentation to discuss argumentative defects in terms that go back to Aristotle's *So-*

phistici Elenchi—in terms that are basically logical. Thus, an argument is bad if its induction is faulty, or its terms are not precisely defined and fixed, or its deductive structures are not properly distributed. The inadequacy of this approach should be apparent from what has already been said about argumentation. The logician's criteria of validity are not those of the rhetorician. Even worse, the usual classifications of logical sins have very little relevance to what actually goes on in argumentation. It will be useful, then, to examine logical failures in terms of concrete, published instances, selecting from a plethora of examples, some of which might be our own.

THE TERMS OF THE LOGICAL STRUCTURE

The premise of this book has been that argumentation has as its primary object the establishment of a particular connection between particular terms. The terms are as important as the connections, and as apt to be misleading.

Writer and reader must have approximately the same meanings for the terms used in discourse: this is the first requirement for communication. This is the writer's responsibility. Unless a definition is offered, a word ought to refer to those experiences to which the ordinary reader would apply it. "Fascist," for instance, ought to refer to an individual who, in his convictions, has some central relationship to the beliefs annunciated by German and Italian leaders prior to the Second World War. (Reasonable men might, of course, disagree within limits about what constitutes a central relationship.)

The problem of terms is usually discussed as though it were a matter of "connotation"; a word, having acquired a bad or good "connotation" from being used in a particular context for some length of time, is applied in another context, taking its goodness or badness along with it. But the problem is simpler than this; it is a matter of mislabeling, not according to some absolute criterion of rightness, but according to one's audience. Most people would define a fascist, for instance, by a series of qualities—racist, authoritarian, anti-intellectual, militaristic, and so forth. To a communist, the term means something much less specific, perhaps merely someone actively hostile to communism. A communist writing for a non-communist audience and using "fascist" according to his own definition, without specifying what it is, deceives, intentionally or unintentionally.

This explanation does not account for the entire problem, of course. The terms a writer uses are an important part of his basic strategy. For the communist, for instance, "fascist" and "anti-communist" usually mean approximately the same thing, as has been pointed out. The term "fascist" is ordinarily a preferred term because it is a part of the polarizing strategy, widely characteristic of modern ideologies, that tends to sharpen all choices into distinct oppositions. In the same way, the ideologies of the right polarize politics into communist and anti-communist. Insofar as this use of terms represents a way of seeing the world, it is a psychological rather than a rhetorical problem.

The importance of terms is universal. A major element in the quarrel between the liberal arts contingent and the social scientists in any college is a difference of opinion as to the most suitable terms with which to describe human beings and human activity. The social scientists, for their own ends, prefer a mechanistic and passive terminology; the terminology of the liberal arts tends to be dynamic and active. "Conditioning" and "learning," for instance, refer generally to the same activity, which is not changed by reason of the name that is put on it. But the word used will profoundly affect the way in which that activity is regarded.

However much one may dislike one set of terms or the other, a writer is entitled to propose his own point of view, by the terms he chooses, toward the experience he deals with. But he is not entitled to assume the intrinsic superiority of one terminology over another in the matter of truth-telling.

It is commonly asserted that undefined terms are a major fault in argumentative discourse. This is questionable. Certainly, one would ordinarily expect the important terms in an argument to be defined, in one way or another. But very often a major term will be self-evident; it would be pedantry to define "The Civil War" in an argument about it. Even terms with less concrete referents are not liable to cause trouble if they are used consistently within the normative range of meaning.

The ambiguity of terms is apt to be encountered ordinarily in one of two situations. The first can be illustrated by a quotation from Sartre:

> First, what is meant by anguish? The existentialists say at once that man is anguish. What that means is this: the man who involves himself and who realizes that he is not only the person he chooses to be, but also a lawmaker who is, at the same time, choosing all mankind as well as himself, can not help escape the feeling of his total and deep responsibility. Of course, there are many people who are not anxious; but we claim that they are hiding their anxiety, that they are fleeing from it.[1]

As a human being of mature years, the reader must know what the feeling "anguish" is. But what is the "anguish" which one does not know one has? Existentialist writers habitually use grandiloquent (the word is Sartre's—or Sartre's translator's) words with two senses, one experiential and the other somehow beyond experience. And much of the time one does not know which sense is intended.

The second source of terminological obscurity is illustrated by two passages, one from the beginning of a chapter by Sir Julian Huxley and the other from the end.

> It is easy to confuse the two ideas of progress and improvement; so ... I want to remind you of a few salient points. There are all kinds of biological improvement. ... But improvements are not something ready-made, they are trends in time. And most of them turn out to be finite; ... Occasionally one line of advance continues after related lines have come to a stop; and then you get what I called successional replacement, where a later deployment replaces an earlier one as a dominant type. ... Putting the matter in another way, there is continuity of improvement between one group and its successor, as for instance between reptiles and mammals. We need a term for the sum of these continuities through the whole of evolutionary time, and I prefer to take over a familiar word like progress instead of coining a special piece of esoteric jargon.

In this passage, Sir Julian defines "progress" in terms of "improvement"; it is the sum of improvements as these are reflected in successive species. But in the second passage the meaning is quite different:

[1] Jean-Paul Sartre, *Existentialism and Human Emotions* (New York: Philosophical Library, 1957), p. 18.

And so, in human life, the fact of progress is linked with the problem of destiny, in its dual sense of something to be obeyed and something to be fulfilled. Man alone is conscious of destiny; human organization is so constructed as to make men pose the problem of existence in this form. Ever since he first began, man has been groping to discern the features of his destiny more clearly. In the light of the evidence now available, he could come to the realization that his destiny is to participate and lead in the creative process of evolution, whereby new possibilities can be realized for life.[2]

In this second passage, "progress" is being used in its normative sense, as something good, as something worth human effort. Huxley has shifted his usage; the mere word "progress" is being used as a bridge between an account of what is and a desire to intrude an "ought." In the first meaning of the term there is no implication that human effort is required, because "progress" is defined as a condition of things; in the second, "progress" has become something desirable and hence a proper human goal.

But the greatest hazard in the use of terms is not vagueness or ambiguity; it is Platonizing. Is *The Death of a Salesman* a tragedy? Can an octosyllabic poem be a sonnet? Such questions, which are omnipresent in human discourse, inevitably presume that there is some sort of Platonic archetype of the form in question against which a particular example can be measured for its purity. There isn't, or at least no one has succeeded in establishing them to anyone else's satisfaction. Whether or not *The Death of a Salesman* is a tragedy depends upon how we define "tragedy." We may argue that it is inconvenient to regard it as such, according to a particular definition, but we cannot argue that it is or is not.[3]

Nevertheless, this sort of argument abounds in almost every field. Thus a contemporary linguist, referring to a difference of

---

[2] Julian Huxley, *Evolution in Action* (New York: New American Library, 1957), pp. 99, 117.

[3] Where conventional definitions exist, of course, the case is different. Law, for instance, is permeated with conventional definitions from which lawyers habitually argue. But these arguments are not about the nature of things; they are about the relationship of an instance to a convention.

opinion between Max Müller and Samuel Butler as to whether animals have languages, writes:

> Müller and Butler did not argue about the facts of animal behaviour which Darwin had described. Their disagreement arose more directly from differences of opinion about the correct definition of the term "language." To-day our definitions of human language are more precise, so we can say with correspondingly more precision why Butler was wrong.[4]

But this is nonsense. There is simply nothing in the universe that can tell me that the hoot of an owl must or must not be included in a definition of "language." Words are human inventions, functioning to relate experiences that seem to have something substantial in common according to human convenience. Precision is certainly a useful characteristic of a definition, but it is useful only because it enables a reader to understand with greater certainty what a writer wishes to tell him. There is no criterion by which the truth of a definition, precise or not, can be measured, since we do not have a Platonic heaven of ideas to tell us infallibly how experiences with the world ought to be classified.

Arguments from such definitions can be positively pernicious. Sir Julian Huxley begins the book from which the two previous quotations have been taken with the declaration, "Science has two functions: control and comprehension" (p. 9). The jaundiced reader knows that before the paragraph is over Sir Julian will assert the positive obligation upon evolutionary science to exercise due control—which he does. This is to derive a most far-reaching principle of action from a very simple definition, as though there were something loose in the universe that could be called science utterly and absolutely, of which evolutionary science was simply an exemplar, bound to act in a way laid down by the Platonic principle. Similarly, Professor Eysenck argues that science tries to explain, psychoanalysis tries to understand, therefore psychoanalysis is un-

[4] George A. Miller, "The Psycholinguists," *Encounter*, XXIII (July 1964), 35*n*.

scientific.[5] The question is, of course, from what kinds of activities we propose to abstract our definition of science in the first place. If psychoanalysis is one of them, then obviously psychoanalysis is scientific. And there is nothing to tell us whether or not to include it. It is a matter of convenience (and ethos).

This is not to say that one should simply define words as one pleases. The more closely a defined term approaches normal usage, the better communication will be (since it is hard to keep an eccentric definition in mind), and that is presumably the point. A word that is frequently redefined will finally not mean anything at all.[6] But our definitions, no matter how precise, cannot tell us anything about the structure and ordering of the universe. They are human ways of grouping experienced phenomena, and there can be no criterion for them beyond human usefulness. They cannot lead us to truth.

THE CONNECTION OF TERMS

"Facts," as these are usually defined, are reasonably easy to come by in human affairs, and, if we are respectful of them, useful ways of grouping them can be arranged, too. But connections between such groupings—the relationships between terms—these are something else. Western philosophy has been puzzling about the possibility of relating terms with confidence more or less continuously for almost two hundred years, since the time of David Hume, and more or less unsuccessfully. Writers of argument have been troubled by the problem for a good deal longer than that.

The writer of argument does not have, of course, the same problem as the philosopher or logician. His objective is probability, not truth, and he knows that the reader's experience, and not ultimate reality, is the test of probability. But his problems are no less

---

[5] H. J. Eysenck, *Uses and Abuses of Psychology* (Baltimore: Penguin Books, 1953), pp. 226–227.

[6] "Humanism" is an example. Originally designating certain attitudes particularly characteristic of the fifteenth and sixteenth centuries, the term became fashionable in this century, with the result that we now have ninth-century humanism, scientific humanism, evolutionary humanism, and four or five others. The consequence is that "humanism" as a designation tells us very little about the attitudes to which it now refers.

for that, and if the nineteen or twenty-three or thirty "fallacies" customarily listed in logic books do not absolutely coincide with the failures commonly found in argumentative essays, they do not necessarily outnumber them.

Induction.   As has been pointed out, "induction" is something of a misnomer when applied to argumentation. The writer of an argument does not draw a sufficient number of concrete instances from reality to support his generalization, even in a probable manner. Instead, he usually offers one or two concrete instances which, he hopes, will function to recall for the reader his experience of a great many examples. The reader's experience, as a consequence, makes the generalization probable or improbable; "experience" here would of course include generalizations previously derived from reading and tested against experience. But one example is as good as twenty if it permits the reader to authenticate the generalization from his own experience.

This process would seem to be largely immune to criticism. The writer offers his examples; the reader finds them consistent with his own experience or he does not. But most readers, it would seem, do not read with sufficient attention to make these judgments in all cases, and writers are tempted to offer evidence that does not function by either logical or rhetorical criteria. We find, as a consequence, many arguments that are in fact pseudo-inductive.

A good example of a pseudo-inductive argument is to be found in Owen Barfield's *Saving the Appearances.* Concerning Copernicus' heliocentric theories, he remarks,

> Secondly, it is generally believed that the Church tried to keep the discovery dark. Actually Copernicus did not himself want to publish his *De Revolutionibus Orbium,* and was only eventually prevailed on to do so by the importunity of two eminent Churchmen.[7]

The second sentence, seeming to bear some sort of proof relationship to the first, is actually a non sequitur. Two swallows do not make a spring, nor two churchmen a church, particularly before

---

[7] Owen Barfield, *Saving the Appearances* (London: Faber and Faber, n.d.), p. 50.

the seventeenth century. Nor do these churchmen function to recall for the reader his own experience with the history of Copernicus; *Saving the Appearances* is not written for readers acquainted with Copernican history. The second sentence is a piece of pseudo-induction, functioning merely as amplification.

Deduction.   In argumentation, deduction is as shaky a process as induction. The writer wishes to connect two terms in a probablistic fashion by means of a third term, or, to put it another way, he wishes to argue for the probable truth of one statement by putting it in a class of conceded statements. The terms themselves may give trouble, as has been seen. The relationship itself may fail in one of several ways. It may fail because the statement appealed to, the major premise, is in fact the statement to be demonstrated, the conclusion, slightly disguised. This is a circular argument, in the logician's terms. Or it may fail by appealing to a major premise to which very few people would attribute any general validity if they confronted it directly. The part-whole fallacy of the logicians can stand for this whole genre—"if a little is good, a lot is better." The passage quoted below presents an interesting variant of this fallacy.

The interest in the development of the human psyche from early animal stages, the attitude to the question whether there are transitions in development between man and animal, or whether, on the contrary, there are essential differences is, in this post-Darwinian age, still actual. As shown by a recent survey, differences in intelligence, symbolic function, and the dependence on the dominance of the instincts were cited as fundamental arguments, and interpreted sometimes as betokening essential differences, sometimes as differences of degree. But the only qualitatively new idea which Aristotle or the Fathers of the Church had not already mooted, is Freud's observation that the appearance of a sexual latency period is an exclusively human phenomenon. In any case, biology has not yet been able to answer in the affirmative Freud's question whether latency occurs in the higher animals. We may, therefore, assume "that the formation of the latency period was the most essential phenomenon in decisively determining the difference between man and animal."[8]

[8] Lajos Szekely, "On the Origin of Man and the Latency Period," *The International Journal of Psycho-Analysis,* XXXVIII (March–April 1957), 99.

A wild enthymeme is floating around here, or rather two of them, but even in this case one is hard put to know how a logician would isolate the problem. The first argues that Freud's definition of man or whatever, represented by the last sentence, is true because it is the only new definition. The major premise has to be whatever is new is true, which would certainly simplify the job of our intellectual pioneers even if it were approximately, argumentatively valid. The second enthymeme, beginning "In any case," necessarily implies that whatever is biologically unique to man (or presumably any other species) is decisive in determining the difference between him and all other animals. Here again, this is simply a bad argument; if man were the only animal to have fingernails instead of claws, that would not make fingernails particularly decisive for anything.

It is worth observing that this paragraph occurs in the introduction. The writer was not primarily concerned to prove the importance of "the latency period"; he wanted to use it as an assumption. He fell into the obvious confusion of the quoted paragraph because he didn't want to deal with the validity of his assumption and couldn't simply acknowledge it for what it was.

Precisely the same dilemma undid the author of the following passage, in an article discussing what variety of linguistics ought to be taught in English courses.

The historical emphasis on validity or correctness seems entirely appropriate even though it does no homage to the popular pre-occupation with behavioral goals and outcomes as the basis for the evaluation of curricula. The issue is not whether the information contained in a given linguistic description can be taught and learned successfully, for surely there is no description which is so difficult that it cannot be taught and learned in some form, but precisely one of the status of the information itself. One might hope to diminish the centrality of the content, thereby making it unnecessary, perhaps, to choose among the various linguistic descriptions, by demonstrating the utility of one or the other description in the teaching of literate skills, e.g., composition. But this hope should not be taken too seriously since the most recent account of empirical research in this area indicates the inconclusiveness of all such demonstrations.

Reviews of educational research, however, have continually emphasized that instruction in grammar has little effect upon the written language skills of pupils. The interpretation and curricular applications of this general conclusion have ranged from the view that grammar and usage should not be taught in isolation from written composition to the position that formal grammar merits little or no place in the language curriculum.

Thus, the validity of proposed linguistic descriptions remains the most pertinent consideration.[9]

In short, the relative "validity or correctness" of systems of linguistics ought to determine which are to be taught because all systems of linguistics are more or less useless. So runs the latter part of the argument.

Again, this argument is a piece of inept ground-clearing. Dr. Rosenbaum wants linguistics taught in English classes, and later on in the essay he gives some reasons for wanting this. But in setting up an *expeditio* that would permit him to select the linguistic system of his choice from a surplus of possibilities, he inadvertently stumbled on an argument that made it unlikely that a sensible man would read further to find out what Dr. Rosenbaum's reasons were.

The two passages quoted above are, after all, arguments; they relate terms in a syllogistic structure even though the implicit premises making the relationship possible are perhaps not what the writers would have cared to affirm explicitly. One encounters, not infrequently, arguments failing to make even this minimal connection:

The decay of the relations between science and culture, and the concomitant withdrawal of science into the purely technical sphere, is often supported by the specious and ambiguous argument that science is, and must be, ethically neutral. In its most trivial and individualistic sense, that scientists do not mind which way their experiments come out, this is clearly untrue; nearly all active scientists more or less passionately hope to be able to prove or disprove some particular theory on which they are working. But that is irrelevant to the function of science as a cultural force. It is much more important that scientists must be ready for their pet theories to turn out to be wrong. Science as a whole certainly

[9] Peter S. Rosenbaum, "On the Role of Linguistics in the Teaching of English," *Harvard Educational Review*, XXXV (Summer 1965), 333–334.

cannot allow its judgment about facts to be distorted by ideas of what ought to be true, or what one may hope to be true.[10]

It is impossible to make a coherent statement out of this, or even to classify its radical defectiveness. It might be helpful to know what Professor Waddington meant by "ethics," but it is difficult to imagine a definition that would make sense out of the passage. If anyone ever asserted that "science is ethically neutral because scientists don't care how their experiments turn out," it would have been the better part of wisdom to ignore him.

In short, the common logical problems in argumentation are not so much defective connections as the absence of any connection at all, or pseudo-connections. The writer of an argument frequently appeals to more abstract principles or to experience, by deduction or induction. He does not, and cannot, prove anything by this move, and he cannot be judged by logical criteria concerned with proof. The reader accepts or rejects the arguments thus made on the basis of probability, judged by his own experience. So long as connections are really made, one cannot speak of defectiveness.

But there are many times—and particularly when he is trying to get something out of the way—when a writer fails to make any real connections at all. His inductive instances do not make any real connection with his point, or his deductive structures lack a middle entirely, or whatever. In these instances the reader with the best will in the world cannot assent to the proposition; there is literally nothing to assent to. Defective rhetoric of the logical variety is found when we could not reasonably agree even if we wanted to.

The Dodges

The student who goes looking for defective rhetoric of the kinds described above is likely to be surprised by its scarcity. Amid

[10] C. H. Waddington, *The Scientific Attitude* (2nd edn.; Middlesex: Penguin Books, Ltd., 1948), p. 30.

much defective rhetoric the particular shapes of logic are sometimes difficult to find.

To be sure, the writer's problems are almost always logical ones, in some sense. The terms that he wishes to join to each other do not fit, and statements of fact that ought to be self-evident are not so. But the writer ordinarily responds to these logical problems rhetorically. He does not allow his difficulty to manifest itself as it is; he attempts to make things better by nonlogical means. He resorts to a "dodge" of one kind or another.

This is understandable if we consider, again, the writing process. The writer knows where he wants to go and he knows, at least roughly, the steps by which he may get there. But if one or more of these steps proves to be inadequate, he will know that also. He may not be utterly conscious of the problem; usually he will not be. But he will sense, on some intellectual level below the entirely conscious one, something awry. And he will attempt to improve his situation without changing his basic argument. This can only be done by some kind of evasion.

Writers are ingenious in these matters, and the dodges they have invented are without number. What follows must be regarded as a survey only of a very rich field. We can properly begin with a consideration of ethos dodges, which in bulk far outnumber all other kinds.

ETHOS ARGUMENTS

In Chapter I it was pointed out that ethos is an inescapable dimension in argumentation; the writer, being present to the reader in some fashion, must define himself for the reader. Furthermore, a writer is entitled to whatever ethos he chooses. (The reader has the right to reject it also.) But ethos is a prerequisite to persuasion; it should not be a means. The line between the two uses of ethos is a fine one, and writers frequently find themselves on the wrong side of it.[11]

---

[11] It should be noted in passing that a writer frequently signals, inadvertently, his own uncertainties by some sort of excess in ethos. A psychologist, for instance, writes,

In our dealings with people we can hardly be said to proceed on a haphazard basis of pure chance (sic). Experience teaches us to expect certain reac-

Ethos can function argumentatively in several ways. The most obvious way is as a kind of premise, illustrated by the remark of the cigarette company executive who declared, "If we were convinced that cigarettes were harmful, we wouldn't be in the cigarette business." Reformulated, the statement asserts, "Cigarettes are harmless because we sell them." The major premise is, obviously, an assertion of the superior moral character of the speaker. This is an ethos appeal. Similarly, the then-Vice-President Richard Nixon was given to "I can assure you" statements about the then-President Eisenhower's health, moral fitness, integrity, and dedication to the national interest; in such statements the persuasive element was the assumption that the speaker was the best possible person to arrive at objective and impersonal estimates of the characteristics in question.

Both statements illustrate ethos functioning argumentatively. The cigarette manufacturer would establish the harmlessness of cigarettes by a direct appeal to his own character, to the sort of person he was. Vice-President Nixon used his own character as evidence for statements about President Eisenhower.

In the above instances, ethos functions by providing implicit premises. More commonly it carries an argument by continually and obtrusively reminding the reader of the speaker's authority.

---

tions from certain types of people; close acquaintance may enable us to predict with considerable accuracy the reactions of our friends, or of members of our family. We may know quite well that Mary is a bit old-maidenish, so that it is better not to tell risqué stories in front of her, while Joan is a bit of a fly-by-night who can always be relied upon to liven up a party. Dick is reliable and so honest that one would not be well advised to discuss in front of him ways and means of obtaining income tax relief which departed ever so little from the paths of rectitude, while Fred is forever cutting corners. . . . (H. J. Eysenck, *The Uses and Abuses of Psychology* [Baltimore: Penguin Books, 1953], p. 223.)

Where did all of these people come from? Mary and Joan and Dick and Fred (and four more!) are ostensibly introduced to support a statement which hardly requires so much demonstration, even if these little thumbnail sketches constituted such support. In fact, Professor Eysenck is nervously stroking the reader with homely examples. It is surely no accident that this passage occurs in an attempt to argue the superior scientific virtue of behaviorism at the expense of the more popular psychoanalysis.

Excessive attention to ethos is perhaps always an indication that the writer is uncomfortable with his argument.

Very often this reminder is set up as an argument—really a pseudo-argument. The following passage was used to support a plea for continuance of the space program:

> In space, we face a radically new and different situation than the world has ever confronted. When the human race decided it wanted to go out on the surface of the sea, it developed a ship.
>
> The ship represented ocean technology and developed the kind of power that Portugal held for a while, that Spain finally took away, and that England ultimately mastered.
>
> It was English sea power that in a sense stabilized the world for a little more than 400 years. But it was basically a mastery of the technology of the oceans that became the base of the power position for those who held it.
>
> And the same mastery required that those who did not have the same capability adjust to the power position of those that did.
>
> It gave the nations with sea power the capability to open up new areas, like the United States, and new territories, and enabled them to bring back resources and incorporate them in the home civilization.
>
> Air power was somewhat different. . . .[12]

On the surface, this is an argument by analogy, as are most appeals to history. But an analogy works argumentatively by juxtaposing a relationship which the writer wishes to establish, X_1-X_2, to one which is more familiar to his audience, Y_1-Y_2. Dr. Webb's analogy cannot be that sort of argument. The relationship of technology to national power, or peace, or whatever (Dr. Webb is exceedingly vague about this) in the past cannot be more familiar to the reader he has in mind than that relationship in the present. If the members of Dr. Webb's presumed audience knew something of history, they would be offended by this cavalier and superficial treatment. Hence the passage is not really aimed at persuasion by argument at all. Its real function is to reassure the audience by displaying the knowledgeability of the writer. As an examination of the whole article would readily show, Dr. Webb's presumed audience was so large, and his conception of it so vague, that he was unable to assume a

[12] James E. Webb, "Why the Race into Space?", Associated Press Release, April 24, 1966.

major premise on which a genuine argument might be constructed. The appeal to ethos almost inevitably followed from this difficulty.

But the most common misuse of ethos works through diction— it is jargon. Ethos is, of course, omnipresent in human discourse. Any extended passage of argumentative prose will set up a particular character for the writer as well as a conception of some experience, which the reader is to be persuaded, hopefully, to accept. If there were no ethos, the reader would not know how to respond to the conception the writer advocates. Furthermore, this ethos is very much a matter of diction, as well as characteristic figures. But all ethos ought to be supportive. Jargon can be usefully defined as language in which ethos is allowed to interfere with the communication that ought to be the primary purpose of the writer.

To put it another way, all language proposes a way of looking at experience. An unusual language, or a technical vocabulary, is proper if it proposes a useful and novel way of looking at experience. The glossary of rhetorical terms that is the center of this book, for instance, is justified, is worth learning, if it permits one to see argumentative discourse in a new and useful way. No technical language can justify itself on any other basis.[13] A technical language becomes jargon, on the other hand, when the ethos implicit in such a language becomes more important than the primary communication, when the diction is selected by the writer primarily for the role it creates rather than for the understanding of experience that it conveys.

Jargon as thus defined can be illustrated by a single sentence from a recent book on psychiatry:

[13] The usual justification, advanced by social scientists particularly, is that a technical language is somehow more precise than ordinary language. (See H. J. Eysenck, *Uses and Abuses of Psychology* [Baltimore: Penguin Books, 1953], p. 225, for a typical appeal to this theory.) But this justification reflects a metaphysical muddle. It assumes that the world of human experience, and human beings themselves, are composed of little bits of invariable things bearing invariable relationships to each other. The trick of knowing ultimate reality, then, lies in giving each of these little things one name, each class one name, and so forth. This view of reality is not tenable in the twentieth century.

There are three types of ego states: Parent, Adult, and Child, which reside in or are manifestations of corresponding psychic organs: exteropsyche, neopsyche, and archaeopsyche.[14]

The reader must perhaps concede to Dr. Berne his "ego states" as an inference from certain kinds of behavior, and even his "psychic organs" as a personification of "ego states." But what, precisely, does the labelling of these psychic states accomplish? An "exteropsyche" must be a psyche derived from the outside, a "neopsyche" something arising within the context of the human being, and an "archaeopsyche" something left over from the past. In short, parent, adult, and child. And these latter terms are far more meaningful, more specific, even for the professional, surely, than the former. What do the Greek constructions contribute to the parent, adult, child conception—besides affirming Dr. Berne's good standing in a profession excessively given to Greek constructions? In short, his ethos?

The sentence quoted above is an example of inflated diction working to set up ethos; equally common is the discourse inflated by verbosity. A passage from another psychology book, this time of behavioral persuasion, will serve to illustrate:

Adaptation he [Piaget] defines as a balance between assimilation and accommodation which tends towards states of equilibrium (although there may be disequilibrium throughout any stage or under certain conditions even at the level of greatest maturity). "Assimilation" is a term derived from the physico-chemical function, characteristic of every living creature, in which substances from the environment are absorbed and changed in order to sustain the organism.

At the behavioural level assimilation is the modification imposed on the environment by the activities of the organism; the organism does not remain passive towards its environment—it manipulates and changes it. Accommodation refers to the fact that the organism is changed by the

---

[14] Eric Berne, *Transactional Analysis in Psychotherapy* (New York: Grove Press, 1961), p. 75. It should be pointed out that Dr. Berne's impulse in this book, and even more in his later one *(Games People Play)*, is very much away from the ethos created by technical jargon. What remains should perhaps be forgiven as a necessary concession to a very ethos-conscious profession.

action of the environment upon it. Thus a chimpanzee grasping and manipulating a wooden stick, as in Köhler's experiments, must accommodate to the size, weight, and strength of the object, and while handling the stick cannot do certain other actions. However much it assimilates— in the sense of using the stick to get food—it must accommodate itself to certain limits dictated by the situation.[15]

The concrete example of the chimpanzee betrays the simplicity of the conception and the waste of words in its explication. For most people, "balance" implies "a state of equilibrium"; how one could "tend" to the other is hard to see. "Assimilation" as it is defined in the second paragraph is sufficiently close to ordinary usage to need no historical introduction; the "physico-chemical function" of the first paragraph is mere scientizing and irrelevant. "Accommodation refers to the fact that" is a very long way around to a simple definition. In short, the passage is inflated; a decent regard for the reader would have cut it in half or eliminated it altogether.

In some writing the ethos-jargon is so out of control that one suspects the act of writing has become merely an act of self-display, like a courtship dance by a castrated peacock. Sometimes such jargon is symptomatic of some conceptual difficulty; it is an unconscious or half-conscious attempt to support a weak argument. Perhaps most often it is used to conceal the triviality of what is being said. Thus, in commenting on senility, a writer remarks, "As in all brain disorders, the emergent symptomatology will be related to the premorbid personality of the person." This is hardly to say more than, "The problems one has when he is old will be related to those he had when younger." But of course, who would want to proclaim anything so obvious? A technical language can at least momentarily obscure the obvious.

Defective Pathos

The instant one abandons Aristotle's misleading dichotomy between thought and feeling, the idea of pathos becomes a peculiar

[15] Robert Thomson, *The Psychology of Thinking* (Baltimore: Penguin Books, 1959), p. 90.

one. How does one go about rousing emotion apart from the content of what is said? There are perhaps only two means to pathos available to the writer. The first is to lower the level of abstraction of one's discourse. Feeling originates in experience, and the more concrete writing is, the closer it is to experience, the more feeling is implicit in it. The C. S. Lewis essay, previously analyzed, well illustrates this approach to pathos. The tropes that appear at the end of major sections are designed to elicit from the reader a full human response to the point made by making its implications sensuous. This approach to pathos might be badly handled, in which case it would be simply ineffective. It is difficult to see how it would be defective as that word is being used here.

The second way in which a pathetic appeal can be made is by simulating in ourselves the emotion we wish from our readers or hearers. If someone with whom we have some basic sympathy becomes angry, we are very apt to become angry too. This is of course the basis for the pathetic appeal of traditional oratory. But seen from this point of view, traditional pathos is merely a variety of ethos. This fact is apparent in the peroration of almost every traditional speech. The speaker steps forward in a role that is ordinarily a modification of the one assumed to that point, and takes for himself a stance toward the subject which his audience will presumably assume with him. Lincoln, at the end of his Second Inaugural Address, says:

> With malice toward none, with charity for all, with firmness in the right as God gives us to see the right, let us strive on to finish the work we are in. . . .

This is a stance, and hence it is ethos; it is pathetic only in that it is proposed, implicitly, as an appropriate stance for his readers.

Classical rhetoricians specified the peroration as the proper place for pathos, and it is difficult to see how it could be defective if it were so confined. It is almost always defective when it intrudes itself into the body of the speech or essay, by the criterion previously proposed for defective ethos—it gets in the way of communication.

Nevertheless defective pathos of this second source is difficult to define. All argument, all discourse, necessarily sets up an attitude toward its subject, a stance, and this attitude or stance necessarily includes a way of feeling as well as a way of seeing. Since any attitude, and the feeling it includes, is partial, all discourse invites us to feel a certain way about the experience in question, and not another. Pathos intrudes, however, when there is some further demand for feeling, when the feeling is felt to be added onto the experience. An example will perhaps clarify the distinction:

Although Freud was later to develop new and improved therapeutic techniques, the "talking-out" or free-association method provided him with a great deal of knowledge about the underlying causes of abnormal behavior. *With true scientific curiosity and zeal,* he began to probe deeper and deeper into the minds of his patients. His probing revealed dynamic forces at work which were responsible for creating the abnormal symptoms that he was called upon to treat. Gradually there began to take shape in Freud's mind the idea that most of these forces are unconscious.

This was the turning point in Freud's scientific life. Putting psychology and neurology aside, he became a psychological investigator. The room in which he treated his patients became his laboratory, the couch his only piece of equipment, and the ramblings of his patients his scientific data. *Add to these the restless, penetrating mind of Freud, . . .*[16]

The impulse to look upon Freud's activities with entire approval is apparent in every line, but this is a part of the perspective of the writer and his own business. The underlined phrase in the first paragraph and the clause in the second, on the other hand, are excessive. They stand outside the account, explicitly demanding the admiration of the reader. They are pathetic.

In traditional argumentation the mark of defective pathos was usually a cluster of response-demanding figures, such as the exclamation, the apostrophe, and the rhetorical question, and these are still used at times for a pathetic effect. Much more common today, however, is the hyperbolic and adjectival style which has become characteristic of literary criticism.

[16] Calvin S. Hall, *A Primer of Freudian Psychology* (New York: New American Library, 1954), pp. 15–16. (Italics added.)

The impossible is happening in this *dream-like* scene: even the lines of stratification in the rock move with life *as if vibrated by the wind like an aeolian harp.* With the recollection of this *rich* image of Romanticism, *we realize* that the wind *not only* creates the music of the present, *but* its omnipresence in nature creates the music of all time, as represented in the stratification of the rocks. The harp's power, which according to popular belief will sound at the millenium, *prepares us* for the metamorphosis about to be accomplished.[17]

The italicized elements, the adjectives of the first part and the dramatic devices of the last, in sum make for a kind of hyperbolic tone which is pathetic in intention because it demands a response in excess of that which most readers would feel to be appropriate.

In general, pathos is much less of a problem in argumentation than is generally assumed. Most examples of "emotional writing" found in textbooks—which ought to represent defective pathos— are really examples of self-indulgent ethos. The sentimental lady reporter and the political ideologue write from stances toward experience that most of us would reject because they are taken for the immediate pleasure they give, with little regard for the content of the experience that is presumably the subject of the discourse, or the consequences of those stances. But if the stance is conceded, the writing is no more inherently pathetic than that coming out of any other stance.

DODGES HORIZONTAL AND VERTICAL

The impulse to appeal to ethos and pathos when one is in trouble, and particularly the former, is obviously a powerful one in the distressed human breast, but it is not overpowering in all instances. The writer has other resources. It will be sufficient to finish this chapter with a simple list, with illustrations, of some of the more common ones.

The Self-Evident Dodge.   One of the ways a writer can bridge an awkward hiatus in an argument is to propose his difficulty as a

[17] Donald Tritschler, "The Metamorphic Stop of Time in 'A Winter's Tale,'" *PMLA*, LXXVIII (September 1963), 426. (Italics added.)

paradox so self-evidently true that it does not even need support. An example of the self-evident statement that isn't self-evident at all is found in *The Myth of Sisyphus:*

> The absurd does not liberate; it binds. It does not authorize all actions. "Everything is permitted" does not mean that nothing is forbidden. The absurd merely confers an equivalence. . . .[18]

One should perhaps remember that this is a translation, but in English at least "Everything is permitted" means something like "nothing is forbidden" unless the writer gives us compelling reasons for believing that this is not the case. Camus gives no reasons. He makes an important step in his argument by means of an equivalence that is no equivalence at all.

The "Prove I'm Wrong If You Can" Dodge. One familiar gambit of the writer who wishes to hang something on an unprovable assertion is to decline the attempt at proof, to insist, rather, that cavillers take the burden of disproof upon themselves. A passage by T. H. Huxley illustrates this dodge nicely.

> For it is obvious that our knowledge of what we call the material world is, to begin with, at least as certain and definite as that of the spiritual world, and that our acquaintance with law is of as old a date as our knowledge of spontaneity. Further, I take it to be demonstrable that it is utterly impossible to prove that anything whatever may not be the effect of a material and necessary cause, and that human logic is equally incompetent to prove that any act is really spontaneous.[19]

As Huxley well knew, it is equally impossible to prove that everything *is* the effect of material and necessary causes. In this matter, everyone was, and is, entitled to pay his money and take his choice. But Huxley's impulse is to turn an assumption into something more, even if it meant a mouth-filling and confusing sentence that must have distressed him.

[18] Albert Camus, *The Myth of Sisyphus and Other Essays* (New York: Alfred A. Knopf, 1955), p. 50.

[19] Alburey Castell, ed., *Selections from the Essays of T. H. Huxley* (New York: Appleton, 1948), p. 20.

The "You're One, Too" Dodge.   This dodge, like the previous
one, amounts to a kind of sidestepping. A consideration that ought
to have no persuasive force whatsoever is introduced as though it
were a decisive consideration. The passage illustrating it concerns
St. Augustine's rhetorical theories.

Indeed, if we read what St. Augustine says about these figures with
either modern romantic expectations or modern rationalistic expectations, it seems ridiculous. However, we should realize that romantic
metaphor would have appeared laughable, or, perhaps, lamentable, to
him and that he would have regarded the modern scientific conscience
as a form of slavery.[20]

Whether or not St. Augustine would have found modern rhetoric
"lamentable" is not really germane to the question of whether or
not his theories were ridiculous. Professor Robertson obviously
does not want us to find St. Augustine's theory ridiculous, but the
only relationship that might be established between the first statement and his answer to it in the second would be some total relativ-
ism—"Nobody is ridiculous because everybody seems so to someone else"—which he surely would not want either.

The "Somebody Might Object to That" Dodge.   The essence of
this move is the introduction of some third party into an argument
to establish a position that is too weak to be defended by the writer
personally. The illustration is from an *expeditio* in which T. S.
Eliot proposes to narrow the modern choice to his version of a
Christian society and chaos:

If, then, Liberalism disappears from the philosophy of life of a
people, what positive is left? We are left only with the term "democracy,"
a term which, for the present generation, still has a Liberal connotation
of "freedom." But totalitarianism can retain the terms "freedom" and
"democracy" and give them its own meaning: and its right to them is not

[20] Saint Augustine, *On Christian Doctrine,* intro. and trans. by D.
W. Robertson, Jr., Library of Liberal Arts, No. 80 (Indianapolis: Bobbs-
Merrill, 1958), p. xv.

so easily disproved as minds inflamed by passion suppose. We are in danger of finding ourselves with nothing to stand for except a *dislike* of everything maintained by Germany and/or Russia. . . .[21]

At the risk of being proven to have "minds inflamed by passion," we must object that this kind of cavil could be raised about any generalized position whatsoever. "We are left only with the term 'Christianity,' a term which still has, for the present generation, the connotation of 'charity.' But Torquemada undoubtedly called himself a 'Christian,' and assumed himself to be in a state of 'charity,' and his right to them, etc."

The Vertical Dodge.   All of the above quotations are examples of what might be called the horizontal dodge. The writer, confronted with a difficulty, sidesteps it by introducing a consideration that could be regarded as persuasively relevant only by someone who was half asleep. But the writer in trouble has another option; he can set up a vertical dodge.

All argumentative discourse tends to change its level of abstraction from time to time; this is perhaps even necessary to readability. But the writer changing his level of abstraction needs to be watched closely. He may change it for legitimate reasons; on the other hand, he may change it because the argument has become sticky.

One can, of course, dodge up or down. The poor widow whose livelihood depends on twenty-three shares of AT&T and a small life-insurance policy is a standard down-dodge. Her invariable appearance whenever the subject of high profits is introduced is an evasive tactic with which everyone must be familiar.

The up-dodge usually takes the form of personification or allegory. Burke in his *Reflections* provides a convenient example:

Your constitution, it is true, whilst you were out of possession, suffered waste and dilapidation; but you possessed in some parts the walls and, in all, the foundations of a noble and venerable castle. You might

---

[21] T. S. Eliot, *The Idea of a Christian Society* (New York: Harcourt, Brace and Company, 1940), p. 17.

have repaired those walls; you might have built on those old foundations.[22]

This is not just fancy writing. Since the French monarchy, in its vain attempt to establish the constitution Burke was talking about, at one point advertised for antiquaries who could tell them what it was, Burke's retrospective optimism was surely forced. The applicability of Burke's thesis to France was one of the weakest arguments in the *Reflections,* and what is more, Burke surely knew it. The small allegory quoted above functioned for him as a bridge over a tender spot in his argument.

Conclusion

As was said in the beginning, this investigation into defective rhetoric is a survey, not an enumeration. Writers are entitled to the arguments that they choose and, it is to be hoped, believe to be true, just as readers are at liberty to withhold their assent to these arguments. What has been illustrated here are not arguments with which one can disagree, but arguments that are finally not arguments at all. Confronted with some difficulty, the writers who have furnished these illustrations have either failed to establish essential positions at all or have failed to make real connections where connections were required. In some instances these failures are manifest; more often they are concealed by some sort of move that is really irrelevant to the point.

It should be pointed out again that defective rhetoric is seldom adventitious. Writing is intentional; the writer has a point to make, and he has a series of intermediate positions to establish between premise and conclusion. Defective rhetoric almost invariably reflects some difficulty in one or more of those intermediate positions. This difficulty in turn reflects on the validity of the argument itself. The student who would learn to read argumentation properly should learn to look for the problem of which the defect is merely a manifestation.

[22] Edmund Burke, *Reflections on the Revolution in France,* Library of Liberal Arts, No. 46 (Indianapolis: Bobbs-Merrill, 1955), p. 40.

Chapter VIII

A Defective Essay

The following essay is not the worst one at hand, by any means; arguments of a lower order of competence are to be found in almost every issue of major journals. But this essay very well illustrates how a conceptual problem, in different disguises, can plague a writer through the greater part of an essay. It perhaps also has some pedagogical value as an illustration of the hazards of a certain kind of ethos. There has been no attempt to indicate all of the rhetoric; only those figures having some relevance to the point of this analysis have been marked.

CRITIQUE OF PSYCHOANALYTIC CONCEPTS AND THEORIES
B. F. Skinner[1]

[1] (1) Freud's great contribution to Western thought has been described as the application of the principle of cause and effect to human behavior. (2) Freud demonstrated that many features of behavior hitherto unexplained— and often dismissed as hopelessly complex or

(2) *Accumulation* —"and often dismissed" is a *correctio*.
(3) *Accumulation* —"unsuspected,

[1] B. F. Skinner, "Critique of Psychoanalytic Concepts and Theories," *Scientific Monthly*, LXXIX, No. 5 (November 1954), 300–305. This essay was originally delivered as a contribution to a symposium on scientific method. Reprinted by permission of *Science*.

obscure—could be shown to be the product of circumstances in the history of the individual. (3) Many of the causal relationships he so convincingly demonstrated had been wholly unsuspected—unsuspected, in particular, by the very individuals whose behavior they controlled. (4) Freud greatly reduced the sphere of accident and caprice in our considerations of human conduct. (5) His achievement in this respect appears all the more impressive when we recall that he was never able to appeal to the quantitative proof characteristic of other sciences. (6) He carried the day with sheer persuasion—with the massing of instances and the delineation of surprising parallels and analogies among seemingly diverse materials.

in particular" is another *correctio*. (4) *Accumulation* —"accident and caprice" is a doublet *synonymia*. (5) and (6) *Antithesis*. (7) "With the massing" is *accumulation*.

This is a "some say" introduction, as the "has been described" clearly warns the reader. The position set up is to be refuted or modified in some important way. The *accumulations* running through the first four sentences are somewhat heavy; the *correctios* are probably a response to this heaviness. The ethos that Skinner establishes is a judicial one; he praises not Freud's achievement but his precocity, and such praise is patronizing. (This ethos might profitably be compared to that of the Lewis essay.)

In passing, the *accumulation* of the last sentence is worth noting as an illustration of the discontinuity this figure can encompass. If we were to reverse the order of the elements, the effect would be comic. ("He carried the day with the massing of instances and the delineation of surprising parallels and analogies among seemingly diverse materials—with sheer persuasion.")

The last two sentences ought to be transitional; having set up what others say, Skinner needs to get to what he has to say. In fact, they are not.

[2]   (1) This was not, however, Freud's own view of the matter. (2) At the age of seventy he summed up his achievement in this way:

(1) and (2) *Antithesis*. (2) *Exemplum*. (4)

My life has been aimed at one goal only: to infer or guess how the mental apparatus is constructed and what forces interplay and counteract in it.

"not necessarily ... but nevertheless" is *antithesis*. (4) to (8) *Definition*.

(3) It is difficult to describe the mental apparatus he refers to in noncontroversial terms, partly because Freud's conception changed from time to time and partly because its very nature encouraged misinterpretation and misunderstanding. (4) But it is perhaps not too wide of the mark to indicate its principal features as follows: Freud conceived of some realm of the mind, not necessarily having physical extent, but nevertheless capable of topographic description and of subdivision into regions of the conscious, coconscious, and unconscious. (6) Within this space, various mental events—ideas, wishes, memories, emotions, instinctive tendencies, and so on—interacted and combined in many complex ways. (7) Systems of these mental events came to be conceived of almost as subsidiary personalities and were given proper names: the id, the ego, and the superego. (8) These systems divided among themselves a limited store of psychic energy. (9) There were, of course, many other details.

This paragraph has a broken back. The first two sentences promise that Freud's view of his own activities is to follow. But this subject is dropped with a transitional sentence (3) and we get instead a quick *definition* of Freud's system. (There is no point in calling it an *asyndeton*, since the brevity of the list has no rhetorical function.) The subject of Skinner's paper being Freudianism, this *definition* is very much in order. It is the first two sentences of the paragraph that are out of place, but these in turn are a response to the last two sentences of the previous paragraph. These seemed to be transitional on first reading; since they don't transit to anyplace in particular this cannot have been their real function. If they do not constitute a *paralipsis,* they are paraliptic (to coin an expression). They are there because Professor Skinner could not resist a swipe at Freud in passing. The effects of defective rhetoric do not always appear immediately.

[3]   (1) No matter what logicians may eventually make of this mental apparatus, there is little doubt that Freud accepted it as real rather than as a scientific construct or theory.   (2) One does not at the age of seventy define the goal of one's life as the exploration of an explanatory fiction.   (3) Freud did not use his "mental apparatus" as a postulate system from which he deduced theorems to be submitted to empirical check.   (4) If there was any interaction between the mental apparatus and empirical observations, it took the form of modifying the apparatus to account for newly discovered facts.   (5) To many followers of Freud the mental apparatus appears to be equally as real, and the exploration of such an apparatus is similarly accepted as the goal of a science of behavior.   (6) There is an alternative view, however, which holds that Freud did not discover the mental apparatus but rather invented it, borrowing part of its structure from a traditional philosophy of human conduct but adding many novel features of his own devising.

(1) *Paralipsis* (what have logicians to do with Freud's view of his own theory?) set up in an *antithesis;* "real rather than"—*antithesis.* (2) *Sententia.* (3) *Accumulation.* (3) and (4) *Antithesis.* (4) "If there was"— close to a *paralipsis.* (5) and (6) *Antithesis.* (6) *Paralipsis.*

This paragraph resumes the subject promised at the beginning of the previous paragraph and abandoned. That Freud regarded his system as true is proven by a *sententia.* (One wonders about the status of *sententias* in behaviorism.) The paragraph reads as though it were a *prolepsis,* as though Skinner were saying, "What I am about to say about Freudianism cannot be dismissed out of hand because Freud regarded his constructs as reflecting the fact of human psychology." What follows, however, makes this reading impossible.

One should notice the remarkable presence of two *paralipses* introducing irrelevantly derogatory opinions in one paragraph; the last two sentences of the first paragraph have the same flavor to them. In part the impulse to this figure stems from the ethos Professor Skinner has adopted, or rather a conflict between ethos and intention. The judicial role is an analytical one—the pipe-smoking scientist concerned with facts only. But even this early in the essay it is apparent that Skinner does not like Freudianism, does not like it at all. But this dislike cannot be expressed within the given ethos; hence it takes the form of dissenting judgments vaguely attributed to someone other than the referee giving the speech.

[4] (1) There are those who will concede that Freud's mental apparatus was a scientific construct rather than an observable empirical system but who, nevertheless, attempt to justify it in the light of scientific method. (2) One may take the line that metaphorical devices are inevitable in the early stages of any science and that although we may look with amusement today upon the "essences," "forces," "phlogistons," and "ethers" of the sciences of yesterday, these nevertheless were essential to the historical process. (3) It would be difficult to prove or disprove this. (4) However, if we have learned anything about the nature of scientific thinking, if mathematical and logical researches have improved our capacity to represent and analyze empirical data, it is possible that we can avoid some of the mistakes of adolescence. (5) Whether Freud could have done so is past demonstrating, but whether we need similar constructs in the future prosecution of a science of behavior is a question worth considering.

(1) *Antithesis*—"was a scientific construct rather than." (2) *Accumulation*—"although we may look . . . these nevertheless" example set up in an *antithesis*. (3) and (4) *Antithesis*. (4) "If-Then" *enthymeme;* "if we have learned . . . if mathematical"—*accumulation*. (4) "Mistakes of adolescence"—*personification* of science. (5) *Antithesis*.

It would appear that we now must alter our estimate of the rhetorical function of the previous paragraph. Together with this one, it perhaps comprises an *expeditio:* "Freud thought that his system was true, but that isn't so; others think it useful, but *that* isn't so." The conclusion left would be that, being neither true nor useful, it ought to be abandoned. The difficulty with this analysis is that the refutations of truth and usefulness are so gingerly handled. We don't know why Freudianism isn't true, except that there is an alternative view. The last sentence seems to promise that usefulness will be dealt with in more detail than truth has been, but this proves to be illusory.

[5]   (1) Constructs are convenient and perhaps even necessary in dealing with certain complicated subject matters. (2) As Frenkel-Brunswik shows, Freud was aware of the problems of scientific methodology and even of the metaphorical nature of some of his own constructs. (3) When this was the case, he justified the constructs as necessary or at least highly convenient. (4) But awareness of the nature of the metaphor is no defense of it, and if modern science is still occasionally metaphorical, we must remember that theory-wise it is also still in trouble. (5) The point is not that metaphor or construct is objectionable but that particular metaphors and constructs have caused trouble and are continuing to do so. (6) Freud recognized the damage worked by his own metaphorical thinking, but he felt that it could not be avoided and that the damage must be put up with. (7) There is reason to disagree with him on this point.

(1) "And perhaps even necessary"—*correctio,* in effect. (2) "And even" —another *correctio.* (3) "or at least"—another *correctio.* (4) "But awareness" —*sententia;* "if modern science" —an implicit *enthymeme.* (5) *Antithesis.* (6) and (7) *Antithesis.*

This paragraph is hard to describe in sober terms. The first sentence would lead one to expect that Professor Skinner is going to decide the conditions under which constructs are permissible; he would then be in a position to show that Freud's use of them was outside the prescribed conditions. But what follows reads as though he could not bear to make such a concession to human frailty. Sentence four, as a consequence, implicitly contradicts sentence one, and sentence five then contradicts sentence four. The paragraph

ends with the same sort of vague suggestion that things might be
otherwise as the previous paragraph did.

The reader's impression at this point is surely that Professor
Skinner is trying, without success, to get a critique under way. He
doesn't like Freudianism, is patronizing of it as a matter of fact, but
he is having a hard time formulating a position that would make
a critique possible. Instead of developing a rational argument, perhaps with the help of "mathematical and logical researches," he
alternates between genteel hints at the inadequacy of Freud and
paralipses.

[6] (1) Freud's explanatory scheme followed a
traditional pattern of looking for a cause of
human behavior inside the organism. (2)
His medical training supplied him with powerful supporting analogies. (3) The parallel
between the excision of a tumor, for example,
and the release of a repressed wish from the
unconscious is quite compelling and must
have affected Freud's thinking. (4) Now, the
pattern of an inner explanation of behavior
is best exemplified by doctrines of animism,
which are primarily concerned with explaining the spontaneity and evident capricious-
ness of behavior. (5) The living organism is
an extremely complicated system behaving in
an extremely complicated way. (6) Much of
its behavior appears at first blush to be absolutely unpredictable. (7) The traditional
procedure had been to invent an inner determiner, a "demon," "spirit," "homunculus,"
or "personality" capable of spontaneous
change of course or of origination of action.
(8) Such an inner determiner offers only a
momentary explanation of the behavior of the
outer organism, because it must, of course, be
accounted for also, but it is commonly used to
put the matter beyond further inquiry and to
bring the study of a causal series of events to
a dead end.

(1) and (2) A
disguised *enthy-
meme.* (3)
Example. (4)
Example. (5) to
(7) *Enthymeme.*
(6) *Accumulation.*
(7) "A demon"—
accumulation.
(8) *Enthymeme;*
"Such an inner . . .
but it is com-
monly"—
antithesis.

The *enthymeme* of the first two sentences really implies that Freud thought as he did *because* he was a doctor; this may or may not be the case, but the argument is clearly *ad hominem*. A similar *ad hominem* argument is set up in sentences five through seven, directed this time against people who believe in homunculi and personalities and things. The argumentative strategy that gets "homunculus" and "personality" in the same list, and hence treats them as of the same order, was unknown to classical rhetoricians; a modern writer has called it "giving a dog a bad name."

[7]   (1) Freud, himself, however, did not appeal to the inner apparatus to account for spontaneity or caprice because he was a thoroughgoing determinist. (2) He accepted the responsibility of explaining, in turn, the behavior of the inner determiner. (3) He did this by pointing to hitherto unnoticed external causes in the environmental and genetic history of the individual. (4) He did not, therefore, need the traditional explanatory system for traditional purposes; but he was unable to eliminate the pattern from his thinking. (5) It led him to represent each of the causal relationships he had discovered as a series of three events. (6) Some environmental condition, very often in the early life of the individual, leaves an effect upon the inner mental apparatus, and this in turn produces the behavioral manifestation or symptom. (7) Environmental event, mental state or process, behavioral symptom—these are the three links in Freud's causal chain. (8) He made no appeal to the middle link to explain spontaneity or caprice. (9) Instead he used it to bridge the gap in space and time between the events he had proved to be causally related.

(1) *Pseudo-enthymeme;* "spontaneity or caprice"—*synonymia.* (1) and (2) *Antithesis.* (4) *Antithesis.* (6) *Accumulation.* (7) *Accumulation.* (8) and (9) *Antithesis.*

The previous paragraph and the present one together make up a *distributio;* "Other people used animism in this way, Freud in this." If the reader feels (as this reader does) that nothing substantive was gained in introducing animism in the first place, then the previous paragraph is another *paralipsis,* and the connection with this one is spurious. Otherwise both paragraphs would have to be regarded as having further definition as their end. This reading would in turn suggest that after seven paragraphs we are still concerned to find out what Freudianism is.

[8] (1) A possible alternative, which would have had no quarrel with established science, would have been to argue that the environmental variables leave *physiological* effects that may be inferred from the behavior of the individual, perhaps at a much later date. (2) In one sense, too little is known at the moment of these physiological processes to make them useful in a legitimate way for this purpose. (3) On the other hand, too much is known of them, at least in a negative way. (4) Enough is known of the nervous system to place certain dimensional limits upon speculation and to clip the wings of explanatory fiction. (5) Freud accepted, therefore, the traditional fiction of a mental life, avoiding an out-and-out dualism by arguing that eventually physiological counterparts would be discovered. (6) Quite apart from the question of the existence of mental events, let us observe the damage that resulted from this maneuver.

(2) and (3) A peculiar figure— probably an *expeditio.* (4) *Accumulation;* "dimensional limits" —*synonymia?* (does the first word add anything to the meaning of the second?); "clip the wings"—*abusio.* (6) "Quite apart" —*paralipsis.*

Again (and it is aggravating to have to make the same point so often) we have a paragraph whose argumentative function is totally obscure. The first four sentences are probably, again, *paralipsis.* They are characteristically vague; it is impossible to identify the figure in sentences two and three because one does not know what the sentences, together, mean. Apparently we know too little of the nervous system to justify behaviorism, and too much to support Freudianism. What then? The point is not supported in any way, nor is our inadequate (or excessive) knowledge of the nervous system brought to any application. The paragraph promises an alternative to Freud but does not develop such an alternative. And all of this is, again, a dead end; the last two sentences simply return to the subject matter of the previous paragraph.

[9]   (1) We may touch only briefly upon two classical problems that arise once the conception of a mental life has been adopted. (2) The first of these is to explain how such a life is to be observed. (3) The introspective psychologists had already tried to solve this problem by arguing that introspection is only a special case of the observation upon which all science rests and that man's experience necessarily stands between him and the physical world with which science purports to deal. (4) But it was Freud himself who pointed out that not all of one's mental life was accessible to direct observation—that many events in the mental apparatus were necessarily inferred. (5) Great as this discovery was, it would have been still greater if Freud had taken the next step, advocated a little later by the American movement called Behaviorism, and insisted that conscious, as well as unconscious, events were inferences from the facts. (6) By arguing that the individual organism simply reacts to its environment, rather than to some inner experience of that environment, the bifurcation of nature into physical and psychic can be avoided.

(3) and (4) *Enthymeme.* (4) and (5) An "if-then" argument. (6) *Accumulation* and implicit *enthymeme.*

We seem to have moved into the second section of the body of the essay; at least Freudianism is finally confronted directly, and specific objections are raised to it. It is significant that this confrontation does not take place until the alternative to Freudianism, hinted at several times, is also made explicit—behaviorism. The essay is really concerned with the defects of Freudianism as compared with behaviorism.

But one cannot describe the first part of the paragraph as argumentative. It might be paraphrased as "Introspection constitutes a problem because, even according to Freud, it leaves some mental events unobservable." The major premise that we would have to derive for this if we were to make an argument out of it, "Anything that leaves events unobservable constitutes a problem," might be true. But Skinner wants to argue that we should abandon Freudianism; is the fact that it contains a problem relevant ground? Every science has a problem or two, including behaviorism.[2]

But the fact that Freudianism has a problem is then linked, arbitrarily and oddly, to a manifest argument whose paradigm is, "If some is good, more is better." This is included by Aristotle among the fallacious enthymemes, of course (*Rhetoric* II. 24. 3.).

There follows a series of paragraphs that make similar points in a similar fashion. It will be economical to consider several of them at once. The rhetoric of these paragraphs, as indicated in the margins, should be particularly noted.

[10] (1) A second classical problem is how the mental life can be manipulated. (2) In the process of therapy, the analyst necessarily acts upon the patient only through physical means. (3) He manipulates variables occupying a position in the first link of Freud's causal chain. (4) Nevertheless, it is commonly assumed that the mental apparatus is being directly manipulated. (5) Sometimes it is argued that processes are initiated within the individual himself, such as those of free association and transference, and that these in turn act directly upon the mental apparatus. (6) But how are these mental processes initiated by physical means? (7) The clarification of such a causal connection places a heavy and often unwelcome burden of proof upon the shoulders of the dualist.

(3) *Accumulation.* (3) and (4) *Antithesis* in *accumulation.* (6) Close to a *rhetorical question.* (7) "And often unwelcome" —a *paralipsis.*

[2] One problem that behaviorism has is that it cannot be defended without recourse to language that reflects the very mentalism it would do away with—"observes," "explain," "advocated" occur in this paragraph.

[11] (1) The important disadvantages of Freud's conception of mental life can be described somewhat more specifically. (2) The first of these concerns the environmental variables to which Freud so convincingly pointed. (3) The cogency of these variables was frequently missed because the variables were transformed and obscured in the course of being represented in mental life. (4) The physical world of the organism was converted into the conscious and unconscious experience, and these experiences were further transmuted as they combined and changed in mental processes. (5) For example, early punishment of sexual behavior is an observable fact that undoubtedly leaves behind a changed organism. (6) But when this change is represented as a state of conscious or unconscious anxiety or guilt, specific details of the punishment are lost. (7) When, in turn, some unusual characteristic of the sexual behavior of the adult individual is related to the supposed guilt, many specific features of the relationship may be missed that would have been obvious if the same features of behavior had been related to the punishing episode. (8) Insofar as the mental life of the individual is used as Freud used it to represent and to carry an environmental history, it is inadequate and misleading.

(4) to (7) *Accumulation* of sentence three. (5) to (7) *Example* of sentence four. (7) *Accumulation* of previous point.

[12] (1) Freud's theory of the mental apparatus had an equally damaging effect upon his study of behavior as a dependent variable. (2) Inevitably, it stole the show. (3) Little attention was left to behavior per se. (4) Behavior was relegated to the position of a mere mode of expression of the activities of the mental apparatus or the symptoms of an underlying disturbance. (5) Among the problems not specifically treated in the manner that was their due, we may note five.

(2) "Stole the show"—decayed *abusio*. (3) *Accumulation*. (4) *Accumulation*.

[13] (1) The nature of the act as a unit of behavior was never clarified. (2) The simple *occurrence* of behavior was never well represented. (3) "Thoughts" could "occur" to an individual; he could "have" ideas according to the traditional model; but he could "have" behavior only in giving expression to these inner events. (4) We are much more likely to say that "the thought occurred to me to ask him his name" than that "the act of asking him his name occurred to me." (5) It is in the nature of thoughts and ideas that they occur to people, but we have never come to be at home in describing the emission of behavior in a comparable way. (6) This is especially true of verbal behavior. (7) In spite of Freud's valuable analysis of verbal slips and of the techniques of wit, and verbal art, he rejected the possibility of an analysis of verbal behavior in its own right rather than as the expression of ideas, feelings, or other inner events, and therefore missed the importance of this field for the analysis of units of behavior and the conditions of their occurrence.

(2) *Accumulation.*
(3) *Antithesis* in *accumulation.*
(4) Example.
(5) *Antithesis* in *accumulation.*
(6) "Verbal behavior in its own right rather than" —*antithesis.*

The excessiveness of this rhetoric is both positive and negative. The positive excess is the extraordinary amount of *accumulation* and *antithesis*. The obverse side of this profusion is the total lack of any *enthymeme*. In fact, there has been no significant *enthymeme* in the essay to this point, if one wishes to forgive Professor Skinner the part-whole argument noted above. We have all kinds of statements implying that Freudianism is awful, but what constitutes awfulness in specific instances is nowhere considered.

The second paragraph of this section, beginning "The important disadvantages," is typical. It may be that when Freud introduces considerations of "conscious and unconscious experience" he loses "specific details" of the initial experience. It may be. But why is the reader supposed to regard this as a particularly heinous fault? When the behaviorist regards mental life as nonexistent it may be that he loses some specific details too.

The deficiency is even more serious in the first of the five problems proposed (quoted immediately above). Why is "the emission of behavior" particularly "well represented" when it is represented as simply "occurring"? What *reason* does the reader have for accepting such a position? None that Skinner has given him.

We may as well look at the rest of the Freudians' problems, although some excision is in order.

[14] (1) The dimensions of behavior, particularly its dynamic properties, were never adequately represented. (2) We are all familiar with the fact that some of our acts are more likely to occur upon a given occasion than others. (3) But this likelihood is hard to represent and harder to evaluate. (4) The dynamic changes in behavior that are the first concern of the psycho-analyst are primarily changes in probability of action. (5) But Freud chose to deal with this aspect of behavior in other terms—as a question of "libido," "cathexis," "volume of excitation," "instinctive or emotional tendencies," "available quantities of psychic energy," and so on. (6) The delicate question of how probability of action is to be quantified was never answered, because these constructs suggested dimensions to which the quantitative practices of science in general could not be applied.

(4) and (5) *Antithesis*. (5) and (6) *Antithesis*.

[15] (1) In his emphasis upon the genesis of behavior, Freud made extensive use of processes of learning. (2) These were never treated operationally in terms of changes in behavior but rather as the acquisition of ideas, feelings, and emotions later to be expressed by, or manifested in, behavior. (3) Consider, for example, Freud's own suggestion that sibling rivalry in his own early history played an important part in his theoretical considerations as well as in his personal relationships as an adult.

(2) *Antithesis*.
(3) *Example*.

(There follows a lengthy section in which it is asked, in effect: "Didn't Freud *really* just learn behavior patterns instead of developing sibling rivalry?")

[16] (1) An explicit treatment of behavior as a datum, of probability of response as the principal quantifiable property of behavior, and of learning and other processes in terms of changes of probability is usually enough to avoid another pitfall into which Freud, in common with his contemporaries, fell. (2) There are many words in the layman's vocabulary that suggest the activity of an organism yet are not descriptive of behavior in the narrower sense. (3) Freud used many of these freely—for example, the individual is said to discriminate, remember, infer, repress, decide, and so on. (4) Such terms do not refer to specific acts. (5) We say that a man discriminates between two objects when he behaves differently with respect to them; but discriminating is not itself behavior. . . . [Further examples of "repressing" and "deciding" are added.] (6) The difficulty is that when one uses terms which suggest an activity, one feels it necessary to invent an actor, and the subordinate personalities in the Freudian mental apparatus do, indeed, participate in just these activities rather than in the more specific behavior of the observable organism.

(2) *Antithesis.*
(3) *Example.*
(5) *Antithesis.*
(6) *Antithesis.*

[17] (1) Among these activities are conspicuous instances involving the process of self-control—the so-called "Freudian mechanisms." (2) These need not be regarded as activities of the individual or any subdivision thereof—they are not, for example, what happens when a skillful wish evades a censor—but simply as ways of representing relationships among responses and controlling variables. (3) I have elsewhere tried to demonstrate this

(2) *Antithesis.*

by restating the Freudian mechanisms without reference to Freudian theory.[3]

[18] (1) Since Freud never developed a clear conception of the behavior of the organism and never approached many of the scientific problems peculiar to that subject matter, it is not surprising that he misinterpreted the nature of the observation of one's own behavior. (2) This is admittedly a delicate subject, which presents problems which no one, perhaps, has adequately solved. (3) But the act of self-observation can be represented within the framework of physical science. (4) This involves questioning the reality of sensations, ideas, feelings, and other states of consciousness which many people regard as among the most immediate experiences of their life. (5) Freud himself prepared us for this change. (6) There is, perhaps, no experience more powerful than that which the mystic reports of his awareness of the presence of God. (7) The psychoanalyst explains this in other ways. (8) He himself, however, may insist upon the reality of certain experiences that others wish to question. (9) There are other ways of describing what is actually seen or felt under such circumstances.

(2) and (3) *Antithesis.* (4) *Accumulation.* (6) to (8) *Enthymeme.* (9) *Accumulation.*

[19] (1) Each of us is in particularly close contact with a small part of the universe enclosed within his own skin. (2) Under certain limited circumstances, we may come to react to that part of the universe in unusual ways. (3) But it does not follow that that particular part has any special physical or non-physical properties or that our observations of it differ

(2) and (3) *Antithesis.* (7) *Antithesis.*

[3] The reference is to Skinner's *Science and Human Behavior* (New York: The Macmillan Co., 1953).

in any fundamental respect from our observations of the rest of the world. (4) I have tried to show elsewhere how self-knowledge of this sort arises and why it is likely to be subject to limitations that are troublesome from the point of view of physical science. (5) Freud's representations of these events was a particular personal contribution influenced by his own cultural history. (6) It is possible that science can now move on to a different description of them. (7) If it is impossible to be wholly non-metaphorical, at least we may improve upon our metaphors.

So end Freud's troubles, or at least this list of them. The lack of any argumentative figures is again striking. The major figure is the *antithesis,* which is chiefly used to contrast the Freudian procedure to its disadvantage with the behaviorist one. But the nature of that disadvantage is never explicitly indicated. It is taken for granted as self-evident.

And yet over and over one feels Skinner reaching for an argument. The assertion in sentence four of Freud's second problem, "The dynamic changes in behavior . . ." sounds like a premise. But its relationship to sentence six, which would have to be the conclusion, is quite obscure. (The "because" of the latter sentence signals an explanation.) The first part of problem four treats an implicit definition of behavior as though it were behavior itself, and hence could be used to determine what is not behavior, but the sentences do not add up to an argument. The last sentence of the first paragraph, beginning "The difficulty . . ." gives a sort of reason for rejecting words like "discrimination" (or "feeling it necessary" for that matter) but it is impossible to get a significant *enthymeme* out of it, with or without what precedes. The major premise would have to be sentence six, "The use of terms which suggest an activity makes it necessary to invent an actor." What would be proven by it?

The fifth Freudian problem is also bare of clear-cut argumentation, with the possible exception of a part-whole fallacy set up by sentence five, having for its major premise, "If the mystic's perception of God can be explained in other ways, then all perceptions can be explained in other ways."

In general, the technique in this section is to pick specific instances in Freudian psychology that are different from behaviorism, and to use these differences as being somehow self-evident defects. But since the obvious point of the essay is to persuade the reader that behaviorism is superior, Professor Skinner can only go from one circle to another.

The next paragraph functions as a conclusion to all five problems, apparently.

[20]   (1) The crucial issue here is the Freudian distinction between the conscious and unconscious mind. (2) Freud's contribution has been widely misunderstood. (3) The important point was not that the individual was often unable to describe important aspects of his own behavior or identify important causal relationships but that his ability to describe them was irrelevant to the occurrence of the behavior or to the effectiveness of the causes. (4) We begin by attributing the behavior of the individual to events in his genetic and environmental history. (5) We then note that because of certain cultural practices, the individual may come to describe some of that behavior and some of those causal relationships. (6) We may say that he is conscious of the parts he can describe and unconscious of the rest. (7) But the act of self-description, as of self-observation, plays no part in the determination of action. (8) It is superimposed upon behavior. (9) Freud's argument that we need not be aware of important causes leads naturally to the broader conclusion that awareness of cause has nothing to do with causal effectiveness.

(3) *Antithesis.*
(4) through (6) *Narratio.* (7) through (8) *Antithesis.*

Again, we have chiefly two *antitheses,* a piece of *narratio* and, in sentence nine, Professor Skinner's favorite argument, a part-whole one.

The concluding sections of the essay can be considered briefly:

[21] (1) In addition to these specific consequences of Freud's mental apparatus in obscuring important details among the variables of which human behavior is a function and in leading to the neglect of important problems in the analysis of behavior as a primary datum, we have to note the most unfortunate effect of all. (2) Freud's methodological strategy has prevented the incorporation of psychoanalysis into the body of science proper. (3) It was inherent in the nature of such an explanatory system that its key entities would be unquantifiable in the sense in which entities in science are generally quantifiable, but the spatial and temporal dimensions of these entities have caused other kinds of trouble.

(3) *Accumulation* and transition.

This is surely one of the most puzzling paragraphs in the history of essay-writing. The long transitional sentence beginning the paragraph and summarizing the essay to this point, is like a roll of drums leading to the climactic, "the most unfortunate effect of all." But this most unfortunate effect is whisked before the reader's eyes in a way that is almost surreptitious. It is stated once, then amplified with a sentence that abruptly and awkwardly drops off with a transition into the next paragraph. Every instinct of the writer would have been to weight this most important point, to contrast it with other options, to argue its importance. In the earlier part of the essay, Professor Skinner has shown no reluctance to weight his assertions by *repetitions* and *antitheses*. Why he should have here dealt with his most important point in such a hugger-mugger fashion is a supremely mysterious fact which could only be explained by an appeal to mythical entities like mental states.

[22] (1) One can sense a certain embarrassment among psychoanalytic writers with respect to the primary entities of the mental apparatus.

(2) *Accumulation.*
(3) *Accumulation.*
(3) and (4) *An-*

(2) There is a predilection for terms that avoid the embarrassing question of the spatial dimensions, physical or otherwise, of terms at the primary level. (3) Although it is occasionally necessary to refer to mental events and their qualities and to states of consciousness, the analyst usually moves on in some haste to less committal terms such as *forces, processes, organizations, tensions, systems,* and *mechanisms.* (4) But all these imply terms at a lower level. (5) The notion of a conscious or unconscious "force" may be a useful metaphor, but if this is analogous to force in physics, what is the analogous mass that is analogously accelerated? (6) Human behavior is in a state of flux and undergoing changes that we call "processes," but what is changing in what direction when we speak of, for example, an affective process? (7) Psychological "organizations," "mental systems," "motivational interaction"—these all imply arrangements or relationships among *things,* but what are the things so related or arranged? (8) Until this question has been answered the problem of the dimensions of the mental apparatus can scarcely be approached. (9) It is not likely that the problem can be solved by working out independent units appropriate to the mental apparatus, although it has been proposed to undertake such a step in attempting to place psychoanalysis on a scientific footing.

tithesis. (5) *Antithesis* in *rhetorical question.* (6) *Antithesis* in *rhetorical question.* (7) *Antithesis* in *rhetorical question.* (9) "Scientific footing"—*abusio.*

Here, surely, is the emotional center of the essay. As the series of rhetorical questions makes clear, here if nowhere else the writer felt himself on sure ground. Even in this paragraph, however, the vagueness of sentence eight, a crucial and climactic sentence, throws away much of the force of the paragraph. What are the "dimensions of the mental apparatus"? One would have thought, from what has gone before, they could be determined with a tape measure.

[23] (1) Before one attempts to work out units of transference or scales of anxiety, or systems of mensuration appropriate to the regions of consciousness, it is worth asking whether there is not an alternative program for a *rapprochement* with physical science that would make such a task unnecessary. (2) Freud could hope for an eventual union with physics or physiology only through the discovery of neurological mechanisms that would be the analogs of, or possibly only other aspects of, the features of his mental apparatus. (3) Since this depended upon the prosecution of a science of neurology far beyond its current state of knowledge, it was not an attractive future. (4) Freud appears never to have considered the possibility of bringing the concepts and theories of a psychological science into contact with the rest of physical and biological science by the simple expedient of an operational definition of terms. (5) This would have placed the mental apparatus in jeopardy as a life goal, but it would have brought him back to the observable, manipulable, and preeminently physical variables with which he was in the last analysis dealing.

(2) and (4) Implicit *antithesis*.
(5) *Antithesis*.

Little needs to be said of this concluding paragraph, except to point out that the *antithesis* between Freudianism and something else is repeated for the last time—this time in connection with a further term that is to be a basis for choice, a relationship with the established sciences. The term is not proposed in a fashion that could be called argumentative, however. The concluding *antithesis* is a curious one—it is hard to see how a mental apparatus might be a goal—but it probably reflects the behaviorist's own fundamental dualism, between those who are willing to sacrifice everything, including Aristotle's strictures on the part-whole fallacy, to scientific method, and those who are not. The *antithesis* would thus be a kind of strategic appeal to the audience's emotional desire to be *au courant*. This is sound theoretical strategy, as old as rhetoric itself.

The first characteristic to be accounted for in this essay is its vagueness. In part, as was pointed out, this is the result of an ethos that doesn't fit very well. The result is a curious kind of oscillation. In Freud's fifth problem, for instance, we find the forthright statement that Freud "misinterpreted," but two sentences later it turns out that "the act of self-observation can be represented" as such and such. This isn't very forthright at all; the question is, should it be? After a couple more forthright, manly statements, the paragraph (18) ends with the extraordinarily tentative statement that "There are other ways of describing what is actually seen or felt under such circumstances." This tonal uncertainty probably is a result of a conflict between Professor Skinner's attitude toward Freud and an ethos that prohibits such an attitude.

The vagueness of the diction is perhaps also ultimately a function of ethos. "Good" words, like "dimension," "dynamic," and so forth, are used over and over again with little concrete significance. Their function is emotive, to give the illusion of life to a deplorably static and dull scientific construct—more or less for the same reason that we send flowers to funerals.

But the vagueness is not merely a matter of ethos or diction. It is inherent in the argument itself. To begin with, the essay suggests that Professor Skinner was not sure about his own intentions. The title promises a consideration of "psychoanalytic concepts and theories"; the conclusion recommends behaviorism as a substitute. The relationship between the two intentions was not, the rhetoric suggests, squarely faced. It is only in paragraph eight, after four vague references to unspecified alternatives, that behaviorism is explicitly referred to at all, and then Skinner introduces it as gingerly as an old maid carrying out a dead mouse.

Scientific method is handled with the same sort of fastidiousness. It is only in paragraph twenty-two, after repeated hints and allusions, that the superiority of behaviorism is asserted to be its consonance with scientific method. It is then hastily dropped.

But what is Skinner's point? The superiority of behaviorism is obviously its consonance with science; his thesis must depend on a minor premise something like, "because behaviorism permits the use of the methods of the physical sciences." The essay suggests that Professor Skinner is sensitive enough to be unhappy with such a reason, or at least with the public declaration of such a reason. The confusion between horse and cart is too obvious. Physicists surely devise methods with an eye on the objects of their inquiry. This would seem to be the sensible, and even the scientific, procedure. What Skinner would recommend is that we choose a psychology, not according to the object of our inquiry, but according to its consonance with the method developed for other inquiries. That is what he recommends, but not very clearly or forthrightly.

But there is still another problem. What is the conclusion of his enthymeme, the major clause of his thesis? It would have to go something like this:

Behaviorism is ⎯⎯⎯⎯⎯ than Freudianism because its postulates permit the quantifying methods of the physical sciences.

But how to fill in the blank? Almost every paragraph is troubled into vagueness by the problem. "Better" is probably the most common implication, but it is in itself vague. "More convenient?" That is not very persuasive; science is not supposed to pick its postulates for their convenience. The word that the writer would surely like to use is "truer." But the truth of behaviorism is hardly established. So the essay is troubled from beginning to end by a great hole in its thesis where "truth" ought to be.

This analysis is of course based on the premise that the essay is a forensic argument, that it is designed to persuade. The possibility that it is not forensic, but epideictic, must also be considered. An epideictic argument is not really directed to persuasion; its function is to reinforce community solidarity by rehearsing the familiar and celebrating the virtue of the virtuous, as the in-community has already defined that virtue. If the essay is in reality epideictic, all comments are beside the point and the foregoing analysis is in vain. But the essay pretends to be something else.

One further caution. The foregoing analysis is an attempt to relate the deficiencies of an essay to the intentions that led to them, as these are revealed through an analysis of its rhetoric. It is not an analysis of Professor Skinner, who may have written admirable essays in situations where the intentional ambiguities that plague this one did not exist.

Part IV

Reportorial Writing

Much modern prose discourse is obviously not argumentation, nor is it yet history or fiction. It lies someplace between the straight narrative of the latter and the formal parts-relationships of the former. It is not history or fiction because it does not have a line of action whose significance is intimately concerned with the temporal relationships established. It is not argumentation because it does not relate concepts to each other explicitly (although it may contain subordinate arguments). This third kind of writing will be called "reportorial," because it frequently presents itself as high-level reporting.

It is easy to point to examples of reportorial writing. In such magazines as the *Reporter, Harper's,* or *Atlantic Monthly,* most articles, whether they are discussions of the war in Vietnam or the industrialization of Red China, are reportorial. So are discussions of particular sports when there is an attempt to do more than describe a game. Literary criticism is largely reportorial, as are most articles in journals of psychotherapy.

The mark of such reportorial articles is that they are engaged in the elaboration of a single term. The writer of an argument might have for his central thesis the opinion that "The policy struggle going on in the Kuomintang reflects tensions created by the Russo-Chinese split." The central concern of a reportorial writer, on the other hand, might simply be an explication of "The policy struggle going on in the Kuomintang." Argumentation relates terms; reportorial writing explicates a central term.

Simply because reportorial writing is not argument does not mean that it may not be persuasive. But it persuades by a different method. It persuades by proposing a particular point of view toward its subject. In effect, the reportorial writer says to the reader, "Let's look at the Vietnamese war (or human nature, or whatever) from this point of view." This strategy can be a very powerful persuasive approach. Anything of any consequence can be regarded from several points of view, and the point of view one assumes is apt to be decisive. To take another contemporary instance: the civil rights movement could be demolished by someone taking a strictly legalistic point of view in describing its activities. A moral point of view might lead to quite another attitude.

Of course, not all reportorial articles are usefully regarded as persuasive. An article on social change in Nepal, for instance, is not apt to have any significant effect on an American or European audience. But whether or not a particular specimen is persuasive has nothing to do with form; it is purely a question of subject matter. Insofar as a particular subject has relevance for the reader, can potentially be affected by his attitudes, writing about it will be persuasive.

But how is it that one point of view is persuasive for a particular reader, another not? The answer to this question is necessarily complicated. In the first place, ethos plays a very large part in reportorial writing, perhaps even larger than in argumentation since the reader has fewer checks on the process of persuasion. The gaps in an argument can be detected, but it is very difficult to check on the writer who proposes to command assent by telling us, for instance, the "facts" of Vietnam. The reader's estimation of the writer's character must be critical to his judgment of the writer's account of anything.

But the ethos for serious reportorial writing today is very narrow. The stance of the reporter is that he is just giving us the "facts." In practice, this stance works out to an ethos of "judiciousness." This ethos requires that the writer set himself up as impersonally as possible, as a disinterested observer simply trying to find out what the particular "facts" might be. He must particularly manifest his awareness that every situation has several sides. He can then proceed to present it, essentially, from the point of view that he thinks is the correct one. In short, the essence of the reportorial ethos is that the writer present himself as what he cannot possibly be—an impartial observer.

The reportorial writer is of course not completely confined to this ethos. Among groups outside the main traditions of the time —the right wing, for instance—the prophetic ethos is common. Reviewers frequently have somewhat more room. We have tolerated the personal ethos of a strong personality from time to time; the late H. L. Mencken is an example. But by and large, the more serious a writer proposes to be, and the more he approaches the central attitudes of the time, the more he must incline to judiciousness and impersonality.

But there is more to reportorial persuasion than ethos. Equally judicious—that is, equally skilled—writers can be found on both sides of most major questions. How, then, does the individual choose? What functions to persuade besides ethos? It is perhaps most useful to see the further element in persuasion, the test that the individual applies to a particular account, as falling someplace upon a scale between two poles.

The first pole might be called experiential. Do the writer's comments about a particular situation agree with my experience in similar situations? Does this description of the motives of various groups in Vietnam, for instance, square with what I already know, or believe, about human beings and their behavior? Reporting that makes this claim to validity really extends our experience by relating it to new situations. It may modify previous generalizations to some extent, but it is the congruity between the new and the old that is persuasive.

The importance of this experiential test can be illustrated negatively by recourse, again, to politics. The occasional attempts of the radical right to communicate with the political center (and vice versa) on particular issues are futile because the two groups bring a radically different interpretation of experience to the encounter. Hence, what seems a self-evident reading of a particular situation to one group will be self-evident nonsense to the other. A book such as *None Dare Call It Treason*,[1] for instance, arises out of a certain reading of experience. Its author, Mr. John Stormer, surely sees his own life as a conflict between a very sharply distinguished, and highly motivated, right and wrong; the book is simply an extension of that reading to matters not directly experienced, to recent political history. For those whose own experience reflects Mr. Stormer's, *None Dare Call It Treason* was undoubtedly a deeply satisfying explanation of modern history. For those whose experience did not, it was meaningless.

The second pole might be called analogical. This type of reportorial writing seizes on a pattern that is believed to be visible in certain activities and extends it to other activities, by analogy.

The best illustration of the analogical method at work is seen in the late nineteenth-century social movement called Social Darwinism. Darwin proposed a belief about the world, a belief in evolution through the struggle of natural selection. This was not a matter of anybody's experience; it was a deduction (and perhaps a valid one) from evidence that the ordinary literate man had never even encountered. Social Darwinism extended this belief to human society. Dozens of writers described human society in Darwinist terms as though they were discovering Darwinist principles in it. But in fact they were imposing them on it. Social Darwinism was a product of analogical thought.

These are not mutually exclusive ways of looking at the world and writing about it. Darwinism could be experienced in human society in part, and hence the Darwinist analogy was not utterly irrelevant as a point of view, although it was limited. On the other hand, it is likely that all human thinking about particular situations contains analogical elements. But a particular piece of reporting can be more or less experiential, more or less analogical. And it is probably the better part of wisdom to suspect the analogy when one detects it.

[1] John A. Stormer, *None Dare Call It Treason* (Florissant, Missouri: Liberty Bell Press, 1964). As was pointed out before, one reads one's experience as one wants to, at least in part.

Obviously, there is no "art" of reporting in the way that there is an "art" of argument. It is a bastard form of writing because it borrows structures and techniques haphazardly from other kinds of writing. This does not mean that it may not require a great deal of skill to manage successfully. But it does mean that one cannot understand it as one can argumentation. There is not much to do with it except to show how it works in specific examples, which the next chapter will undertake to do.

Chapter IX

Some Reportorial Texts

Reportorial writing is defined as discourse engaged in elaborating one central term; the practical consequence of this characteristic is that there are no intrinsic structuring elements to give shape to the whole. Argumentation, it will be remembered, derives its structure, first, from the overt relationship between writer and reader, which requires that beginning and ending be formal elements of the overall structure, and, second, from the logical relationship that necessarily prevails between the terms of its thesis. A long argument may have other elements, of course—a *narratio,* a *reprehensio,* and so forth—but these will be subordinated to the main structural elements provided by the reader-writer relationship and by the thesis. And it is particularly the thesis, with its logical relationship between its terms, that makes it possible for an argument to move.

Reportorial writing, on the other hand, is an expansion of a single term. This term may have a number of subordinate elements, but they will bear no necessary relationship to each other. If my subject is the Vietnamese crisis, for instance, I may find it desirable to discuss the topography of the country, its history, the character of its ruling junta, and four or five other subtopics. Each of these subordinate elements may have its own intrinsic order, the narration, description, exposition, and so forth of books on writing, but they will have no necessary relationship to each other.[1]

And yet movement is a law of life for the reportorial writer as well as for the writer of argument. The reader-writer contract is the same; the reader agrees to follow the line of discourse laid out by the writer as long as it promises to get somewhere, which means as long as it seems to be moving. The writer of argumentation derives this movement from his thesis. The reportorial writer has nothing comparable to provide movement for his essay. Thus the primary art of the reporter[2] is the art of inventing pseudo-connections and consequently pseudo-movement.

The art of the pseudo-connection is a difficult one for those who would learn to use it, but it presents no great difficulty for the student whose object is merely understanding. It consists in the manipulation of various devices, some strictly rhetorical and others not, to give an illusion of either the temporal connectedness of narrative or the logical connectedness of argument. These devices are for the most part simple enough, and it will be sufficient merely to watch some of them in operation.

The first example of reportorial writing is very short and very simple. Furthermore, the persuasive intent is minimal.

A NEW DISEASE[3]

1) From time to time new diseases make their appearance. Some are attributable to social or scientific progress—to contact with new products of chemical industry or adventure into new physical conditions. In others the origin is obscure. The latest of these is of a particularly distressing kind. It is a form of blindness in both eyes practically confined

---

[1] Much of the futility of many freshman writing courses is caused by teaching these subordinate elements of nonfictive discourse as though they were genres of writing capable of independent existence.

[2] It should be clear that this word is being used in an abnormal sense, to designate the writer of reportorial writing. Newspaper reporters, unless they are columnists, work from their own formulae. These formulae have little to do with the kind of writing described in this chapter.

[3] Ffrangcon Roberts, "A New Disease," *The Spectator,* Vol. 189 (December 19, 1952), p. 837. Reprinted by permission of *The Spectator.*

to premature babies. From its main characteristic, the formation of fibrous or scar tissue behind the lens, it is called retrolental fibroplasia. From this tissue strands extend across the interior of the eyeball to the retina, and these on contracting cause retinal detachment.

2) In labelling a disease "new" caution is needed. Some diseases are new only in the sense that new methods of diagnosis or treatment bring them to light. The classical example is appendicitis. Others are merely pre-existing diseases separated out from an ill-defined group by better understanding of their nature. Retrolental fibroplasia belongs to neither of these categories. Since the eye, by virtue of its transparency, lends itself uniquely to direct examination by means of the ophthalmoscope, an instrument which has been in use for many years, it is inconceivable that the previous existence of this condition could have been overlooked. It is, without doubt, a new disease.

3) Although sporadic cases of somewhat similar conditions had been recorded since 1820, it was unknown as a definite disease until 1942, when it was described by an American ophthalmologist. It was first reported in this country [Great Britain] in 1949, and in France and Australia in 1951. Both here and in the United States it has become the commonest cause of blindness in preschool children. In the United States it accounts for one-third of blindness from all causes. In this country, so far, the proportion is smaller, but in the last few years twenty-two cases have been reported from the Oxford area alone and nineteen have been found in 120 inmates of the Sunshine Homes. The incidence varies directly with the degree of prematurity. According to one American series it affects 23 per cent of babies weighing less than 3 lbs. at birth, 7 per cent of those between 3 and 4½ lbs. and 5.5 per cent of those over 4½ lbs. Above 5 lbs. it is rare. All observers agree that the incidence is increasing.

4) The cause is entirely unknown. The disease is not contagious, nor is it due to social conditions or to any discoverable abnormality or infection of the mother. It is first observed shortly after birth, but whether the process starts before or after birth is disputed. The formation of the fibrous mass must be the end-result of an antecedent process. Anomalies of the blood vessels and persistence of embryonic structures have been described, but whether these are causes or associated disturbances is unknown. In any case, to attribute the disease to them is only to push the explanation one stage further back. Some authorities believe it to be part of a more extensive disorder, finding other congenital manifestations, including mental deficiency, in some of their cases. Such concomitants seem, however, to be rare.

5) It has been variously attributed to one or other of the hazards,

natural or artificial, involved in premature exposure to the rigours of post-natal life—incomplete temperature control, vitamin deficiency and digestive or dietetic failure. Premature exposure to light, which would seem a likely cause, is ruled out since the disease is not prevented by covering up the eyes. Treatment of concomitant anaemia by blood-transfusion is equally unsuccessful. Oxygen deficiency, due to persistence of the foetal type of circulation, has been suggested, but so also has the administration of oxygen in too high concentration. Neither increase nor decrease in the amount of oxygen given has proved effective.

6)   These explanations, apart from being disproved by the failure of the appropriate corrections, neglect the fact that this is a new disease superimposed on a condition which has always been with us. In Switzerland, where the treatment of prematurity has long been of a high standard, it is very rare. Though a disease of prematurity, it is not due to prematurity or to any of the known causes of prematurity. Clearly some new factor is involved. The assertion recently made by a Member of Parliament that it is a result of the Health Service is only partly true. The service, by providing more extended facilities for forms of treatment already in use, merely increases the number of potential victims. On the other hand, the statement recently broadcast by the Minister of Health to the effect that decline in infant-mortality is a measure of improvement in national health requires modification.

7)   Infection, probably by virus, has been suggested, and has some evidence in its favour. It would explain the remarkable geographical variation in incidence which is found not only in different parts of the same country—it is twice as high in Illinois as in New York—but also in different hospitals in the same town. It would also explain the observation that, apart from twin-pregnancies, it has never been seen twice in the same family, a fact which suggests that the mother acquires immunity on the first occasion. It is now well established that an attack during pregnancy of German measles, an infection once considered harmless enough, is liable to result in abnormalities of the offspring. It may well be that in the condition which we are discussing the mother contracts some infection too trifling to be noticed.

8)   For the established disease no cure has been found. Attempts have been made to restore some degree of retinal function by surgical removal, in part at least, of the fibrotic mass. Radiotherapy has been used, so far without success, in the hope of inducing regression. A method which in some ways has a more rational basis is the administration of the substance known as A.C.T.H. (adrenocorticotrophic hormone), the recently discovered secretion of the pituitary gland which stimulates the suprarenal gland to produce cortisone, a substance which is known to

induce regression of abnormal fibrous tissue. First results were indeterminate, but more recently workers in this country have claimed some success. As in the treatment of other diseases, the assessment of results is rendered difficult by the occasional tendency to spontaneous arrest and regression. The surest way to prevent the disease lies, of course, in preventing prematurity. Meanwhile search for the cause requires, and is indeed engaging, the coordinated energies of obstetricians, pediatricians, and ophthalmologists. The number of cases seen at any one centre being small, collation of experience is essential, and is being undertaken by the Medical Research Council.

9)   This disease, the serious social implications of which require no emphasis, illustrates many of the difficulties encountered in medical research. It demonstrates the increasing complexity of our concepts of disease-processes, the great width of the investigational net which must be cast, the difficulty in distinguishing cause from effect, and the multiplicity of attempted remedies which, so long as the cause remains a mystery, are no more than empirical. Its almost simultaneous appearance in regions as far apart as Western Europe, America and Australia raises the fundamental problem of the genesis of disease. Finally, it proves, if further proof be needed, the sombre and sobering truth that the environment against which man struggles, so far from being constant and static, is ever changing, ever evolving and dynamic, and that on the chessboard of medical science nature is always one move ahead.

Like much reporting, this is a kind of "situation report." Its point is probably merely to tell the readers of the *Spectator* that there is a new disease abroad, but it is set up as though its subject were "the status of retrolental fibroplasia."

The first two paragraphs would probably have to be called introductory, although they do both more and less than an introduction to an argument would. A piece of reporting does not really need an introduction, since there is, usually, neither a writer's presence to establish nor a question to raise. The ordering of these two paragraphs reflects the power of the argumentative convention, since they are set up in imitation of an argument. They are unlike an argumentative introduction in that they define the major term of the essay. But Dr. Roberts, in imitating argumentation, is necessarily driven to setting up a pseudo-problem in these first two paragraphs. They read as though the fact that retrolental fibroplasia is a new disease presents some sort of problem for the rest of the essay. It does not; it is merely the first in a list of facts.

The body of the essay is very readily analyzed. Paragraph three gives the history and incidence of the disease, four through seven speculation about its cause, and paragraph eight discusses its cure. These are of course "aspects of" the subject. Since this example of reporting imitates argumentation (rather than fiction), its divisions are well marked.

The dominant rhetorical figure is, by far, the *praeteritio*. There is a *praeteritio* concerning new diseases in the second paragraph, a long one about causes in paragraphs four through seven, and yet another in paragraph eight. It will be noted that its entire function is to introduce information in some sort of organized form. The *praeteritio* is so useful for this purpose that it might be called "the reportorial figure" without exaggeration. If the *praeteritios* were deleted from a magazine such as the *Reader's Digest,* for instance, its bulk would probably be cut in half.[4]

The conclusion reaches for relevance, as well as for a sense of rounding off the essay, by changing the level of abstraction. In effect, the significance of what has been reported is emphasized by treating it as an instance of a universal situation. Since the essay has not been concerned with retrolental fibroplasia as an example of any of the things it is finally asserted to be an example of, the conclusion is obviously a pseudo-conclusion, owing its shape to argumentation as does the introduction.

The second example is again typical, this time of political reporting. Unlike the previous essay, it derives its structure from history or fiction rather than argumentation.

THE DIVIDED BUDDHISTS OF SOUTH VIETNAM[5]

1) No more welcome political news has come out of Vietnam than Thich Tam Chau's decision to resign his high post in the Unified Buddhist Church after playing the key role in averting a disastrous and irreparable break between the church and the government. He has thus isolated the extremists and opened the way for the creation of a new

[4] The *praeteritio* used as an information-giving device is hazardous; it is an eternal temptation to the writer who would pad a little.

[5] Denis Warner, "The Divided Buddhists of South Vietnam," *The Reporter,* June 16, 1966, pp. 22–24. Mr. Warner is currently *Look's* Asian Correspondent. Reprinted by permission of the author.

moderate Buddhist base in Saigon which may prove of incalculable importance in the September election.

2)   One of the most persistent myths in South Vietnam is that since the downfall of the Diem regime the Buddhists have become so strong and unified that no other force in the country, including the Vietcong, is proof against them. While it is true that militant monks rule the Buddhists of central Vietnam, command a large following among Vietnamese students, and have succeeded in creating political fanaticism out of religious fervor, the movement is anything but united. Nothing in Vietnam is more illuminating or, under the circumstances, more surprising than a close examination of the politics of Buddhism.

3)   Until 1964, Vietnam's largest and most important Buddhist organization was the General Buddhist Association of Vietnam. It consisted of three communities of monks and three lay associations for northern, central, and southern Vietnam, with the "northern" component mainly composed of refugees or former residents of North Vietnam. Although the Buddhists in general strenuously resented their inferior role vis-à-vis the Catholics during the Diem regime, little was heard of their association until May 8, 1963, when eight Buddhists were killed by government troops in a demonstration outside the radio station in Hue.

4)   The incident, which precipitated the Buddhist campaign leading to the downfall of President Ngo Dinh Diem, was set off by an inflammatory speech by Thich Tri Quang, one of the leaders of the association, which the Hue authorities had refused to rebroadcast on the radio. It was followed the next day by an equally strong letter to all Buddhist monks, nuns, and laymen signed by Thich Tam Chau, head of the association's northern section. He wrote that "In recent years, we Buddhists . . . have been buried alive, slandered, exiled, jailed, persecuted, insulted. . . . Let us be united in determination. Let tens of thousands of men act like a single man. Let us be ready to protect our religion and to die for our religion. . . . We must be ready to put on the robe, join hands, look up to the Buddha, and take long strides on the road to martyrdom."

5)   To co-ordinate their efforts, the Buddhists formed the Intersect Committee for the Defense of Buddhism to act as the sole spokesman for the various Buddhist associations then involved in negotiations with the Diem government. Leading the committee were Thich Tri Quang and Thich Tam Chau.

6)   In those fevered months when the Xa Loi Pagoda in Saigon became national headquarters for this early struggle movement, the monks learned a great deal about political power and its manipulation. The guns of the generals finally ended the Diem regime, but it was the work of the monks that made the coup possible. Almost overnight they

.

emerged as a major political force, and it soon became clear that, having tasted power, they were of no mind to return to the serenity of the pagodas and their lives of meditation and prayer.

7) Two months later, the monks were ready to advance a step further. In January, 1964, against the protests of many leading Buddhist laymen, they created the Unified Buddhist Church, consisting of fourteen of the country's sixteen Buddhist sects. In vain the laymen appealed to Thich Tinh Khiet, the Supreme Venerable of the General Buddhist Association, who, now in his eighties, neither reads nor writes the romanized Vietnamese language but only the ancient Chu Nom script, which has not been in general use since the fifteenth century. But the monks had the ear of the Supreme Venerable. He did not respond to the laymen's protests that the Unified Buddhist Church's creation and character had been decided without consulting them or to their charges that the monks were breaking their vows of poverty and using expensive cars and air conditioners. In retaliation the monks dissolved the laymen's association in central Vietnam, and shocked them anew with talk of violent demonstrations.

8) The two main branches of the Unified Buddhist Church were put under the direction of the same two monks who began the agitation against Diem. One branch, the Institute for the Clergy, was run by Tri Quang, and the secular arm, the Institute for the Propagation of the Faith, by Tam Chau. This led to a profoundly significant division within the Buddhist movement. In (sic) also led to the revival, in opposition to the Unified Buddhist Church, of the General Association of Buddhism, which optimistically claims a million adherents, and the Association of Studies of Buddhism, which has a membership of intellectuals and senior Buddhist laymen and monks. However, since these groups believe that Buddhism as such should play no part in the political affairs of the state, their opposition to the political machinations of the Unified Buddhist Church is passive and ineffective.

9) The Institute for the Propagation of the Faith, or Vien Hoa Dao, is housed in a group of wooden barracks near the outskirts of Saigon adjoining the Allied military headquarters. It was built on a former dump, and the surroundings are squalid. Yet cabinet ministers, generals, diplomats, and businessmen regularly pass through its gates to seek advice or make deals. It has become both a marketplace and a pressure point. Hard bargains have been struck over cabinet positions and much money has changed hands there. Governments that fell out with the Buddhists eventually were themselves brought down.

10) The Vien Hoa Dao, organized into departments such as education, youth, laymen, propaganda, social and cultural affairs, and fi-

nance, is the Buddhist government. If its plans materialize, it could some day take over every cabinet post in South Vietnam. Premier Nguyen Cao Ky is well aware that his real battle with the Vien Hoa Dao has just begun.

11) "I was approached by certain venerables who agreed to stop agitation in exchange for key jobs for Buddhists in my cabinet," Ky said in Danang on May 18. " 'Stay in power, you have our confidence,' these people said. And now they are attacking me. Their plan was clear. They wanted the Ministries of Information, Interior, and Defense so they could control the elections."

12) In terms of present political organization, the most important portfolio in the Vien Hoa Dao is that of Commissioner of Youth, a post presently filled by Tri Quang's principal lieutenant, a notoriously corrupt monk named Thich Thien· Minh, who on June 1 was severely wounded by a grenade thrown at his car. Thien Minh is an excellent speaker, a good organizer, and an experienced negotiator. He fought with the Vietminh against the French in central Vietnam, and was arrested as a Vietminh activist in 1950. After that war he is believed to have had connections with the Vietcong and worked in an area under Vietcong domination. In Saigon he has surrounded himself with young monks brought from Hue. Many of the novice monks are believed to be Vietcong sympathizers. Needing no identity cards, students in political difficulty can shave their heads, don a monk's robe, and find a ready refuge in the pagodas. The Badan Pagoda on the outskirts of Saigon is used quite openly by Vietcong returning from Zone D, one of their main bases northwest of the capital.

13) The education portfolio in the Vien Hoa Dao is also held by a follower of Tri Quang, Thich Minh Chau. His younger brother was an attache in the North Vietnamese embassy in Peking in 1963 when Minh Chau attended a Buddhist congress there. He is not regarded as sympathetic to the Vietcong, however, and is even considered right-wing by Tri Quang's standards.

14) Despite the presence of such Tri Quang men in his organization, Tam Chau still controlled the Vien Hoa Dao. He had the backing of perhaps a million refugees and migrants from the North, where he was born in 1921. Tam Chau told me that he had been imprisoned by the Vietminh for three years. During the war against the French he worked with the Catholics in the southern Red River Delta as a chairman of the Religious League Against Communism. While he describes himself only as non-Communist, his associates say that he is vigorously anti-Communist. During one of several interviews I have had with him in recent years, he attacked the concept of neutrality as a solution to

Vietnam's problems. "We just have to look at Laos," he said, "to see what neutrality can mean."

15) These are the two main and contending factions. There are also a number of uncommitted elements. One favors a neutralist policy; another is headed by Thich Quang Lien, who was educated at Yale and who has been interested at times in pushing peace moves. And finally there are the Theravada Buddhists. They have two principal leaders, one of whom is now vice-chairman of the Vien Hoa Dao and the other chief of the department of laymen and leader of the army chaplains. Late in May the support of all these groups was with Tam Chau.

16) Politics in the Vien Hoa Dao has been consistently bitter since its founding in 1964. Tri Quang, who had decided that Tam Chau was weak and pliable, supported his election as chairman and he has never ceased to regret it. At that time, the Unified Buddhist Church monks were unanimous in agreeing that Vietnam should become a Buddhist state and that other religions should be banned. Six months later, realizing the divisive effects such a program would have on the broader political scene, Tam Chau changed his mind and decided to work merely for Buddhist leadership in a society that would also find a place for the Christians and the sects. Tri Quang has never forgiven him. "Tri Quang may say he wants to make friends with other religions, but this is not true," Buddhists told me. "He believes he can turn all of Vietnam, including the North, into a Buddhist state that he will dominate."

17) A year after the first election, Tri Quang wanted to replace Tam Chau as chairman with his own chief lieutenant, Thien Minh, but he could not round up a majority. One way or another, Tam Chau kept his post until his resignation on June 3 and until recently has successfully beaten off Tri Quang's attempts to extend his Hue-based political organization to Saigon.

18) The fight between the two factions has often been vicious, not merely within the Vien Hoa Dao but in the national political arena as well. In return for Tri Quang's promise of support in the 1965 Vien Hoa Dao elections, Tam Chau agreed to back his plans for a new party, at first called the Force of Vietnamese Socialist Buddhists and later shortened by dropping the word "Socialist." Although it was to be an official Vien Hoa Dao party, Tam Chau's laymen were barred from the first meeting. Tam Chau reacted by instructing his ally, the Commissioner for Laymen, to form a separate political party, which was also called the Force of Vietnamese Buddhists. The situation became somewhat ludicrous and both forces were quietly dropped.

19) Tri Quang thereupon tried another tack. He began to concentrate on the organization of his followers in central Vietnam. The

Struggle Movement was the result. It began in Hue, spread to other parts of central Vietnam, then to Dalat, and is now established in Saigon. In all areas it contains Communist elements, and in Saigon the Vietcong pull the strings.

20)   The leader of the Saigon group disappeared about the middle of May, and reports circulated that he had been kidnapped by the police. Two of his aides (who disappeared from Saigon a year ago to escape charges that they were involved in a peace movement) are reportedly hiding out with the Vietcong.

21)   Tam Chau had always intended to match Tri Quang's Struggle Movement with a political group of his own, but until his resignation circumstances forced him to temporize. "You may think I am exaggerating," one Buddhist told me, "but if he does not support the Struggle Movement against Premier Ky, Tam Chau's life may even be in danger."

22)   Since 1963, the two monks have outdone each other in political intrigues. Tri Quang once trapped Premier Nguyen Khanh into promising him a contribution of thirty million piastres. When Khanh turned up with only five million, Tri Quang looked at the gift and commented, "You misunderstand me. I didn't ask for money, but please give it to the Van Hanh university." Khanh made the gift, but from that day Tri Quang fought to get rid of him and persuaded the Vien Hoa Dao to vote unanimously for his dismissal.

23)   That was a Tri Quang coup, but Tam Chau has had several of his own. By committing the Vien Hoa Dao without a vote of the membership, he forced Tri Quang to participate against his will in the campaign against the government of Khanh's successor, Tran Van Huong. With the fall of Huong, however, Tri Quang succeeded in gaining control of the Ministries of Finance, Economy, Education, and Social Affairs in the government of Huong's successor, Dr. Phan Huy Quat. Tam Chau found himself not only without influence inside the government but also with a challenge from Thien Minh, enriched by a government handout of millions of piastres. This time an expedient alliance between Tam Chau and the Catholics, who were even more fearful of Tri Quang's strength, brought the government down.

24)   Inevitably, the rivalry between Tam Chau and Tri Quang spilled over into the Ky administration, which Tam Chau supported and Tri Quang opposed. Ky rewarded Tam Chau by sending him on a goodwill mission to Japan, Korea, and Formosa, and by contributing millions of piastres to the construction of new pagodas in Saigon. Tri Quang did not consult Tam Chau when he sent his Struggle Forces into action against the government in Danang in May. As his campaign developed, he presented Tam Chau with a petition against Ky to sign. "My friend,"

Tam Chau reportedly said, "you ask too much. If you continue to press me, I will split the church and form a committee against the division of the people." Tam Chau rose and left the room, banging the door behind him. It was never fully reopened.

25) The widening gulf between the rivals has been more of a set-back for Tri Quang than for Tam Chau, but Tri Quang's hold on the Buddhists in central Vietnam remains as firm as ever and he is all-powerful in the Institute for the Clergy. He is surrounded by a small group of able monks, several of whom, the Tam Chau faction suspects, have some sort of association with the Vietcong. "If Tri Quang wants to put fifty thousand demonstrators into the streets of Hue, he can do it with a snap of his fingers," a Buddhist told me. "All together, in central Vietnam he can count on one to two million followers."

26) Tri Quang can just as easily keep demonstrators off the streets. I was in Hue when Premier Ky told a group of newspapermen in the Mekong Delta that he would remain in power for another year. Although there are forty-eight separate Struggle Committees in Hue, there was not a single spontaneous protest. Tri Quang was in consultation with Thien Minh, and Tri Quang's followers knew that no move should be made until their decision was handed down.

27) Three days later I was at the Hue airport waiting for a plane, as was Thien Minh, who was surrounded by members of the various Struggle Committees. "Tri Quang has said that he gave the Americans a pledge not to hold demonstrations," one of these young men told me. "But if the Americans do not honor their pledge on elections, then Tri Quang says that he will attack the Americans not merely on policy but on grounds of imperialism." When and if that moment comes, it will be impossible to differentiate between the Struggle Forces and the Vietcong. Even if such a development were confined to central Vietnam, it would be dangerous enough. If it were to spread through all of South Vietnam, it could have disastrous consequences.

28) Many Buddhists in Saigon now understand this. "No one can attack Tri Quang directly, but he can be attacked through Thien Minh," said one Buddhist layman. "Arrest the Vietcong close to Thien Minh. He is vulnerable on many grounds. He is rich, powerful, and unloved. When he had difficulty in raising demonstrators in Saigon in April, he recruited hundreds from the salt market, paying them eighty piastres a day each. Don't forget if it comes to force that Tam Chau has followers who can match Thien Minh's worst efforts in Saigon. The Railway Workers Union, the most powerful of all, is under his control, and he has twenty thousand men, some of them armed and some from the Hoa Hao sect in his 'Knights to Protect the Oppressed Peoples.' "

29) Another Buddhist layman urged that Tam Chau should be encouraged to form a political party of his own. "Then Tri Quang will be neutralized." "Do it with money," said a third. It now appears that Tam Chau has decided to take the plunge.

The real structure of the essay is clear enough on close inspection. After two introductory paragraphs there follow: (1) five paragraphs of history; (2) an analysis of the overall political organization of the Buddhists, through paragraph eleven; (3) an analysis of the organization of the Vien Hoa Dao, through paragraph fifteen; and (4) a collection of specific examples.

Every writer must fight dullness. But the hazard is an acute one for Mr. Warner. A catalog of anything but one's own virtues or accomplishments is inherently dull. Mr. Warner's job is to take the reader through three successive catalogs of information that we presumably ought to have, but will certainly resist, if we know that the delivery of such information is the author's object. Mr. Warner escapes being boring and retains his audience by disguising his purpose.

The opening two paragraphs actually constitute a double introduction. The first is a pseudo-introduction; it sets up the significance of Thich Tam Chau's resignation as the subject of the essay, which it most certainly is not. The real function of the paragraph is to give a sense of immediacy to an essay that really only surveys a situation in existence for some time. The second paragraph introduces the real subject, the political divisions among Vietnamese Buddhists. It will be observed that both paragraphs are declarative rather than problematical in tone; a declaration leads naturally to amplification and reportorial writing.

The first section, paragraphs three through seven, firmly establishes the pseudo-structure of the essay; it constitutes a brief history. The writer does not acknowledge his second section as being a new element in the essay. It is introduced as though it were further history, rather than a catalog: "The two main branches . . . were put under the direction." Sentences three and four, "This led . . . In (sic) also led," continue the fiction of a historical narrative. This fiction being sufficiently established, the writer can then finish off his catalog in three straightforward paragraphs.

The author again blurs divisions within the essay by relating the second and third sections, his two major catalogs, as closely as possible; the analysis of the Vien Hoa Dao follows immediately upon its enumeration. This catalog is the most openly static of the three, although one observes such statements as, "Despite the presence of such Tri Quang men in his organization, Tam Chau still controlled the Vien Hoa Dao"—a statement that implies a narrative.

Paragraph fifteen is particularly interesting. It abandons the pretence of a narrative structure by being a summary of the section that has gone before, but it is implicitly introductory. The reader is assured that, the ground cleared, the history is about to begin.

Of course it does not. Section four, beginning with paragraph sixteen, is actually another catalog of specific instances set up more or less chronologically (how chronologically it is hard to tell), but lacking any real development to a conclusion. Technically this was surely the most difficult section to write, and Mr. Warner works very hard to get a sense of coherent development into his list. He uses two techniques chiefly. First, he works an alternating narrative line —"Tri Quang . . . Tam Chau." Second, he uses transitional sentences that imply a development that is not really there—"The fight between the two factions has often been vicious, not merely within the Vien Hoa Dao but in the national political arena as well."

It should also be noted that he conceals the catalog of this section, which is quite long, by breaking it in two. Paragraph twenty-two opens with a statement clearly signaling a new section of the essay and some progress. But no progress follows; we have instead another series of incidents that simply dramatize the term the essay is engaged in presenting, "The Divided Buddhists of South Vietnam."

Finally, the essay ends very abruptly. It is difficult to end a piece of reportorial writing in any case. Again, convention leads a reader to expect a conclusion to announce the point at which he and the writer have arrived. Since in reportorial writing this ending point is identical with the point of origin, it makes for difficulties. Perhaps Mr. Warner minimized these difficulties by reverting to his opening paragraph with one sentence and shutting up his typewriter. It seems more likely that he had some editorial assistance in his conclusion.

Several general characteristics of the essay ought to be noted. In the first place, the writer proposes to give the "facts" to an audience that needs to know them. And only a handful of an audience of thousands might be expected to be any judge of the authenticity and relevance of those "facts." How are the rest to know that Mr. Warner is not making the whole thing up?

Obviously, the reader's judgment will depend very heavily on his response to Mr. Warner's ethos. This is a perfectly unexceptionable judicious ethos, supported by ten or twelve names of institutions and men which the reader will never remember, but which he will be impressed by, as evidence of the writer's general knowledgeability. The tone is low-keyed and casual, the tone of a man concerned with presenting the situation as it is.

At the same time the author has a very definite point of view, and perhaps he ought to be regarded as the more trustworthy because there is little attempt to disguise it. The reader knows perfectly well that Mr. Warner has no objection to United States participation in the Vietnamese war, that he thinks it can be brought to a successful conclusion, and that he hopes for some kind of rapprochement between Buddhists and the government to this end.

Furthermore, the essay functions to persuade us to the same point of view. Perhaps it would be more accurate to say that the explicit intent of the essay is to convince the reader of the last possibility, that Buddhists and government can perhaps now begin to cooperate. But we are at least to some extent persuaded to accept his whole position by reason of having assumed it to see the Buddhist political situation from Mr. Warner's point of view.

The third example of reportorial writing is openly persuasive in intention; as a consequence, the ethos of the writer is much more sharply defined than is customary for this genre.

HOW CITY PLANNERS HURT CITIES[6]

1) City planners and rebuilders are killing our cities, not on pur-

---

[6] Jane Jacobs, "How City Planners Hurt Cities," *Saturday Evening Post,* October 14, 1961, pp. 12, 14. Copyright, Jane Jacobs. Reprinted by permission of the author.

pose, but because they do not understand how cities work. Their well-meant but ignorant actions, supported by public money and political power, can be fearsomely destructive.

2) We are continually assured that planners are producing healthful city environments for us. But most planners and rebuilders do not recognize a healthful city environment when they see one, much less know how to create one. Consider, for example, a district called the North End, in Boston.

3) Twenty years ago, when I first saw the North End, its buildings were badly overcrowded. Rundown brick houses had been converted into flats. Four- or five-story walk-ups had been built to house immigrants first from Ireland, then Eastern Europe and finally from Sicily. You did not have to look far to see that the district was taking a severe physical beating and was desperately poor.

4) When I saw the North End again in 1959, I was amazed. Scores of buildings had been rehabilitated. Instead of mattresses against the windows, there were Venetian blinds and glimpses of fresh paint. Many of the small, converted houses were now occupied by one or two families instead of three or four. Some of the families in the tenements had uncrowded themselves by throwing two flats together, equipping them with new bathrooms and kitchens. Mingled among the buildings were splendid food stores. Small industries—upholstery making, metalworking, food processing, and the like—rimmed the neighborhood. The streets were alive with children playing, people shopping, strolling and talking.

5) I had seen a lot of Boston in the past few days, most of it dull, gloomy and decaying. This place struck me as the healthiest district in the city. To find out more about it, I went into a bar and phoned a Boston planner I know.

"Why in the world are you down in the North End?" he said. "Nothing's going on there. Eventually, yes, but not yet. That's a slum!"

"It doesn't seem like a slum to me," I said.

"Why that's the worst slum in the city. It has 275 dwelling units to the net acre! [Excluding streets, nonresidential land, etc.] I hate to admit we have anything like that in Boston, but it's a fact."

"Do you have any other figures on it?" I asked.

He did. Statistics showed that the neighborhood's delinquency, disease and infant-mortality rates are among the lowest in the city. The child population is just about average. The death rate is low, 8.8 per 1000, against the average city rate of 11.2.

"You should have more slums like this," I said. "Don't tell me there are plans to wipe this out. You ought to be down here learning as much as you can from it."

"I know how you feel," he said. "I often go down there myself just to walk around the streets and feel that wonderful, cheerful street life. You'd be crazy about it in summer. But we have to rebuild it eventually. We've got to get those people off the street."

6)   My planner friend's instincts told him the North End was a healthful place. Statistics confirmed it. But his training as a city planner told him the North End *had* to be a "bad" place. It has little park land. Children play on the sidewalks. It has small blocks. In city-planning parlance, the district is "badly cut up by wasteful streets." It also has "mixed uses"—another sin. It is made up of the plans of hundreds of people— not planners. Such freedom represents, as one of the wise men of city planning put it, "a chaotic accident . . . the summation of the haphazard, antagonistic whims of many self-centered, ill-advised individuals."

7)   Under the seeming chaos of a lively place like the North End is a marvelous and intricate order—a complicated array of urban activities. These activities support and supplement each other, keeping the neighborhood interesting and vital. The planners would kill it.

8)   The North End is not unique. In city after city, there are districts that refuse to decay, districts that hold people even when their incomes rise and their "status" improves, districts that spontaneously repair and renovate in spite of discouragement by government officials and mortgage lenders. These interesting and vital areas are the ones that have everything possible wrong with them—according to city-planning theory. Equally significant, in city after city the districts in decline and decay are frequently the ones that ought to be successful—according to planning theory.

9)   The Morningside Heights area in New York City is such an example. According to theory, it should not be in trouble. It has a great abundance of park land, campus areas, playgrounds and other open spaces. It has plenty of grass. It occupies high and pleasant ground with magnificent river views. It is a famous educational center. It has good hospitals and fine churches. It has no industries. Its residential streets are zoned against "incompatible uses."

10)   Yet by the early 1950's Morningside Heights was becoming the kind of slum in which people fear to walk the streets. Columbia University, other institutions and the planners from the city government got together. At great cost the most blighted part of the area was wiped out. In the torn-down area a middle-income project complete with shopping center was built. Nearby a fenced-off low-income project was erected. The projects were hailed as a great demonstration in city saving.

11)   After that Morningside Heights went downhill even faster. It continues to pile up new moutains of crime and troubles to this day. The "remedy" didn't work. Dull, sorted-out "quiet residential areas" in cities

fail because they are inconvenient, uninteresting and dangerous. The dark, empty grounds of housing projects breed crime. And it is much the same with dark, empty streets of "quiet residential areas" in big cities.

12) Our cities need help desperately. If places like Morningside Heights are to be helped, the help must be based not on imitations of genteel, "good" addresses, but on understanding the real needs of those who live in big cities. A little involvement with the life of city streets, a little recognition that empty grass festooned with used tissue paper is no treat for anyone, a little common sense—these are the first requirements.

13) The New York City neighborhood where I live is considered a mess by planners. They have plans to sort out its differing land uses from one another and isolate residences from working places with a buffer strip. Such a strip would be useful primarily to muggers. For months residents and businessmen of the neighborhood have been combating the scheme to simplify and regiment the area with Federal funds. Simplification would be the avenue to its ruin.

14) One need only watch the sidewalks to see how the neighborhood is built upon a complicated set of activities. Each day Hudson Street, my street, is the scene of an endlessly varied parade of persons, some of them neighbors, many of them strangers. This scene is all composed of interesting movement and change.

15) I make my first entrance a little after eight A.M. when I put out the garbage can. Around me, droves of junior-high-school students and people coming to work in the district walk by the center of the stage. While I sweep the sidewalk, I watch the signs and rituals of morning. Mr. Halpert unlocking his laundry hand-cart from its mooring to a cellar door. Joe Cornacchia's son-in-law stacking out empty crates from the delicatessen. The barber bringing out his sidewalk folding chair. Mr. Goldstein arranging coils of wire that proclaim the hardware store is open. The primary children, heading for St. Luke's to the south. The children for St. Veronica's heading west. The children for P.S. 41 heading east. Well-dressed and even elegant women, and men with briefcases, emerge now from doorways and side streets. Simultaneously numbers of women in house dresses emerge and pause for quick conversations. Longshoremen who are not working gather at the White Horse Tavern or the International Bar for beer and conversation.

16) As noontime arrives, the executives and business lunchers from the industries in the neighborhood throng the Dorgene Restaurant and the Lion's Head coffee house down the street. If there were no workers to support these places at noon, we residents would not have them to use at night. Character dancers come onstage: a strange old man with strings of old shoes over his shoulders; motor-scooter riders with big black beards

and girl friends who bounce on the back of their scooters. Mr. Koocha-
gian, the tailor, waters the plants in his window, gives them a look from
the outside and accepts a compliment on them from two passers-by. The
baby carriages come out.

17) As the residents return home from work in other places, the
ballet reaches its crescendo. This is the time of roller skates and stilts and
tricycles and games with bottle tops and plastic cowboys. This is the time
of bundles and packages and zigzagging from the drugstore to the fruit
stand. This is the time when teenagers, all dressed up, are pausing to ask
if their slips show or their collars look right. This is the time when anybody you know in the neighborhood will go by.

18) As darkness thickens and Mr. Halpert moors the laundry cart
to the cellar door again, the ballet goes on under lights. It eddies back
and forth, intensifying at the bright spotlight pools of Joe's sidewalk
pizzeria, the bars and the drugstore. On Hudson Street we do not barri-
cade ourselves indoors when darkness falls.

19) I know the deep night ballet from waking long after midnight
to tend a baby. Sitting in the dark I have seen the shadows and heard the
sounds of the sidewalk. Mostly it is snatches of party conversation. When
the bars have closed, it is the sound of singing. Sometimes there is anger
or sad weeping; sometimes a flurry of searching for a string of broken
beads. One night a young man came along bellowing invectives at two
girls who apparently were disappointing him. Doors opened, a wary
semicircle of men and women formed around him; the police came. Out
came the heads, too, along Hudson Street, offering opinion, "Drunk. . . .
Crazy. . . . A wild kid from the suburbs." (It turned out he *was* a wild kid
from the suburbs.)

20) I have not begun to describe the many differences that keep
our sidewalks bustling. Among businesses and industries alone there are
more than fifty different kinds within a few blocks. On Hudson Street,
just as in the North End of Boston, we are the lucky possessors of a complex city order that is anything but the chaos that city planners proclaim
it to be. Such neighborhoods as ours engender intense affection among
those who live or work in them. As a result, they are stable places where
people of many different incomes and tastes remain permanently—by
choice.

21) The true problem of city planning and rebuilding in a free
society is how to cultivate more city districts that are free; lively and
fertile places for the differing plans of thousands of individuals—not
planners. Nothing could be farther from the aims of planners today.
They have been trained to think of people as interchangeable statistics
to be pushed around, to think of city vitality and mixture as a mess.

Planners are the enemies of cities because they offer us only the poisonous promise of making every place in a city more like dull and standardized Morningside Heights. They have failed to pursue the main point: to study the success and failure of the real life of the cities. With their eyes on simple-minded panaceas, they destroy success and health. Planners will become helpful only when they abandon what they have learned about what "ought" to be good for cities.

22)　When they learn how fulfilling life in a city really can be, then they will finally stop working against the very goals they set out to achieve.

This is reporting, not argumentation, because the parts of the essay are not logically related to each other. Its structure can properly be called rhetorical, in fact. The *comparison* is chiefly used to convey a sense of movement on the structural level; on the paragraph level there is heavy dependence on the *antithesis*.

What is to follow is signalled clearly enough by the two short paragraphs of introduction. The tone is declarative and the point is economically stated by several *antitheses* having to do with the ineptitude of planners. The last sentence of the second paragraph describes forthrightly enough what is to follow, examples compared with each other.

Paragraphs three and four obviously set up the first *comparison*. The dialogue of paragraph five could be called the development of a second *comparison*, using paragraph four in a different way. This comparison would be between the fact about the North End and the planners' attitudes toward the fact. Paragraphs six and seven make explicit the point of paragraphs four and five, depending very heavily on *antithesis*.

Paragraph eight is a clever transitional paragraph. The writer separates the *antithesis* she has been working with, between Boston's North End and city planners, and sets up the North End again as though it had been her subject all along. She then sets up a new *antithesis*, between it and the deplorable results of the city planners. This leads inevitably to a new *comparison*, this time between New York's Morningside Heights and her own neighborhood. Paragraph twenty rounds off this second long *comparison* by altering the level of abstraction; it generalizes what has been implicit in the account of her own section of the city. The conclusion in paragraphs twenty-one and twenty-two elaborate somewhat on the *antithesis* of the first two paragraphs.

These examples do not, of course, exhaust the resources of the capable reporter, although they adequately represent the strategies most commonly used. However, where the writer's job is to create relationships that are not inherent in his intention, any method that works is good enough.

It is hard to imagine the modern intellectual world without the reporter, and most of us have our heads stuffed with information he has given us. But reportorial writing obviously poses as many philosophical problems as argumentation. It is no better guide than the latter to sound convictions. In some ways it is worse, because the reader is apt to be unaware of its persuasive intent.

And what are the criteria for estimating the reliability of a particular piece of reportorial writing? There is no defective reporting, as there is defective argumentation, because the reportorial writer does not pretend to reason with you; he gives you the facts. His ostensible intention could be reduced to a list. When is a list bad? When it leaves facts out? But all reportorial writing must leave facts out. The writer may honestly try to select among the facts available to him according to their relative importance. But he has no magic formula for determining this relative importance, and the reader might disagree with the writer's criteria if he knew what they were.

Perhaps the most obvious measure is after all the best one— the kind and degree of intelligence a particular piece of writing reflects. No matter how satisfying the ethos of a particular reporter might be to me as a reader, I will probably do well to be suspicious of him if he is not also reasonably intelligent. This is not a very satisfying criterion, or a very precise one, but it is perhaps all that the reader has.

Appendix

A Finding List

Argumentative Figures

1. *Enthymeme.* A syllogism with a premise omitted. A genuine enthymeme (as distinguished from a counter-statement or explanation) attempts to establish the probability of a statement by appealing, through its premises, to a generalization of a higher level.
2. *Ratiocinatio.* Two or more enthymemes put together so that the conclusion for one functions as a premise for the next.
3. *Exemplum.* A quotation, essentially, although it need not be direct, with the author stated or assumed to be known. It is used to establish a point by appeal to authority.
4. *Example.* The opposite of the enthymeme, in that it attempts to persuade by appealing to the more specific.
5. *Analogy.* Persuades by setting up a parallel, but better known, situation.
6. *Contrarium.* Similar to the analogy, but introduces more probable and less probable; if the less probable is known to have happened, then the more probable can be assumed to have happened also.
7. *Expeditio.* Works by elimination, setting up all possible explanations or whatever, and then showing that all but one is untrue.
8. *Rhetorical Question.* A question to which there is presumably only one answer, which is ordinarily left unstated as obvious.
9. *Definition.* Not really a figure, but one should watch out for it.
10. *Distributio.* A division of a concept and an apportioning of its

parts or a rejection of one of them. A *structural distributio* is a *distributio* upon which a whole argument or question thereafter depends.   .

The Tropes

1. *Translatio.* Two terms, a base term and a figurative one, which are mediated by a third, implicit term. Very often it is a noun modified by another noun made into an adjective, but this need not be the case. The mark of the figure is the implicit, linking term. Also, at times, the figurative term is simply substituted for the base term —"pearls" for "teeth."

2. *Abusio.* Like a *translatio* in that it involves a base and a figurative term, but there is no mediating term obvious. Very often it is an adjective moved from one kind of experience to another.

3. *Metaphor.* Figurative and base terms so extensively related as to be unparaphrasable and too immediate to permit a linking term.

4. *Metonymy.* A word substitution, in which a base term is simply replaced by a word with which it is frequently associated in common experience—traditionally characterized as the abstract for the concrete, container for thing contained, and so forth.

5. *Synecdoche.* A specific form of metonymy, in which a part is substituted for the whole or the whole for a part.

6. *Epithet.* A noun and its adjectives having some special characterizing force, used either in apposition or as a substitution for the name of the thing so characterized.

7. *Pun.* A play on words, in which the obvious meaning of a word or phrase is accompanied by another meaning because of a similarity in sounds or because one word may have two different meanings.

8. *Simile.* Either a comparison or a *translatio* introduced by "like" or "as."

9. *Transgressio.* The use of a word in other than its customary grammatical form—a noun for a verb, for instance.

10. *Paradox.* A statement containing a patent self-contradiction which is yet true or at least is proposed as truth. The *oxymoron* is a paradox coupled in an adjective-noun phrase.

11. *Personification.* The attribution of human qualities to dumb or inanimate things, or the attribution of human character to human states or human characteristics.

12. *Allegory.* An extended trope, usually an *abusio;* ordinarily it works to make an abstraction more concrete and more active. *Personified*

allegory fragments a human consciousness into personifications which then dramatize the mental state of the consciousness.

Stance Figures

1. *Apostrophe.* A turning away from the established audience to another audience, often the gods or personifications. The apostrophe is always meant to have its effect upon the established audience except when it is a dramatic representation of a character who has lost control of himself.
2. *Correctio.* The modification for rhetorical effect of what has just been said by the substitution of a more fitting expression.
3. *Exclamation.* As it is defined in grammar texts, it implies overpowering emotion and demands a similar state of the audience.
4. *Hyperbole.* Exaggeration that is intentional and that is meant to be understood as such.
5. *Irony.* Some sort of perceived disjunction between statement and meaning. *Dramatic irony* occurs when there is a tension in a literary work between what a character knows and what the audience knows. *Socratic irony* locates the disjunction between the real and apparent character of a speaker. *Verbal irony* lies in some sort of perceived tension between what is said and what is thought or meant. Verbal irony sets up an ambiguity, whereas *sarcasm* merely sets up an obvious opposition between what is said and what is meant.
6. *Litotes.* Understatement for rhetorical effect, and which is understood as such.
7. *Paralipsis.* An interruption in the structure of discourse ostensibly by irrelevant material, reflecting an intention on the part of a speaker or writer that does not coincide with the avowed purpose of the discourse.

Other Figures

1. *Accumulation.* Two or more clauses or sentences that say essentially the same thing, for emphasis or clarity.
2. *Antithesis.* Sentences or, more often, clauses set in opposition to each other, ordinarily for the purpose of distinguishing between choices or concepts.
3. *Asyndeton.* A rapid catalog, often with connectives omitted, usually for tonal effect.

4. *Commutatio.* A special form of the antithesis in which a noun-object relationship is proposed in one clause and reversed in the second; the form of the nouns may be altered ("vulgar-vulgarity").

5. *Comparison.* The elucidation of one thing by juxtaposing it to another for purposes of clarity.

6. *Descriptio.* A description with some sort of rhetorical intention.

7. *Gradatio.* Literally, a step figure, usually describing a sequence of actions or a sequence of states or positions that are not connected syllogistically.

8. *Hyperbaton.* Any pronounced distortion of syntax for purposes of emphasis.

9. *Paraphrasis.* A substitution involving some sort of indirection. It may be the substitution of the elaborated and abstract for the simple and concrete in order to elevate discourse; on the other hand, recourse to abstraction is frequently used in order to make the meaning of what is said less immediate to the audience.

10. *Praeteritio.* The introduction of subjects that the writer does not intend to discuss but wishes simply to call to mind, even though the subjects are relevant to his argument.

11. *Repetitio.* The repetition of a word or phrase, sometimes within parallel syntactical structures.

12. *Sententia.* A general principle having weight and assurance; it really proposes itself as a sort of consensus of all mankind.

13. *Synonymia.* As the name suggests, the use of words or phrases having identical or near-identical meanings close enough together for them to act upon each other.

14. *Zeugma.* A phrase in which one word controls two or more dependent words that are not parallel in significance.

Index

* Major references are in bold type.